The Luftwaffe

THE LUFTWAFFE

Its Rise and Fall

BY HAUPTMANN HERMANN

With an Introduction by Curt Riess

G·P·PUTNAM'S SONS, NEW YORK

Designed by Robert Josephy

MANUFACTURED IN THE UNITED STATES OF AMERICA

"...*those who were responsible for the birth of flight thought of it as a new force in the world for peace, for prosperity, and for true internationalism. Here was to come something which would make the world a happier place by a quick form of transport, that would bring us all closer together....*"

Lord Brabazon of Tara
in his Wilbur Wright Memorial Lecture: 1942

NOTE:

Some of the material in this book has appeared in a briefer form in *Esquire*. The author wishes to express his grateful appreciation for permission to elaborate on this material.

TABLE OF CONTENTS

PAGE

Introduction by Curt Riess   ix

Part I: THE SO-CALLED PEACE
   1. The Dream of Flying   3
   2. The Grand Old Man   20
   3. The Other Pioneers   39
   4. Collapse and Rebirth of an Industry   55
   5. The Fifth Columnist   76

Part II: THE LUFTWAFFE IS BORN
   6. Goering in the Limelight   99
   7. Business Not as Usual   107
   8. Secrecy and Bluff   128
   9. Air Strategy   142
  10. Toward War   154
  11. Dress Rehearsal   174

Part III: ANOTHER KIND OF WAR
  12. Big Business   195
  13. Victory—Through Air Power?   208

		PAGE
14.	Trouble in the Air	224
15.	*Ersatz* Invasion of an Island	239
16.	The Russians Don't Play Ball	250
17.	The Receiving End	265
18.	Tomorrow	278
Bibliography		295

INTRODUCTION

"The Luftwaffe—the German Air Force—will no longer have a decisive influence on the outcome of World War II, no matter how long it takes to beat Hitler."

It is more than two years since I first heard these words. The man who spoke them to me continued:

"No doubt, we will hear of the Luftwaffe before the war is over. We will hear a lot. But don't let us be deceived. No matter what happens, the Luftwaffe can never be used as a strategic first-line weapon within the Nazi plan. It can play no role but that of a tactical and auxiliary weapon."

Even now, as I write these words, I wonder how many readers will feel that I am indulging in wishful thinking. Two years ago, when I first was confronted with these ideas, I was absolutely sure that the man who uttered them was talking through his hat. Two years ago—Poland, Norway, Belgium, Holland, and France were defeated and occupied. Two years ago almost everybody in this country—in fact, all over the world—was convinced that the Luftwaffe was a formidable and probably an invincible weapon. True, the British had been able to accomplish the miraculous retreat of Dunkirk; but Dunkirk at that time was not yet recognized as the first defeat of the Luftwaffe. True, also, the Luftwaffe had lost the battle of England—but the defeat, too, was not at all clear in all its implications.

Therefore, the prediction that the Luftwaffe was through was not taken seriously at all two years ago. I know of no instance where the author of this prediction got more of a response than a polite shrug.

In the meantime, the progress of the war viewed from the Luftwaffe angle has confirmed these early prophecies. In spite of a few spectacular successes at the invasion of Crete and the first initial air victories of the Russian war, there can be little doubt that the Luftwaffe is no longer what it used to be—or shall I say what we thought it used to be. It seems, therefore, a good idea for the man who has been so consistently right about the Luftwaffe to write a book showing why we all considered the Luftwaffe unbeatable when actually all the time the Luftwaffe was doomed. One of the most necessary things in a war is to know one's enemy.

The author signs himself Hauptmann Hermann. His real name, well-known in aviation circles in Germany and in this country, is different. It cannot be divulged at present for reasons which have nothing to do with the book and which have everything to do with certain people related to him who are still living in Hitler-occupied Europe.

Hauptmann Hermann was a German flier in World War I. He joined the German air corps in 1916 and flew bombers to the day of the Armistice. At first he flew light daytime bombers, then, after 1917, twin-engined night bombers. He fought very successfully and covered himself with great distinction. After the war he obtained an engineering degree at a German university, remained there as a scientific assistant, and later joined the Junkers Aircraft Company in Dessau. There he became one of the close collaborators and, indeed, one of the close friends of the

grand old man of the German aircraft industry, Professor
Hugo Junkers.

He collaborated on many experiments in Junkers' *Ver-
suchsanstalt*, "Institute for Basic Research," worked in his
German aircraft factory, and later helped to build up the
big Junkers aircraft factory in Fili, near Moscow. Still
later, he held a leading position in the Junkers Airline System inside and outside Germany—till the Nazis came to
power. Needless to say, as an old hand in German aviation,
he was in constant touch with all its leading men.

He has known Milch, Udet, Messerschmitt, Dornier,
Heinkel. He has known them for many years and known
them intimately. There is scarcely a person of any importance today in the German Luftwaffe whom Hauptmann
Hermann does not know.

His interests and activities were restricted to civil aviation. He was not interested in military aviation, and like his
great friend and teacher, Professor Junkers, he abhorred
the very idea of air rearmament. Still, he was much too
much on the inside of German aviation not to see the trend
toward remilitarization in the air, and he learned numerous
details and countless secrets connected with that rearmament.

I once asked him why he, a man who should have seen
much earlier than most people what was coming, did not
get out of Germany immediately when Hitler came to
power. Of course, if he had not stayed till shortly before
the war started, he would not have been witness to many
of the things which he will discuss in this book—matters
which I think are very necessary for us to know.

Hauptmann Hermann has tried several times to answer
my question. Without going too deeply into this relatively
unimportant matter, I will state here that in my personal

opinion Hauptmann Hermann belonged among those in-
curable German idealists who believed that the German
people and especially the honorable men of German aviation would not allow themselves to be manipulated by a
clique of gangsters. Hauptmann Hermann hoped from day
to day, and then from year to year, that the Nazis would
be thrown out by a wrathful people—at any moment. He
quotes many friends inside Germany who were helped
along in their careers by the Nazis, and who expressed the
same hope up to the very day of the outbreak of World
War II. I think that Hauptmann Hermann and his friends
not only underestimated the staying power of the Nazis
but also overestimated the idealism and the high character
of the German people in general and the men of German
aviation in particular. However, this is an open question.

By leaving Germany only shortly before the war, Hauptmann Hermann was able to get a lot of inside information
as to the way the Luftwaffe was built up, the way it was
supposed to function, and finally how it did function. He
has had ample opportunity to use this inside information
for the benefit of our country, of which he hopes to become a citizen one day. Of late, military experts have
shown great interest in his judgment, which, as the war has
progressed, has proved to be right in every respect. Today
he is employed in an American aircraft factory in a capacity which gives him a chance to give us the benefit of
his experiences in Germany. Also, for some time now, he
has been broadcasting for the United States Government
via short wave to Germany. At regular intervals he ad-
dresses the German fliers, demonstrating to them that their
task is hopeless. He shows them the errors that their su-
periors have made and the inevitable end that awaits them.

He knows too much of what is going on inside the Luftwaffe for his broadcasts and prophecies to be disregarded
by our enemy. For all of those who listen to him even
once must realize that he knows his subject.

And I believe that while Goering, Milch, Kesselring,
Stumpff, Sperrle, may listen out of curiosity to the man
who recalls to their minds so many things—matters of
which only a few men have intimate knowledge—they cannot enjoy his broadcasts. In fact, I think his words make
them feel very uncomfortable.

I hope that this book, which deals with many questions
and facts already discussed in his broadcasts, will have the
same kind of effect on them—if ever it reaches them.

Numerous books about air warfare have been published, especially in this country. There have been very
good books and very exciting ones, and some of them—
for instance, the remarkable work of Major de Seversky—
have created a lot of comment.

Still, I feel that Hauptmann Hermann's book is something special. All recent books on aviation have either
preached a fundamental theory or have tried to demonstrate how air strength has been achieved in this country
or in Great Britain. Hauptmann Hermann shows the other
side of the picture. He tells how air strength was achieved
by our enemies. He shows how the Luftwaffe was con-
ceived—long before anybody was thinking of a man called
Adolf Hitler. He shows the men and the conditions which
helped to bring about German strength in the air.

His book is an inside story if there ever was one.

An inside story, then, and why not? After all, one should
know one's enemy. To know our enemy may, indeed, be
the first prerequisite for United Nations victory. And

Hauptmann Hermann is just the right man to help us to make the acquaintance of our enemy. There are many parallels between German air force morale at the end of the last war and the psychological tendencies of the Luftwaffe personnel today. We must know about these things if we expect to draw the right conclusions.

No war against aggression is worth fighting unless we are determined to remove once and for all the underlying causes for aggression. But in order to achieve this it is necessary to study how after the last war similar attempts were stymied. Hauptmann Hermann shows in his book how the Germans managed to circumvent the stipulations of the Versailles Treaty, devised to crush German aviation. He shows how, in fact, the Versailles Treaty proved to be of prime and very practical help to those who immediately set about building up a stronger and more powerful German air force than the one which had existed in World War I.

The first third of the book is devoted to the amazing story of the building up of the German aircraft industry and of rearmament in the air during the years immediately following the Versailles Treaty; and the remaining two-thirds tells the story of the Luftwaffe, which in the beginning was spectacularly successful but which was doomed and has declined steadily.

Why was the Luftwaffe doomed?

Because it never became what it was intended to become from the start. It was intended to be a strategical and operational weapon, a unit operating according to its own laws. It became, very much against the intentions of the head men of German aviation, only a tactical weapon which could not operate except in co-operation with the army.

The second major reason for the decline and doom of the Luftwaffe is the fact that it very rarely was used the way it was created to be used. It was supposed to be used—and, indeed, was built—for short wars, campaigns which were not to follow each other without long intermissions which would give the Luftwaffe a breathing spell. It was built for campaigns like the Polish war or the invasion of Holland, Belgium, and France. The conflict which began with the battle of England in the summer of 1940 was a long-drawn-out war, and it still is exactly the type of struggle for which the Luftwaffe was not built.

Numerous questions in connection with these two main theses are discussed at great length in the book. Questions such as: What could the Luftwaffe have achieved if it had been used the way it was supposed to be used? What could a Luftwaffe built as a strategic weapon—as, for instance, the R.A.F.—have achieved? Under what conditions would it have been possible to create a strategic weapon of the Luftwaffe?

Many other questions are discussed in the book, many answers are given, many stories are told. We make the acquaintance of the great genius of German and international aircraft production, Professor Hugo Junkers. We meet on intimate terms the men whose machines today are some of our toughest enemies: the Heinkels, Messerschmitts, Dorniers. We get an idea of the fantastic publicity tricks with which Goebbels built up the Luftwaffe as a great "frightener" in the mind of the rest of the world, at a time when there actually was not much of a Luftwaffe. We see how many so-called neutral observers—Lindbergh is one—helped Goebbels in this task without knowing it, no doubt. We get an idea of German Luftwaffe and Nazi espionage; we learn why Hitler sent his planes to Spain. We are given many glimpses of the intrigues and difficulties of the men who today are behind the Luftwaffe. Hauptmann Hermann also proves, in figures based on world production, German production, and German losses, why the Luftwaffe will not survive.

You will read that Hauptmann Hermann is by no means of the opinion that we shall never hear about the Luftwaffe again. On the contrary, some of the most sensational pages of the book are devoted to what Hauptmann Hermann thinks the Luftwaffe will do when the Nazis discover that they have lost out. According to Hauptmann Hermann some unheard-of methods of destruction are still in store for the United Nations.

However, I think the important thing that Hauptmann Hermann has achieved in this book—and which alone would justify its writing—is the unmasking of the great Nazi master mind. The initial spectacular successes of the Luftwaffe gave people all over the world the idea that the men in command of the Luftwaffe were supermen, that they could achieve the impossible and the incredible, that there was no use in trying to fight against them and their weapon. That impression, of course, was exactly what the Nazis wanted to create. Nobody yet has tried to destroy that impression from such a sound basis as Hauptmann Hermann does in this book. You will feel very much relieved and slightly embarrassed to have been frightened so long by men who are far from supermen. You will find out that the Nazis themselves have done nothing to build up the Luftwaffe. That everything which was done in that direction, that everything which helped to weld the German air weapon, was done long before they came to power by men who were not Nazis. You will learn that, on the contrary, the Nazis have shown themselves incapable of continuing the work which was started before they came to power and that they have fallen down on the job and missed out on their greatest chance, perhaps their only chance, for world domination.

All this is told more or less as a personal story. It is the personal story of Hauptmann Hermann, who has known them all, who was present at the very birth of the Luftwaffe and watched its slow development. Incidentally—as in the whole history of Hitler, his political warfare and his bloody wars—it was not necessary to have known anybody in German aviation to know what was going on. Hitler, in *Mein Kampf*, predicted what he was going to do; the German army, in countless books and military magazines, predicted what it was going to do; and everything concerning the Luftwaffe during the last fifteen or twenty years has also been written up and published in countless books and magazines and newspapers. A bibliography has been included, selected by Hauptmann Hermann; and those who may not believe him implicitly will perhaps believe those books and brochures printed in Germany. They have been around for a long, long time. If we had read them, we would have known.

But, then, we did not want to know.

Curt Riess.

Washington, D. C., January, 1943.

PART I: THE SO-CALLED PEACE

1. The Dream of Flying

It was the night of September 23, 1918. Our air group was based on two airfields near the French-Belgian frontier. There were two squadrons on our field, the third along with the staff on the other field. I still remember the half-circle of tents silhouetted against the sky, rapidly disappearing in the dusk. I still hear the noise of the motors making a test run and drowning out every other sound. Then we could see a long stream of sparks from the exhaust until the throttle was eased and the engine, after releasing a long blue flame from the exhaust, was idling again smoothly. When all engines had been tested the ignition was cut.

The sudden silence gave us an unreal feeling of peace and of suspense. We were tense when we emerged from the tent of the squadron leader who had given us the meteorological report and the itinerary for our separate take-offs, the route going out and the return, the latest intelligence reports about the anti-aircraft guns, the searchlight defenses, and the information about the hundred and fifty night fighter airplanes that were supposed to defend Paris against us.

For Paris was the target. Our planes were loaded with hundreds of incendiary bombs. Each of them weighed two pounds. They were the same bombs as are used today. Other German bombers were to visit London that night. The idea was to start so many fires with this first incendiary

3

attack that the fire brigades would not be able to put all of them out.

Then we took our seats and I was about to start my motors. But we never took off. Suddenly through the darkness a car came racing, a staff officer jumped out and rushed toward us. Orders from General Headquarters. We were not to take off. That day it had been decided to send a request to President Wilson to start negotiations for an armistice. Incidentally, the request did not leave Imperial Headquarters at Spa till late on October 3—ten days later.

That sudden change in orders came as a severe shock to us. Only a week before we had attacked Paris heavily with high explosive bombs totaling 22 tons, a terrific amount for that time. We had seen the heavy explosions and the fires that we had caused in Paris, and a few days later we were able to read reprints from Swiss papers with exciting reports of the terror we had created. It is true, we had lost a number of our planes, but not as many as in our first night attack on Paris in the spring of 1918, when I had returned alone—eight planes from our squadron had started out—and had seen three of our planes shot down in flames. This time our squadron had lost only two planes—which wasn't too bad.

Then came something that should have tipped us off. We were requested to drop leaflets over the enemy lines. I still have one of those leaflets and on reading it over I understand why we didn't like the idea of dropping them. Up to that point none of us fliers had doubted for a moment that Germany was going to win the war. That, indeed, was our reason for fighting the war. The leaflets which we had to drop were titled "*Pourquoi?*" (Why?) and under this title there were two pages of printed text in

French, in which we, the Germans, asked the French why this war should be continued. We said that we should be only too happy to make peace, but that France was prevented from doing so by England and also by America, which had decided to continue the war until the utter destruction of Europe was achieved. There was some mention of the sufferings of women and children and the enormous sacrifices—and would it do anybody any good? Certainly not the French. So let's make peace. . . .

Well, that hadn't sounded too well. But somehow we never thought that the reason for such leaflets was that our war was already lost. In the beginning of August the Allies had broken the German lines north of the old Roman road from St. Quentin to Amiens, and we had had to move our airdromes steadily backward. Of course, we had no idea at that time that Ludendorff and Hindenburg had already declared that they could not win the war. It was only now, at the end of September, when our so-called "fire circus" was suddenly canceled, that we really became suspicious.

Still, our spirits were unbroken. Even when the backward movement started in earnest. From that night in September until the day of the Armistice we changed airdromes four times and were bombed more and more often by the Allies. Our own night bombing was continually reduced. "The front lines are too uncertain," we were told. They were uncertain, and naturally night bombing was out when you did not know whom you were going to hit. That was the end of the strategic air war as far as we were concerned. We had to assist the infantry on the battlefield. We were sent on reconnaissance. We had to strafe the ground and do some low-level bombing flights

in order to support the "planned retreat" of our troops—
yes, already then it was called that.

The orders for this type of co-operational work were
not as precise as our orders had been all these years. It
was all very confusing. Commanders who asked for our
co-operation didn't know themselves where their troops
were stationed, and we had never been trained in this
kind of observation work. Furthermore, these armed reconnaissance flights became costly. Not that we were not
willing to take risks. But we began to feel that our actions
no longer had any definite purpose, not even to mention a
defined purpose, and that we were just being sent up to
create some illusion of action. That made us mad, and we
began to resent the useless murdering of our comrades and
the damage to our planes. The emergency airports we now
used were not well enough equipped to handle our heavily
loaded bombers. The strain increased.

The worst, of course, was the fact that the Allied air
forces were by now vastly superior in numbers, and their
pilots were confident of the approaching breakdown of
the German war machine. The Allied aircraft were superior also in quality, and the other side knew it only too
well. Inspection of our planes shot down on the other side
had indicated to them that we had no more copper nor
rubber, that the welding work on our steel spars was
faulty, that our fuel—a benzol-alcohol mixture—often contained so much water that the engines began to cough.

We were getting nervous. One night a German anti-
aircraft battery near our airdrome fired at my plane and
with the first salvo shot half my tail off. This was the first
time I had been hit by flak during the whole war. It seemed
highly symbolic to me. What was the use of precisely cal-

culated and daringly executed forays when everything around us was crumbling? What was the use anyhow?

We began to feel frustrated.

We had just changed our airdromes again, and I had to fly my twin-engined bomber eastward to the new airport early in the morning. It was bitter cold in the half burnt out house near our landing field where we spent the night, keeping warm by feeding some Louis XIV chairs to the fire in the enormous fireplace.

Shortly after I had fallen asleep, I heard light artillery and machine-gun fire on the ground. We soon learned that the machine-gun fire came from our troops aiming at reconnaissance parties. I went on sleeping, at least I tried to. Then my chief mechanic rushed in and told me to take off immediately if I didn't want to be captured. I rushed to the airdrome where the mechanics had already warmed up the engines and climbed into the rear gunner's seat. Just before opening up the engines, I heard machine-gun fire from across the field and as I had to take off in the direction it came from, I didn't feel too good.

When I was up about a hundred feet, I saw that the troops who were firing below were wearing British battle bowlers. The British were taking our airfield, and I managed to get away only on my few seconds' head start.

I flew in the direction of Liége. I still wasn't out of danger. My port engine didn't work properly and it overheated rapidly. I could not gain much altitude, what with my crew of three mechanics in the back, and the baggage and the supply of spare parts and tools which we had loaded into the plane. After we had flown about fifty miles, the ailing engine stopped altogether. It was clear to me that a piston had seized.

I found a field near a little village and landed there. We found that a bullet had pierced the cylinder and caused the failure. Immediately upon our landing, a disorderly crowd of young German soldiers swarmed all over the field, shouting at us that the war would be over shortly, that a revolution had broken out in Germany, and that Soviets were being formed by soldiers and workers in order to lead the German army back home.

I didn't believe a word of it. My observer fired a few rounds over the heads of the crowd when some of the soldiers tried to loot our plane for "souvenirs." That didn't look too good to us. Finally, an officer appeared and we requisitioned his car for my observer and the chief mechanic to drive to our headquarters for a new engine so we could fly back. That was at about eight-thirty in the morning.

At three o'clock in the afternoon they came back without an engine. My observer's face was deadly white. "There is no use exchanging the engine," he murmured. "We have to give up the plane and return to the squadron by car." And then, as an afterthought:

"The Armistice has broken out."

The Armistice conditions saw to it that there would be no German air force, even before the peace itself was negotiated.

Article IV demanded the surrender of 2,000 fighters and night bombers. The surrender of half the material had to take place before November 21, the rest of it before December 2. The number of 2,000 was later reduced to 1,700.

Then came a new order from the Armistice Commission, according to which 600 more airplanes had to be surrendered before the first of January, or, if that was impossible, twenty horses should be substituted for each missing plane. . . . By December 12, the Armistice Commission stated that 2,000 planes had already been surrendered or abandoned, but that only 750 fighters and 25 night bombers had been accounted for. The rest of the lot was made up mostly of obsolete planes and training machines. Many of the first-line squadrons had simply not obeyed orders.

Anyhow, that seemed to be the end of the German air force—at least, that's what it seemed in those days. It had not had a long life, so far. It had been created on October 1, 1912, and when the war broke out only 34 units were in service. But on this November 10, when everything was over, 306 squadrons were in existence.

Between 1914 and 1918 the German air force had trained 17,000 men as pilots and crew. Of these 17,000 men, 4,600 had been killed in action, 2,000 had been killed behind the front lines, 4,300 had been wounded, and 3,100 were missing or were prisoners. So there were really only a few of us around when the curtain went down.

But we German pilots would never have given up. In spite of the depressing last weeks the morale of our men did not decline. (The morale of the German army in general did not decline but broke down.) We had not had the kind of mental training that today's Nazi fliers have—a training to die for an ideal or for a Fuehrer. We wanted very much to live. But we had very definite ideas about the kind of life we wanted to live. We had an uncertain craving for something "decent," for something free from all the dirt and dust of the daily struggle. Flying high up in the air, the little things down below seemed unimportant to us and not worth while.

We didn't consider ourselves heroes. We had long ago

given up bragging, and we were ashamed of the way reporters wrote us up. Perhaps when we started to fly we had been "patriotic" and "heroes" and very sentimental to boot. Now we felt that we were only doing our duty, and since the duty was flying we felt it was rather a privilege.

And now it was all over. Or, as my observer and many of my comrades used to say, "The Armistice had broken out."

To tell the truth, we German fliers were by no means happy that the war was over.

We had had a better living than the rest of the army. We had better uniforms. We got better food, we had more time to ourselves. We were an aggressive sort. And we felt ourselves to be an elite.

Yet, the fact that our morale was excellent while the mass of the German army was in a state of demoralization did not have so much to do with material things as with our mentality—the very special mentality of fliers everywhere in the world. I said we felt like an elite. Flying somewhere in the immense ether, often alone, made us feel superior to the little beings down below, to the small business being enacted miles beneath us. We felt somewhat as follows: Here I am all by myself, there are thousands of anti-aircraft guns, there are thousands of searchlights, there are hundreds of fighters after me. And in spite of them all I'll come back....

We had a special sort of pride.

And now that the war was coming to an end, our superiority, though perhaps imagined, seemed to come to an end. What were we going to do? Most of us were very young, in fact most of us had left school in order to become fliers. Now we had no place to go, we had nothing to do.

Even before the war ended we felt nostalgia. We looked for an object for our dreams, an object for our idealism.

I think it was then and there, while we were on our way back to Germany during those first days of the Armistice, that most of us decided to go on flying—no matter what.

It was this decision not to give up flying, this readiness to go on—no matter what the peace conditions might be, no matter what would be allowed or forbidden in the future—it was this psychological willingness on the part of many young German men that formed the basis for what was later to become the Luftwaffe. Though, of course, none of us knew it then or even imagined it.

This nostalgia for something better, for something higher (in the best sense of the word), this passion for flying—which with many of us was almost a sickness—grew stronger and stronger during the next few years of revolution, inflation, and unemployment, when life became all but hopeless and without point for a great part of the German people. For many of us flying became the very meaning of life.

The moment my observer told me about the Armistice I pulled the fuse of the destroyer charge and blew up the fuel tank—according to our instructions never to surrender a plane. When we drove away we saw the black smoke for a long time.

The next weeks—my next weeks—were full of burning planes, of planes reduced to scrap. I don't remember very well all the phases of my return to Germany. I only remember that our ground crews revolted one night and left for Germany with all our supplies and cars and trucks. Finally we managed to repair a broken down truck on which we transported our most valuable instruments, a few supplies, and those of our men who were not fit to march. But long before we reached the German frontier the car broke down. Then we just got out and marched home.

During my retreat I saw planes abandoned in France and in Belgium because they were no longer fit to be flown or had been damaged deliberately by the hostile population or by the revolutionary ground personnel or just because there was no fuel. Also abandoned were immense amounts of spare engines, spare parts, tools, ammunition, instruments—every kind of equipment farther behind in the reserve depots and in the repair centers, nearly all of which were located in the occupied countries. Nobody thought of salvaging all this material; nobody seemed interested.

A great many planes and engines were lost in the Rhineland and, indeed, everywhere in Germany. Training planes and also fighters and bombers which were about to be sent to the front. They were abandoned and pillaged and looted by souvenir hunters and by scrap thieves. Many of the planes which had already been put on freight trains were simply broken to bits—for scrap, for fire wood, by the starving population. You couldn't blame those people. They needed the wood. They needed the few pennies they got for the scrap. And, anyhow, planes to them were the very symbol of war—which they hated above all.

The greatest number of planes was, of course, still concentrated in the factories and in the reserve depots and in training centers. The destruction of most of them started only after Versailles. But during the last weeks of 1918 some of them were already being torn to pieces and smashed with heavy hammers; propellers were broken, precision instruments were shattered, and some of the wrecks were thrown into yards where they rusted for years. It seemed the end. This return to Germany was a nightmare for those of us who loved flying. It was worse, much worse, than all the dangers of war I had been through.

What now?

As I have said, most of us fliers had decided that we would want to go on flying, no matter what. Of course there were some who decided that there was no future in flying in the Republic of Germany and that was that, as far as they were concerned. Ironically enough, those men who immediately after World War I quit flying cold later came back to flying when the Nazis took over, and it was they who made the most noise about their love for aviation and how much German aviation owed to them. In fact, if you listen to them—and they make it difficult for anybody not to listen to them—it was they who were responsible for the rebirth of German aviation after Versailles. The most prominent among this group is Hermann Goering. I shall have something more to say about him later and about his worthy friends.... There was another group that did not see any chance for the immediate continuation of flying—as they understood it. To them flying meant military flying. So they did the logical thing. They went into the new German army, the Reichswehr, as officers, and it was they who during the next years were the hidden forces that fought for the rebuilding of military aviation, not without success, as I shall later show.

And there was a third group of us—I think it was by far the largest—which consisted of young men who just wanted to fly. Since they were mostly so young that they didn't know anything about flying except the flying itself, they decided to learn something about it. They went to universities and technical schools.

I myself belonged to this group. I had always wanted to be an engineer. Now, of course, I wanted to be an aircraft engineer. So I went to a university in the Rhineland to study and take my exams. It felt a bit funny in the beginning to be back in school after I had felt myself to be a master of the air. But I got used to it. And only a few weeks after the end of the war I was just another student.

We looked funny enough, young former soldiers and former fliers that filled the universities of Germany. We were twenty and twenty-one and twenty-two years old, and the poor food of these past few years and, indeed, of the years to come made most of us look thin and frail and even younger than we were. Many of us didn't have any civilian clothes to wear. We wore our old uniforms. We cut the metal buttons from the jackets—that was all. We had no goal but to study as fast and as much as we could in order to make something of ourselves. And all the time we had a dream. It was the dream of flying again.

I remember one day in the spring of 1919 when some of us young students—all former fliers—got together to found a *Verein*, a kind of club. The name I have forgotten, but it doesn't matter anyhow because it was a very innocuous name which didn't mean a thing. It didn't express the one and only goal of our *Verein*, which was to fly again.

As far as our university, or even the whole youth of the Rhineland, was concerned, this was the birth of the glider movement.

This movement was born spontaneously and grew simultaneously in many parts of Germany during 1919 and 1920. I think the only explanation for this amazing fact was to be found in the attitude of the German youth, in its decision to go on flying—no matter what. I do not know why it happened that the Rhoen mountains in central Germany became the Mecca of the new movement, though there had been some glider experiments in the Rhoen even before the war. Probably the Rhoen became the center because it was in the geographical center of Germany and thus easily reached by all the young men, who didn't have the money for long journeys. As it was, the whole glider business, cheap as it was compared with any other kind of flying, presented almost insurmountable difficulties and the greatest sacrifices for us penniless young men. But it didn't matter. Here again was a chance to fly—and, incidentally, to fly without doing something illegal. The Treaty of Versailles had not restricted gliding, for the simple reason that there had been no gliding at the time of Versailles.

Or, to be precise, there had been some gliding but it was too experimental and too obscure for the men who formulated the Treaty of Versailles to know much about it. Of course, the science of gliding goes back to Otto Lilienthal, who made his first attempts from a little mountain in Pomerania as far back as 1891. His first attempts were mainly based on research on the flying of birds. A few years later, Lilienthal was injured in a fall and died. By that time he had achieved something like 300 meters—a fantastic distance for those early years.

The Wright brothers took up gliding in the beginning of our century. They really built the first effective glider, but they went a step further and invented the motor-driven plane. And from then on, gliding was practically forgotten and only considered as one stepping stone in the development of motor-driven planes. So it was only logical that gliding should make its reappearance in a country which was not allowed to possess any motor-driven planes, or at any rate only a very limited number, and whose population was much too poor to afford motor-driven planes.

We started, really, from scratch. A few seconds in the air seemed all we would ever be able to attain. A minute, we thought, would not be so easy to accomplish.

Of course our planes were extremely primitive because they had to be extremely inexpensive. We had to build them ourselves, and we had to get the material ourselves.

During the daytime we studied at universities or worked in factories. And at night we constructed our gliders, using wood and cotton which we collected from our friends, our parents, or sometimes even the owner of a factory who was mildly interested in the new sport. Occasionally the airplane industry came around with some cotton fabrics or even a bit of metal. But that didn't happen very often.

There was also the question of transporting the planes to the Rhoen. We couldn't afford the expensive freight rates of the railway. Therefore, we had to construct our gliders so that they could be taken apart and folded up, which made the rates somewhat less terrific. We took them ourselves into freight cars and hovered over them, defending our contraptions passionately against the mistrustful looks of the railway employees who were pretty sure that we were crazy. In a way, we probably were. So we arrived at the Rhoen. Many of us were so poor that we never thought of paying for a room or even for a bed at the modest inn in Gersfeld near the Wasserkuppe, the highest mountain in the Rhoen. We slept in tents or sleeping bags or whatever we brought along in the way of ersatz. Some of us who brought our gliders in coffin-like boxes slept in those boxes.

That was not as easy as it sounds now, twenty years afterward. The weather was raw; it rained day and night for more than two weeks. So we had to wait in the fog and rain. What we possessed in the way of covers and blankets we used to protect our precious gliders against the rain. We didn't mind getting wet. We sat on the mountain and waited, shivering, looking out for better weather and talking about the future of Germany in general and our own future in particular.

I still remember a sixteen-year-old boy who was with us and who had arrived with a glider made of odds and ends of wood and paper. He was terribly excited and hardly talked to any of us. His name was Peter Riedel. Twenty years later he was to be German air attaché in Washington, D. C.—the last attaché before the outbreak of World War II.

Among those present—at the inn in Gersfeld—were also Professors Ludwig Prandtl and Theodor von Karman, now director of the Guggenheim Institute at the California Institute of Technology. There was also an especially attractive young man with a beautiful wife, who had been an *Oberleutnant* during the war, and seemed very much interested in our doings. His name was Kurt Student. He is today chief of the German parachutists.

Well, finally the rain stopped, the cover of fog tore open, and the atmosphere began to clear. Immediately we started to send our gliders up into the air. Among the many entries was my plane, called "Black Devil" because it was covered with black cotton. For a few minutes I was the happy holder of a world record on the "Black Devil." First, Dr. Klemperer—today an engineer in the Douglas Aircraft Company—tried and achieved a flight that lasted something like 1½ minutes. Then I came along and bettered his record by another half minute. Then Klemperer tried again and set the unheard-of world record of 2½ minutes in the air, which as far as I know was not beaten till the next year.

Records ... sport. Yes, it was only a sport in the beginning. Records and world records were established and
broken, our frail gliders often pancaked. We were jubilant
over improvements in our craft, and in general we had a
lot of fun. None of us then dreamed that our youthful
attempts would be of great military value in later years.

Today, of course, I know. Today I know a lot of things
I would not have believed had anybody told them to me in
1920 or 1921. Today I know that in a way our innocent
gliding in the Rhoen helped to lay the foundation for the
Luftwaffe. It helped instill in those of us who had not been
in the war the excitement of flying. It helped those of us
who had flown to become even more enthusiastic and even
more determined never to give up flying—no matter what.

But soon there were other, much graver developments.
The army became interested in our innocent little sport and
some of us were subsidized. Our attempts were subsidized,
innocently enough, by the Ministry of Traffic, behind
which was, not innocently at all, the army. We were approached with suggestions to experiment along half-mili-
tary lines. Well, we hardly realized what it meant at that
time.

Neither did many of us realize what it meant when years
afterward the Nazi party became violently interested in
gliding and subsidized our sports movement by creating
national competitions with many interesting prizes. Those
prizes were furnished to the Party by a certain industry
which hoped that, once the Nazis came to power, rearmament would start in earnest. At that time I had progressed
far beyond the glider movement. I had become a grown
man and earned my livelihood in the aircraft industry. I
was no longer in touch with gliding and had no idea that

it had become more and more a Nazi movement. I can still
remember the shock I felt when I revisited the Rhoen after
many years, in the summer of 1932. A little monument
had been erected at the spot where we had made our first
attempts, honoring those attempts. And there was an in-
scription that read:

> *"Wir deutschen Flieger*
> *Wurden Sieger*
> *Durch uns allein.*
> *Volk flieg Du wieder*
> *Und Du wirst Sieger*
> *Durch Dich allein."*

(We German fliers became victorious through ourselves
alone. German Nation, you must fly and you will be
victorious through yourself alone.)

That was in 1932, many months before the Nazis came
to power, in fact, at a moment when not many in Germany
seriously believed that the Nazis would ever come to
power. But it was typical Nazi poetry. It proved to me
then that in any case the Nazis had taken over the glider
movement.

But, as so often happens in history, they had taken over
something which they had by no means started. We young
Germans who had traveled to the Rhoen, starving and
freezing, had done it without any idea of a war of re-
venge in the future. We had done it because we wanted
to fly. We had done it because we did not want to give
up our dream of flying. And even now I cannot condemn
this dream of flying, though on it were laid the first
foundations of the Luftwaffe.

2. *The Grand Old Man*

In 1923 I was still studying at my Rhenish university
and also conducting experiments dealing with combustion
in engines. I had become my professor's assistant. He
thought a lot of our experiments, but I had no idea that he
was talking about them outside of the laboratory and was
therefore quite surprised when one day an old gentleman, a
friend of my professor's, appeared and expressed his interest in the experiments.

Of course, I recognized him at once. Anybody in Germany, and I'd almost say anybody in the world who was
interested in flying or engines or anything having to do
with flying, would have recognized him immediately. The
little, wiry man with the miraculously youthful body, the
important head covered with thick white hair, the large
forehead, the blue eyes that sometimes seemed the eyes of
a dreamer and sometimes the eyes of a cynic, the energetic
chin—once you saw him, even in pictures, you could not
forget him.

That was Professor Hugo Junkers.

He was very much interested in the experiments which
were to serve as the basis for my doctor's thesis. For hours
—on that first day and on other occasions—he listened to
my explanations. I shall not go into that now since it is
involved and technical and today of historical interest only.
But I will never forget my excitement on that first visit of
his to my laboratory, the thrill I experienced when he

20

actually sat down with me to discuss my problems, and my astonishment and admiration for him when I realized that within ten or fifteen minutes he understood what I was driving at. He talked about the problem as though he had been pondering its intricacies for many weeks or even months.

He returned the next day. As a matter of fact he came back many days in succession, just to watch me or glance through my notes. He asked pertinent questions, made suggestions, and just by being there helped a lot to clarify points in my mind which somehow I had never been able to clarify for myself.

It was at least a week before he seemed to realize that, quite aside from my experiments, I was there, too—that is, that I existed. He asked me about my life. When I told him that I had been a flier, he raised his eyebrows.

Then he said, "How would you like to work with me?"

How would anyone who was interested in aircraft mechanics and who was a fool for flying like to work for the outstanding man in the world as far as aircraft construction was concerned? I could hardly speak. But Professor Junkers did not expect an answer. He went on talking about the experiment, asking other questions, suggesting other approaches, and he seemed to have forgotten his offer entirely. Only when he left that day, he said, "Good, then you are going to work with me as soon as you have taken your doctorate and you are finished here."

That was his last visit to my laboratory. The next day he left town.

That was in 1923, when the Allies had occupied the Rhineland on account of nonpayment of reparations. It was a wild and exciting time. The heads of German industry, especially of heavy industry, and also the owners of the big coal mines and steel concerns had proclaimed passive resistance. The Government of the Reich, then briefly headed by Dr. Wilhelm Cuno, a rightist and a man closely allied with heavy industry, had backed up this passive resistance. There were acts of sabotage in the Rhineland, a few train wrecks occurred, and the Allies took measures to prevent further sabotage. One of the measures consisted of forcing professors and university assistants to travel on every train that was run through the Rhineland or the Ruhr district—as preventive hostages. Many a night I studied for my thesis sitting in a third-class compartment in one of those trains between Cologne, Dusseldorf, Aachen, Duisburg, etc. Occasionally I slept, too, but only occasionally.

It was all very weird, strange, nightmarish.

Then I finished my thesis and I wondered what next. At that time it was practically impossible for any of us to travel from the occupied Rhineland into Germany proper. So I looked around for a job in the Rhineland. One day a Belgian officer connected with some kind of a commission tipped me off that I was going to be arrested the following night with a few dozen other university men. I was not very much afraid or even unduly excited because I knew that we would be released eventually. But eventually—that might mean weeks or months, and I did not feel like losing weeks or months. It was then that I decided to get out of the occupied zone.

I escaped. There was no chance for me to negotiate the "frontier" between the Rhineland and the rest of Germany. But the Belgian officer helped me to get from the Rhineland into Holland; from there I caught a train to Berlin. And from Berlin I went to Dessau, where the Junkers company was.

I didn't ask for Junkers himself. I asked for a job. I got a job. I was put into a department which was preparing to build a factory in or near Moscow. After a few weeks I was made assistant to the chief of the department, and later on I was made liaison engineer. I traveled to Moscow quite frequently during the next six months or so.

I saw Junkers occasionally when he went through the building in which I was working, but he did not seem to see me. We never talked. After about six months I was put in charge of building a repair plant for the factory. Three months later, I was taken over by the department of "air traffic" which then had just started to be developed.

Late in 1924, an American who was very much interested in our air traffic plans appeared in Dessau. He came with a personal introduction from Henry Ford to Junkers. One morning the Professor came to my office together with the American. It was only then that he saw me for the first time.

"Don't I know you?" he asked me and went on, "Of course, I know you. I remember your experiments very well. Why didn't you come and ask me for a job?"

"I have a job," I said. And I told him I had thought it might be better if I first proved what I could do and then got in touch with him.

Junkers nodded. He liked that. A few days later he asked me to come to his office. That was the first of a number of talks. He told me what he thought and he asked my opinion. We became better and better acquainted. We became friends. He trusted me. During the next ten years or so we never lost contact with each other. Sometimes I traveled for him, in Russia or the Near East or in Africa, and he would send me a wire asking me to go back to consult with him. Sometimes, when he took a vacation, he would telephone me and have me come to Bad Gastein, an Austrian spa, and we would talk for hours and hours about all the problems connected with aviation and the aircraft business.

I still can see him: his energetic and serious face, his wiry, mobile body, his sometimes dreamy and sometimes ironic eyes. He was a strange kind of person, an eccentric. He loved old clothes and especially old hats, and it was almost impossible for Frau Junkers to get him to buy a new suit. If he did he wouldn't wear it anyhow. He had a passion for sun baths. If he could spare an hour or so he would get out of his office, slip into his trunks, and lie in the sun on his private terrace. Sometimes he would call us for conference onto his sun terrace.

But even there he was never without his little notebook. He carried it everywhere. I think he must even have gone to bed with it. He was forever taking out the little notebook and writing something into it, some new idea which more often than not had nothing to do with the conversation he was carrying on at the particular time. Every now and then his secretaries would get hold of the precious little volume, hover over it for hours, trying to make out what he had written, and transfer all the jottings to little cards which were indexed and cross-indexed for further reference. Those little cards were really the foundation stones for some of Junkers' most important inventions.

In Gastein he and his wife used to live on a strict diet. He ate a lot during the day but in the evening he ate only an apple and half a slice of bread with butter. Why, I never found out. But he insisted that I either share this diet or remove myself from his table. Of course, I chose to starve.

It was a great honor for me to be invited to Gastein. Ordinarily, Junkers didn't like seeing too many people. He was always afraid of the celebrities who traveled to

Dessau and wanted to be entertained. He was equally afraid of the people who came to Dessau just to meet him—as a celebrity. Often he would simply hop into a plane and fly away from it all to his little bungalow in Bayrisch Zell. But if and when he decided to be the host, he was a wonderful host. The reason he didn't like people was that he didn't like to talk in generalities. He loved to talk problems and new solutions. He had, of course, to give many lectures. He wasn't a very good speaker because he didn't care for effect. But what he had to say was extremely stimulating to those who understood. It was interesting to note to what degree his urge to create something new, to use approaches that had never been tried out before, and his contempt for routine as such were mirrored in his language. He hated nothing so much as ready-made phrases and clichés, and if you used them you really made him angry. Every one of us who collaborated with him was very careful to watch his language.

Junkers had a family of twelve children, and he was a good father, though a very unconventional one. He never tried to interfere in the personal affairs of his children. His oldest daughter Hertha is pretty well known in this country, since in 1928 she became the President of the Junkers Corporation in the United States. She later married a Nazi farmer. Another daughter married a Communist. Junkers didn't mind.

There was a period when he named every new plane after one of his children. Then he gave up. "I can't produce children that fast," he laughed.

In a way, we, his close collaborators, were just as much his children as his real children. He always insisted that a technical product could never be created by a single person without using all the resources which had previously been created by others, and without the collaboration of a great number of human brains. He didn't like the word "employee." We were his collaborators or his friends. "Every effort is collective," he once said. That made him the opposite of practically everybody else in the aircraft industry. All the other aircraft geniuses were stars, or at least tried to act like stars. Junkers invariably played down his own importance and played up the work of his collaborators. He considered the fact that he owned the company or certain parts of it more or less a technicality. "I'm only a trustee," he said.

Once, when publicly praised for his inventive genius, he answered in his shy and humble way, "To each great invention there may be a contribution of genius. But it amounts to hardly more than 5 per cent. The other 95 per cent is sweat."

He was, however, by no means jovial or patriarchal in his relations with his collaborators. Neither was he expansive with his family. He had a theory as to how to achieve the most fruitful collaboration. According to him, it came about through the creation of a *Gefälle* (a gradient). He liked nothing better than to pit his children against each other, to have them disagree, because he thought that by airing and having to fight for their points of view they would become clearer in their own minds and would arrive at something constructive. His procedure was exactly the same with us, his collaborators. Therefore, the meetings with him were by no means nice, quiet gatherings. They were extremely stormy. With almost fiendish joy he would incite us to prove each other wrong, to prove that the plans of this or the other one were impossible and why. He would induce us to go to extremes. Then, when we were all excited and pleaded our cases passionately, he would listen to us carefully and seemingly calmly, only to get excited himself after a short time, to start shouting himself and banging his fist on the table.

Then, suddenly, he would calm down, take out his notebook, make a few entries, smile, and very lucidly sum up the situation. He never had a personal grudge against any of us on account of a disagreement with our ideas. He did not mind when we went out on a limb in one way or another—on the contrary, he loved it. He said that the presentation of an idea or a project that was absolutely unworkable very often could lead to the finding of something workable. And he was right. Sometimes, with the aid of his notebook, he would come back to suggestions made years before in such conferences, and while they had then looked silly and utterly fantastic, they didn't look silly any more.

He didn't handle us gently. Nor was he easy on himself. When he sent his first expedition to South America—that was in 1923—to show his first passenger plane, F 13, he sent his son Werner along. When Werner was killed in a crash there, he felt the loss as keenly as any father. But much later he told me, "I think I was right. Have I the right to risk the life of other people's sons if I don't want to risk the life of my own son?"

He was consistent. Seeing us not as employees but as collaborators meant that he saw us as human beings with responsibilities and a right to our own opinions. That is, he saw us as free people. He was democratic, and not only inside his factory. He was a democrat through and through. He belonged to the Democratic party until 1930, when he became disgusted with politics in general and with the Democratic party in particular, because it was no longer democratic.

He was consistent. Because he was a true democrat, he was a true internationalist. He was for international co-operation in all fields. He was for the brotherhood of all peoples in the world. And that, for him, was by no means a hazy dream. He was very matter-of-fact about it. In fact, he thought that aviation could play a decisive part in bringing about such an international commonwealth.

Once he told me, "The airplane will become a weapon of happy humanitarianism that will carry blessings to all people and all nations and that will bring back blessings from all peoples and all nations." He thought that by making the world smaller, the plane would help the nations of the world to become better acquainted with each other and thus to understand each other.

Small wonder that Professor Junkers was thrown into a rage when, shortly after World War I was over, he was asked by certain men in the German government—I shall have more to say about them later—to design his passenger planes so that they could easily be converted into bombers.

Professor Junkers was consistent. Since he considered all his inventions collective inventions, he was very much against exploiting the people who worked for him. The workers, the technicians, everybody. He was against exploitation anyhow. He was against industrial activity for profit's sake alone. He thought it immoral. He thought it interfered with his duty of social responsibility. He thought it the duty of an industrial leader to see to it that his collaborators were not dismissed when profits ran low. And he insisted on raising the living standard of the workers, not only because he knew that would mean good business, but also urged by his strong sense of social responsibility.

He felt strongly that the capitalistic system was bankrupt. To build up an industry only for the profit of a few
leaders seemed unethical to him. He felt that there was no
reason for the so-called economic cycles, the periods of
depression and of prosperity. Because they were caused
neither by corresponding fluctuations on the production
side nor by fluctuations in the basic demand. The only
groups which, in his opinion, caused these cycles were
financiers—or, as he termed them, "money manipulators"—
bureaucrats, and politicians, whom he referred to as "para-
sites on the body of creative and productive humanity."
Though he did not like politicians, he sometimes talked
these things over with them. But he never got an honest or
reasonable statement of their case from them, nor did he
from the Communists or the Nazis or the so-called German
Democrats.

"We can hope to solve these questions only if we approach them scientifically," he once told me. "The only
basis from which to start is responsibility. And those politicians don't know what that means."

His anti-capitalistic conceptions seemed even stranger
since he was a very rich man—in fact, one of the richest
men in Germany. He was financially independent, something very rare in the aircraft industry, which is dependent
upon enormous capital investments and was even more so
in the early days than now, since there were fewer markets
and fewer returns on the money invested. He was independent mainly through the profits from two of his
companies—the IKO, a factory that made bath heaters,
and the JUMO, the motor factory. A short outline of
Junkers' life and of his great achievements should make this
clearer.

Junkers was born in 1859, in Reydt, of an old Rhineland family. In 1888, after his graduation from the technical university in Berlin, he became an assistant to Wilhelm Oechselhaeuser, who had founded the powerful Continental Gas Company in Dessau and was trying to find new possibilities for his company. Oechselhaeuser charged Junkers with the development of gas engines, a task in which Junkers showed his outstanding scientific and technical talent and his profound understanding of economics. A few years later Junkers broke away and founded his own company to manufacture bath heaters, and in 1897 he became professor of thermodynamics at the technical university at Aachen, where he stayed until 1911. It was there that he collaborated with Professor Reissner, who started his test flights with a duck-type aircraft with an elevator in front. (Reissner is today in the United States.) On February 1, 1910, Junkers took out his now famous flying-wing patent, which was to become basic not only in his own work but also in the development of the modern cantilever monoplane throughout the whole world.

Later he left Aachen and returned to do research in Dessau. In 1913, he formed the Junkers Motor Works in Magdeburg, near Dessau, where he developed his stationary double-piston Diesel engine. In 1915 he built his first all-metal cantilever monoplane of steel sheet construction. In 1917, he was forced by the High Command—this was in the middle of the war—to form the Junkers-Fokker Works for the production of Junkers all-metal military aircraft in Duralumin sheet construction. Immediately after the war, however, he formed his own Junkers Aircraft Company in Dessau, and by spring of 1919 had brought out on the market the first all-metal airplane designed for purely civilian use, with a cabin for four passengers and a cockpit for two pilots. This was the F 13 which has already been mentioned.

F 13 was to become famous all over the world. General Billy Mitchell, for one, was so enthusiastic about it that he ordered the first batch for the newly created United States mail service. The planes were delivered in the summer of 1919.

In 1922, Junkers prepared to build a big aircraft factory in Fili, near Moscow—an adventure which was to prove fateful. He also obtained a concession for airlines in Soviet Russia. The next year he formed another Junkers company for the construction of his gasoline aero-engines and of the first Diesel aero-engine to fly successfully after 1929. In 1924, he consolidated his airline division in the Junkers Air Transport Company, and put on the market the first three-engined all-metal passenger plane, G 24. Only a year later, he was forced to give up his vastly expanded airline undertaking, with the German government on the receiving end, at a time when he owned the greatest aircraft manufacturing and operating organization in the world. It was a plot which, in a way, can be considered the most important turning point in the development of the Luftwaffe, and which I shall refer to again at greater length.

In 1926 Junkers built his three-engined transport plane, G 31, which had been perfected on the basis of performance records of planes in the Junkers airlines, and in 1929 he brought out the highly successful Ju 52, which incorporated the improvements based on experiences of Junkers airlines in Persia and the Middle East. (Ju 52, although now 14 years old, is still considered the best German transport plane.)

This may suffice as a short biography of a very successful self-made man. He made most of his money with his gas stove, which he had invented when he was trying to find new ways of using gas. He also made a great deal selling licenses abroad, for instance, the patent of his first monoplane, for which America, among others, paid license fees up to 1937. Later, he received large sums of money from the export of Junkers planes all over the world.

In a way it always seemed to me that Junkers very much resembled Henry Ford. Both were self-made men, both were extremely successful, both had revolutionized their particular branch of production. Once, during one of our lengthy conversations in Bad Gastein, I talked with Junkers about Ford. Junkers had met Ford personally, I think it was in 1928, shortly after a Junkers plane achieved the first east-west Atlantic crossing. Junkers admitted readily that Ford had done civilization a great service. He admired Ford's mechanical devices and his manufacturing methods. He disliked the subjugation of long-due developments to considerations of mass production. He deplored the fact that Ford was only a businessman with no interest in scientific progress.

He never tried to hide the fact that he disliked Henry Ford as a person. He was amazed and repelled by Ford's intolerance, his anti-Semitism; he despised him for his lack of social sense and responsibility. Junkers' criticism of the American industrialist was not so much directed against his dismissal of men when business slackened as against his annual practice of laying off thousands while he re-tooled for a new model. Junkers felt there was something wrong with an industrial leader who was, as the Professor saw it, indifferent to the economic security and the human dignity of the individual.

But, then, in spite of his success in business, Junkers really was not a businessman at heart.

In his company all his love belonged to the research institute. He was never interested in production for itself; he was interested only in getting the experience, in finding out whether the lines developed in the research institute came up to the requirements of the practical. He felt the same way about his airlines; for him they were a testing ground.

He always went on learning. He was never arrogant. He never professed to know things. He was almost humble in his scientific and technical discussions.

Strangely enough, especially in a scientist, he was a great gambler. He liked to stake everything on one card. He risked everything in order to get ahead. But, of course, that made him a pioneer, though to others he may have seemed a visionary. That helped him not to get bogged down with the old and tested but to create new and revolutionary ideas and to revolutionize the whole business and science of aircraft.

Junkers forever preached and practiced suspicion of what he termed unalterable facts, petrified theories, and most of all the men who stuck to them. On the other hand, no abstract solution ever satisfied him. An idea, a machine, an organization, or even a social concept did not satisfy him unless it could be made to work, unless it was made to work. And he never allowed himself or others to freeze such solutions. If the economic usefulness of any development seemed to wear out, and even before that point was reached, he constantly tried to improve and to adapt his products as well as his organization and his ideas. Thus, research and change, eternal change became his first concern. Therefore, he was never interested in mass production for its own sake, but only for the sake of improving the product according to its functions. Whenever he could, he left the mass production of his inventions to others.

There is a fundamental, almost dramatic logic in all the inventions of Junkers. They are all organically connected, and each successive invention is only the logical consequence of the preceding one.

When he was first put in charge of developing new uses for gas, back in 1888, he tackled the problem typically by separating it into its component parts and solving each of them separately. At that time there existed no reliable instrument to calculate the caloric value of fuel. Therefore, he first designed such an instrument, using the lamella principle (employment of many thin scales or plates for the purpose of increasing surface space), and it became a device of such fundamental importance that it was adopted everywhere. And Junkers started building that instrument, the Calorimeter, in his own factory at Dessau.

His research into the thermo-dynamic fundamentals of combustion, heat-flow, and heat-transfer then brought him to the point of designing his gas engine with two pistons moving against each other in one cylinder. That principle proved so successful that it was later adapted to the Junkers stationary Diesel engine, to the Junkers truck-aero-Diesels, and found its final expression in the revolutionary free-piston engine Diesel compressor which, without crankshaft, connecting rods, valves, and ignition, is the simplest and most trouble-free piston engine ever designed.

But this development was only one of many that started with the Calorimeter. In the basic research which led Junkers to the invention of the Calorimeter he had, of course, studied the element of heat flow and heat exchange. The complete heat exchange in his Calorimeter gave him the idea of employing the same principle of lamella design in the manufacture of a bath stove heated by gas and automatically regulating the optimum flow of gas and water. Later his bath stove was adapted to liquid fuels and electricity as well as to solid fuels.

There is a direct connection between these inventions and Junkers' subsequent persistent use of thin sheet-metal constructions in all his airplanes, and his lamella roof construction and in the pre-fabricated houses he developed in the thirties.

In investigating the flow of the heated gases, Junkers tried to find the best shape for his lamella for heat transfer. In his typical, methodical way, he designed for himself a wind tunnel to investigate the resistance of bodies of different shapes (that was around 1910).

By that time, Professor Eiffel of Paris had already made his aero-dynamic investigations to determine wind pressure—as a prerequisite to building his famous tower. In his classic book *The Resistance of the Air*, he had published his results, showing that the thinner the profile, the smaller the resistance it would offer to inflowing gases.

Junkers did not accept that generalization, which, indeed, would not have fitted the principle of his bath stove. That is, the flow of the heated gases around the lamella with the least possible resistance. He investigated the limits within which Eiffel had carried through his tests and found that under certain conditions thick airfoil profiles would be superior in wind resistance to thin ones. He not only adapted that new knowledge to his bath stoves, but with his intuitive vision also saw the immense importance of that scientific principle for aircraft—at a time when he had not yet had anything to do with aviation. He recognized the fallacy of aviation pioneers in building aircraft with thin wings, bracing them with a maze of struts and wires, and then putting the engine, pilot, and passengers into the open air stream, thus creating a resistance which even at the low speed of those days prevented many planes from getting into the air at all.

Thus, before working at all in aviation, he arrived at the basic patent of 1910 for the flying wing, a thick cantilever wing inside which were carried engine, passengers, and loads and which was supported entirely by internal rigging which would not add to the drag. Air resistance had to be reduced to a minimum to keep down the engine power required as well as the amount of fuel to be carried. Thus from economic considerations the foundation for modern aircraft was created.

Between 1919 and 1934 the inherent soundness of all of Junkers' inventions and developments became continually more manifest. It is ironic that when he was finally recognized internationally as the greatest genius of modern aviation, he was finished as far as Germany was concerned. The Nazis, of course, could not use a man with such democratic, international, and pacifist ideas.

But the Nazis were by no means the only ones who fought Junkers. Junkers had had to fight all his life. It started in 1898 when the young Professor talked about his revolutionary double-piston engine in the *Schiffsbautechnische Gesellschaft* (Association of Ship Builders). He proposed that his new engine be used in ships. The engineers present were impressed, but immediately realized that anybody who aided Junkers would have to fight the big ship-building companies, which had no desire to adopt a new engine because it would mean the writing off of great investments in existing machinery. It was then that the forces of big business started to fight Junkers, whom they pronounced a "menace" and "too individualistic." This struggle never really ceased. But even more serious was the simultaneous campaign of the German army against Junkers.

The old Professor once said to me that his life was really one long succession of fights with the army. He complained that the army had tried to thwart the whole direction of his ideas and of his work and to subdue his spirit.

It started in 1915 when the army experts ridiculed his efforts to build the first all-steel airplane. They not only criticized that particular project, but tried to discredit Junkers entirely. When his first steel plane flew, and proved to be superior in every respect, the German War Ministry could no longer afford to overlook it. But the generals said, "Junkers may have good ideas, but he is not a flier and not a practical man." So they forced him to take a partner, Anthony Fokker, and to form the Junkers-Fokker Works.

Junkers and Fokker were fundamentally so different in their outlook and conceptions that clashes inevitably occurred all the time and interfered with any really constructive work either of them tried to carry out. They separated shortly afterward.

Almost until the end of the war there were only wooden planes. Junkers built the first steel airplane in 1915. He also built a *Panzer* plane to be used against infantry which flew low and was protected against anti-aircraft. All in all, he built 227 of these planes, not a single one of which had been shot down at the end of the war.

This amazing record did not render Junkers more sympathetic to the army. His great inventive genius seemed lost to them after the war when he came out openly for pacifism and international brotherhood and protested vigorously at the very idea of rearmament. It was on account of this that the army continued its fight against Junkers. It was the final result of many of the army's intrigues that Junkers finally lost his air traffic company. And it was the final victory of the army over Junkers that he was forced to build planes for military use.

This was undoubtedly the greatest tragedy in his life until the Nazis came to power.

3. *The Other Pioneers*

I have written at such length about my old friend and teacher, Professor Junkers, for many reasons, one of which is the curious fact that the Nazis recently have tried to build up a legend that Professor Junkers was one of them. They who did everything to crush him and who, in my opinion, are as responsible for his death as if they had killed him outright, have now the unbelievable impudence to claim this man and to falsify his history and to create a lie. Now, at a time when the Nazis unfortunately are deriving so many advantages from Junkers' inventions, at a time when many types of Junkers aircraft are in the sky to destroy those who fight for democracy and peace and tolerance, somebody should stand up and tell the world that the man who created those planes would be today, as he was all his life, on the side of those who have to fight them.

Another reason why I have written at such length about Junkers is that he really must be considered one of the men who—in spite of himself—helped build the Luftwaffe. If one looks at the enormous spectacle of the rise and fall of the Luftwaffe as a dramatic play, he might be termed the tragic hero.

But aside from all that, I think that any story of aviation in the twentieth century which doesn't reserve one of its important chapters to Junkers would be a falsification of history. He was—and I am not speaking only as his friend, because I know that most of the experts in American aviation are of my opinion—one of the outstanding geniuses of aircraft development after 1910. Of course, there were many other great talents among the pioneers of German aviation who, voluntarily or involuntarily, directly or indirectly, helped to create the Luftwaffe. But they were all overshadowed by far by Hugo Junkers.

I have known them all, Focke, Klemm, Messerschmitt, Dornier, Heinkel, Rohrbach, etc. Sometimes I think I have forgotten them, as I have tried to do very often and very earnestly. But then I open the newspapers and I read about the four-engined heavy bomber of Focke-Wulf, the FW 190 fighter, and the Me 109 and Me 210, the Do 217, the Flying Pencil, the He 111 and He 113 and He 177, the newer four-motored bomber, and I know that I'll never forget them.

One of them, of course, is missing. One of them who was among the most gifted of the pioneers in German aircraft development is no longer represented in the air over Europe. I refer to Dr. Edmund Rumpler.

He had the great misfortune to be born a Jew, and that alone meant that he was doomed when the Nazis came to power, although Goering and Udet liked him very much. However, he never gave up. He stayed in Germany and continued to work on new ideas and new constructions. Shortly before I left Germany for good, he had just finished his design of a cast-iron crankshaft for an aero-engine, very similar to the 1,000-horsepower design he had started to work with in the 1920's. He was very much alone then. He had sent his family out of Germany, I understand, but somehow he could not bring himself to leave, though there was only misery in store for him. Friends have told me that he died shortly before he was to be deported to Poland. I can only say that I hope this is so.

Rumpler became world famous in 1908 when he built a strange airplane called *Die Taube* (the pigeon), which became the most popular airplane in Europe before the war. During the war the improved *Taube* became one of the three standard types used by German flight squadrons. He built other successful war planes such as the Ru C1, a reconnaissance and fighter plane, and the Ru C5, a long-distance reconnaissance plane. The speed and the ceiling of the latter were so superior that it made possible long distance reconnaissance deep into enemy country without protective escort.

Shortly after World War I Rumpler began to lose interest in airplanes. He concentrated more and more on motor cars, and he designed and built in 1928 the first really streamlined car in the world.

Of all the pioneers of German aviation or, let us say, of post-war aviation, Hanns Klemm resembled Junkers the most by far. He, too, wanted to build for peace and not for war. He, too, was an idealist. But he was more sentimental than Junkers, more uneven, and much less of a personality.

Born in 1885, he was a civil engineer until World War I, joined Dornier in 1917, and there learned how to build planes. Early in 1918 he became chief designer of the new aircraft factory of the Daimler Motor Company, and designed two fighter planes. Immediately after the war he switched over to motor cars and became the technical director of the Daimler Body Works. But his interest in aircraft had been stimulated. He switched back again in 1919 and designed and built his first low-powered, light airplane, L 15, equipped with an American 12 horsepower Harley Davidson motor. That was the beginning of a development of which the fruit was to be a great number of airplane models purely for civilian use.

Klemm is a small wiry man, typically Swabian, that is, a square-headed man who always wants his way. He is excitable, and his red mustache seems to bristle, and his eyes behind gold-framed glasses alternately blink and glitter. He speaks with a strong Swabian accent. He is a stern Protestant and has never done and would never do anything that conflicted with his religious beliefs. Small wonder, then, that this rugged individualist has been at loggerheads with the Nazis again and again. He is one of the few men who have never been afraid to tell Goering or Milch exactly what they thought of them and their ideas.

He is not interested in politics. He is interested, though to a lesser degree than Junkers, in humanity. The very idea behind the small planes he built was "a plane for every man."

He never allowed anybody to advise him about the running of his plant. It was all very individualistic. Because he could only work that way, he left the employ of the Daimler people immediately after he had built his first planes and in 1926 started his own company in Boeblingen, near Stuttgart.

In spite of the heavy pressure brought to bear upon him by the Nazis, he declined to build warplanes until the beginning of World War II. When approached by Goering, he pointed out that he would lose his international market and that the Nazis did not want this since his export brought much foreign exchange into Germany. In 1928 the Klemm-Aeromarine Corporation in New Jersey started building Klemm planes in the United States. In 1932 the British Klemm company was formed. In 1939 he sold all his rights in a new design and its production methods to the United States. His sports planes were sold all over the world and were a huge success.

Only once, in 1934, did the Nazis succeed in forcing him to knuckle under and do something about military aviation. They made him build a factory in Halle for all-metal war-planes. But he only stayed till the factory was completed and the planes began rolling off the production line. Then he turned the whole factory over to Fritz Siebel, who was a good friend of Goering's and always willing to take over a smoothly running business. Then Klemm went back to Boeblingen and civil aviation.

Professor Heinrich Focke was the opposite of Klemm, at least externally. He despised loud talking. He was always humble and very much detached, and if you talked business with him or prices he was visibly pained. He was a gentle person and looked much younger than his years. The Nazis didn't like him too well. He was too soft-spoken. He didn't like show enough.

He became interested in airplanes while he was still going to school. It was also at school that he formed his life-long friendship with Georg Wulf, who became his enthusiastic collaborator and his chief pilot.

During the war, Focke worked as an engineer for the German air corps and Wulf served as a pilot. In 1924 they founded, with the help of Bremen financiers, the Focke-Wulf Corporation. They built various transport planes and then returned to manufacturing the so-called *Ente, canard* type; they made it a successful twin-motor plane. In 1927 Wulf crashed in one of these and was killed. Focke later left his company and devoted himself to the development of his helicopter, which in 1937 broke all world records for helicopter flights. It was flown to Berlin and demonstrated in the *Deutschland Halle* (a kind of Madison Square Garden) by a girl pilot. The plane hovered at different altitudes, flying sideways and backward and proving an enormous success.

Focke was not at all interested in military aviation, which meant that the Nazis ultimately were not interested in him either. The many planes which the Focke-Wulf company designed and built for the Luftwaffe before and during the war have nothing to do with Focke himself. Since the outbreak of the war he has devoted himself solely to research and new developments.

Junkers, Klemm, and Focke were all either not interested in or opposed to German rearmament in the air. Rohrbach, Messerschmitt, and Heinkel, on the other hand, were interested in aviation almost entirely from the rearmament angle. In the middle, between the two groups, was Dr. Claude Dornier.

Dornier was a remarkable man. Every time I had anything to do with him he made me feel that he was a personality like Junkers and Klemm. He was a strong individualist. But there was something missing. I think that, deep down in his heart, Dornier himself did not believe in Dornier. He had a great many good ideas, but somehow everybody had the feeling and I think Dornier himself had the feeling, too, that he was the eternal runner-up. If Junkers had not been around, Dornier would undoubtedly have been the first man. But there was Junkers.

Dornier lacked self-confidence. He didn't appear to be a happy man, but looked sullen, sulky. He was always in a bad humor. He was tall and very thin, and he had an intelligent face, but there was something almost sinister about him. He carried himself badly, his shoulders were always stooped, and there was a heavy scar across his chin. Something emanated from Junkers, something which inspired everybody. Nothing went out from Dornier.

Immediately after the war, he asked the German government to subsidize him and his works. I don't think he did it because he wanted to make money. I believe his lack of self-confidence, his unsureness of himself, led him to take this step. During the first few years after Versailles, Dornier went to Switzerland and Denmark to build planes. Later he sold his licenses to Japan, to the United States, to the Dutch East Indies, to Italy, to Spain. In fact, no German engineer has sold more licenses abroad than he. He should have been immensely successful. But somehow he wasn't.

Dornier came from the Zeppelin Airship Company, where he had been an engineer since 1910. A development of special metal sections and of metal propellers soon brought him into close contact with Count Zeppelin himself, who made him in 1912 chief of the department for developing an airship for transatlantic service.

When the war started, Zeppelin made him chief of a new company which was to develop giant flying boats with Duralumin construction. It was thus that Dornier came—in another way than Junkers—to the all-metal airplane.

The most widely used of the Dornier planes was the *Wal*, originally produced seventeen years ago. It was a twin-engined flying boat. The *Wal* was developed into the Do 18, which was fitted with two Junkers Diesel engines. Dornier increased the weight of his planes gradually to ten tons, and with them the regular German airmail service across the Atlantic was started in 1934. Improved versions of the original *Wal* were the Do 14, Do 18, Do 22, Do 24,

and Do 26. After building a much bigger four-engined
super-*Wal* in 1926, Dornier designed and built the Do X
in 1929. It was a 60-ton boat, the biggest that had ever been
built up to that time. Owing to the lack of powerful engines at that time, the Do X had to be equipped with
Curtiss "Conqueror" engines, twelve of which were arranged with their twelve propellers on top of the wings,
and this faulty arrangement was responsible for its poor
performance. In 1931 the famous plane was flown to the
United States, and it lay at anchor for many months in
Long Island Sound before its captain, Friedrich Christiansen—a famous German pilot of World War I and one of
the most infamous Nazis of today—could muster enough
courage to take it back. In fact, it was only due to the
energy of the well-known former flier, Anthonie Strass-
mann, that the Do X ever started again.

Upon its arrival in Germany Do X was dismantled and
put into a museum. Today Dornier is building mostly land
planes for the Luftwaffe, especially for long-distance reconnaissance and for bombing—the Do 17, Do 19, Do 23,
and Do 215 being the most important ones.

Dr. Adolf Rohrbach was one of the German aviation
men who staked everything on the militarists. And he
always depended upon the militarists. When the general
staff dropped him, he was finished.

Maybe he did so because he looked so much like an
officer. He was tall, slim, a grand seigneur, very popular
with women, a man of the world, elegant, dashing, amusing—if he wanted to be. He made others around him look
petit bourgeois. They were, of course, compared to him,
petit bourgeois. He needed considerable amounts of money,

not only for his plant but also for his private life. No matter how much money he got, he never had any.

He started, like Dornier, in the Zeppelin Company, and
was Dornier's collaborator during the war. Afterward he
built for the Zeppelin airplane works in Staaken near Berlin a four-motored airplane for civil aviation, a beautiful
giant high-wing monoplane, in all-metal construction with
the engines in the leading edge of the wing, which was so
thick that a mechanic could crawl to the engines while in
flight.

The engines were 260 horsepower Daimler Mercedes
engines from the war. The Inter-Allied Control Commission insisted that the plane, which had been built to ac-
commodate eighteen passengers, be dismantled as a "military plane."

But Rohrbach's fame was established. With that one
plane he became one of the most prominent German airplane designers. It was not difficult for him to find private
persons to finance him, and the government, too, subsidized
him. So, in 1922, he formed the Rohrbach Metal Aircraft
Company in Berlin, with a branch in Copenhagen—in order
to evade the Inter-Allied Control Commission.

Until 1927 he built various models of huge all-metal
flying boats, all of them high-wing cantilever monoplanes
of sweeping lines and very good to look at.

As soon as the War Ministry decided that his planes were
highly promising as far as speed and seaworthiness went,
he was heavily subsidized. Then catastrophes began to occur at demonstrations, pilots were killed, and the Reichstag
got very excited about the War Ministry spending money
on such ventures. The War Ministry, too, decided that
Rohrbach's boats were not sturdy enough, and that much

of their maneuverability had been possible only at the sacrifice of structural strength.

By that time Rohrbach had become very arrogant in his demands for subsidies. So finally the army dropped him. Rohrbach then devoted himself for some time to studying new aircraft projects, the most interesting of which was a paddle-wheel airplane.

After the Nazis came to power he formed another company, but the army never again trusted him enough to subsidize him in a big way. He died before the outbreak of the war.

Willy Messerschmitt was the exact opposite of Junkers. He never dreamed of peace, but always of war. He was not in the least interested in humanity. He was interested only in destruction. He never cared for the happiness of other people. As a matter of fact, the lives of others didn't mean anything to him.

Messerschmitt was not in the war as he was too young. When it was over he studied to become an engineer and became interested in the glider movement. I remember Messerschmitt's first glider models; they were very much like the Me's of today. His tendency even then was to achieve superior performance by sacrificing weight and thus security.

Messerschmitt was born and raised in the Bavarian town of Bamberg, very near the Rhoen mountains. An event early in Messerschmitt's life, which I witnessed, seems to me very symptomatic of him. In 1921 he appeared with a model which his best friend flew in the Rhoen. There was a crack-up in mid-air, and Messerschmitt's friend was killed.

I think if that had happened to most of us, we would not

have gone on in aviation. I am convinced, for instance, that men like Klemm or Junkers would never have gotten over such an early tragedy. But Messerschmitt was different. I remember exactly how he looked when the catastrophe occurred. There was a fierce look in his eyes. He pressed his lips together. His hands went nervously through his mop of dark hair. When we wanted to talk to him to comfort him, he turned on us and suddenly shouted, "You can't say it was my fault. I have nothing to do with it. It was his fault."

He was actually angry with us. And in the years after that he was a man who shouted a lot and behaved boorishly with his employees and collaborators. I always think that he tried thus to hide the fact that he was not too sure of himself.

His best friend was not the only one to be sacrificed. Many of the finest German test pilots perished trying out Messerschmitt models during the next twenty years or so. Practically every model he designed crashed before he made changes in it. But this never seemed to touch him. His ambition was overpowering. And army circles didn't mind either because his planes were very promising from the military point of view. The War Ministry subsidized him heavily almost from the beginning.

Messerschmitt was an early Nazi. He was a close friend of Hess, and later of Goering, at a time when nobody thought the Nazis would ever wield any power. Today, both Goering and Hess are silent partners in the Messerschmitt enterprise.

Of course, at that time, the Nazis couldn't help Messerschmitt financially. But there were other people who did. People from so-called "patriotic" circles, men of heavy industry who were looking forward to general rearmament. Many of the trusted friends of these industrialists were holding key positions in airline companies, and thus it was arranged that Messerschmitt could count on subsidies in one form or another.

Messerschmitt started modestly enough with a small company of his own in his home town of Bamberg, building gliders and then small low-powered all-metal cabin planes for a Bavarian airline.

From 1926 on, the army subsidized him. It was then that he was able to take over the Bavarian Airplane Works in Augsburg, which once had belonged to the flier, Udet, who had built them with money provided by his rich father-in-law. There is no denying that from the very beginning and in spite of their deficiencies and the great risks they involved as far as human lives were concerned Messerschmitt's planes were something outside of the traditional lines, and they rightly attracted the attention of the German army and, indeed, of international observers. Even his low-powered racing planes, while extremely flimsy and dangerous, had to be admired for their slimness, their grace, and their aero-dynamically highly efficient lines.

Messerschmitt acquired international fame when in 1936 his beautiful low-wing, so-called "passenger" plane, the Typhoon, was flown all over the world by officers of the Luftwaffe. Of course, the Typhoon was by no means a passenger plane. It was the embryo of a fighter plane and the predecessor of the famous Me 109. Anyhow by that time, and since 1935, Messerschmitt was concentrating exclusively on military planes. The "commercial" models that he brought out were, of course, nothing but camouflage, as were the contracts which his company signed with German airlines.

If there is any man in German aviation who is more important to the German Luftwaffe and its effort than Messerschmitt, it is Ernst Heinkel. Like Messerschmitt he was never interested in anything but military aviation. He built his planes for rearmament purposes solely. He wasn't interested in science, and he wasn't and isn't interested in people.

Heinkel is now fifty-five years old, but he looks much older. He is small, bald, and fat. He wears thick-lensed glasses, speaks a broad Swabian dialect, and is outwardly anything but what may be termed the Aryan ideal. He started flying before World War I and he began designing airplanes in 1913. During the war he managed to design and build some excellent float plane single-seater fighters, which brought down many British flying boats over the North Sea and the Channel.

After the war he joined the Caspar Works as chief designer. His firm succeeded early in getting so-called "development orders" from the army. It was all very hush-hush. In 1922 he formed his own company in Warnemuende, and in 1932 he added a plant in Rostock—both on the Baltic. Ever since the Nazis have been in power, he has expanded and expanded again and again.

Like Junkers, Heinkel was always an excellent engineer. But that is about all he had in common with Junkers.

From the very beginning he was in close contact with the Nazis, probably not so much for ideological reasons as for business reasons. Hitler rewarded him not only with immense orders, but also by appointing him a *Wehrwirtschaftsfuehrer*, "Regional Leader of the Defense Industry," giving him the Golden Party Badge, and, finally, the title of Professor.

He is an unpleasant person to work with, and most of

his engineers have not stayed very long with him. He has no consideration for other people or their dignity. He has been involved in a number of scandals, all of which had to do with women. Shortly before the outbreak of the war, he had an outright brawl with one Nazi Reichsstatthalter of his region because the Nazi bigwig wanted one of Heinkel's pretty private secretaries loaned out to work for him. When Heinkel refused, the Nazi tipped the Gestapo off and had the girl arrested on a charge of espionage. Heinkel really didn't care. All he cares about is business.

From the very beginning, that is, immediately after World War I, he was able to get the War Ministry interested in him; he never had difficulty in obtaining large subsidies. He built anything and everything that he was asked to build by the War Ministry. Some years he brought out as many as six or even eight models, and none of these were at that time built in series. It was only when the Nazis came to power, or shortly afterward, that he got down to mass production in earnest.

While Junkers early arrived at his long-range view as to the structural and aero-dynamic features and followed it without deviation in scientific experiments and reasoning, Heinkel experimented in all fields. In other words, while there was one great line in the whole work of Junkers, and even in the life-work of men like Messerschmitt, Dornier, Rohrbach, and, of course, Klemm, Heinkel's versatility was amazing and bewildering. He designed and built land planes and float planes and a flying boat and an amphibian; he designed and built monoplanes and biplanes, braced and cantilever. He designed and built everything from low-powered sports planes to high-powered four-engined bombers, even bigger than the Flying Fortresses. He designed and built elementary and advance trainers, in-

tercepters, and long-range single-seater fighters, reconnaissance planes, torpedo bombers, catapult planes, light,
medium, and heavy bombers, with one, two, and four
engines and all sorts of combinations. His structural designs were not confined to one school of thought. He built
wooden planes, with fabric and plywood covering, planes
with steel structure and fabric covering, light alloy struc-
tures of all descriptions with all sorts of coverings, and,
finally, stressed-skin-shell constructions in his modern
craft, and with which method and material he now seems to
have found his bearings. (As against the old type of airplane
construction where the frame carries the entire load and is
covered by a non-stressed skin—like any vertebrate—
stressed-skin-shell construction carries most of the load
within the skin itself, like a beetle or a tortoise.)

The one common line in all his output is the exclusively
military aspect. Even the famous He 70, which for some
time was used as a high-speed passenger plane, was a study
for military design which has since been continued in a
long series of aero-dynamically highly efficient planes. In
all his designs, Heinkel has been progressive, pioneering,
bold, modern.

He is an amazing man, no doubt about it. He is disagree-
able and a dubious character, and I have never found
anybody in German aviation or, for that matter, in the German Luftwaffe, who liked him. But he is a genius. He is an
inventor par excellence. He invents all the time. He invented the explosive rivet now used in this country, too.
Lately he has found time to interest himself in jet-propul-
sion, on which he has taken out some patents. (Jet propulsion, similar to rocket propulsion, does away with
propellers and gains forward movement by a backward
ejection of gases through one or more jets.)

Junkers found the fundamental; Junkers had the ideas; Junkers built the wonderful machinery that he thought would help to make the world a better place. Heinkel used those fundamentals, used anybody's ideas, used anybody's patents or findings or production tricks, in order to create as many and as dangerous weapons as he could. He did everything in his power, he used aviation and his imagination and his inventive genius to make this world a place not fit to live in.

The Luftwaffe could never have been created without these two men. It is almost symbolic that in order to create the Luftwaffe, a man like Junkers had to be crushed and a man like Heinkel had to be made big, rich, and powerful.

4. *Collapse and Rebirth of an Industry*

In 1914, the German aircraft industry consisted of fifty aircraft companies and ten aero-engine companies. By the end of 1918, when the war ended, the industry consisted of thirty-five aircraft companies and twenty aero-engine companies. By 1917, when America entered the war, Germany was producing roughly one thousand planes a month. In the fall of 1918, the production had been brought up to around two thousand planes a month. Germany's "America program"—the production program devised after the United States' entry into the war—had foreseen more than that. Still, two thousand planes was no small number at that time. Of course, compared with the standards of today, the planes were flimsy contraptions. The frames were mostly wooden, with fabric stretched precariously around them. The speed ranged between 100 and 150 miles an hour, but the maneuverability and the load-carrying capacity were quite astonishing.

I have already mentioned the fact that during the last months of the war our planes showed more and more the lack of materials and of skilled labor. And, of course, with an average of fifty planes shot down a day and fifty planes put out of action through crash landings and losses in training schools—which was the picture toward the end of the war—the German aircraft industry could not have continued much longer to keep the German air corps up to the strength it possessed at the time the war was over.

The fact that the construction of airplanes at that time involved much fewer working hours than it does today can be illustrated by reviewing the number of workers employed in some of the more important factories during the war. Rumpler employed 7,000 workers, Junkers 2,000 workers, Dornier 5,000 workers—nothing at all compared with the number employed today in big plants both in Germany and the Allied countries.

Then came the Versailles Treaty and in it the paragraphs contained in Part V under the heading "Military, Naval and Air Clauses," Articles 198 to 202, and in Part XI, under the heading "Aerial Navigation," Articles 313 to 320, devised to crush German aviation. The paragraphs concerned with aerial navigation dealt mostly with international passenger traffic and made sure that the Allied powers would enjoy the same rights as German aviation over German territory or German territorial waters. As I shall show later, it was precisely these articles that finally made it possible for German aviation to get rid of many of the limitations of the Treaty.

I am including Part V of the Versailles Treaty here, since it is my belief that it is of more than purely historical interest. We should study this well. Part V, Articles 198 to 202, did more to help Germany rebuild its airpower and consequently its Luftwaffe than anything else. If, after the end of this war, there should be another attempt to get the Germans out of the air—as undoubtedly there will and must be—Allied experts should read this Part V with particular care.

It is a perfect blueprint—a perfect blueprint of what

should not have been done, and of what never must be done again. Because, as we shall see later, it was not enough.

The Treaty of Versailles

Part V. Section III

Air Clauses

Article 198.

The armed forces of Germany must not include any military or naval air forces.

Germany may, during a period not extending beyond October 1, 1919, maintain a maximum number of 100 seaplanes or flying boats, which shall be exclusively employed in searching for submarine mines, shall be furnished with the necessary equipment for this purpose, and shall in no case carry arms, munitions or bombs of any nature whatever.

In addition to the engines installed in the seaplanes or flying boats above mentioned, one spare engine may be provided for each of these craft.

No dirigible shall be kept.

Article 199.

Within two months from the coming into force of the present treaty, the personnel of the air forces on the rolls of the German land and sea forces shall be demobilized up to October 1, 1919; however, Germany may keep and maintain a total number of 1,000 men, including officers, for the whole of the cadres and personnel, flying and non-flying, of all formations and establishments.

Article 200.

Until the complete evacuation of German territory by the Allied and Associated troops, the aircraft of the Allied and Associated Powers shall enjoy in Germany freedom of passage through the air, freedom of transit and of landing.

Article 201.

During the six months following the coming into force of the present treaty, the manufacture and importation of aircraft, parts of aircraft, engines for aircraft, and parts of engines for aircraft, shall be forbidden in all German territory.

Article 202.

On the coming into force of the present treaty, all military and naval aeronautical material, except the machines mentioned in the second and third paragraphs of Art. 198, must be delivered to the Governments of the Principal Allied and Associated Powers.

Delivery must be effected to such places as the Allied Governments may select, and must be completed within three months.

In particular, this material will include all items under the following heads which are or have been or were designed for warlike purposes:

Complete aeroplanes and seaplanes, as well as those being manufactured, repaired or assembled

Dirigibles able to take the air, being manufactured, repaired or assembled.

Plant for the manufacture of hydrogen.

Dirigible sheds and shelters for every kind of aircraft.

Pending their delivery, dirigibles will, at the expense of Germany, be maintained inflated with hydrogen; the plant for the manufacture of hydrogen, as well as the sheds for dirigibles, may, at the discretion of the Allied Powers, be left to Germany until the time when the dirigibles are handed over.

Engines for aircraft

Nacelles and fuselages.

Armament (guns, machine guns, light machine guns, bomb-dropping apparatus, torpedo-dropping apparatus, synchronization apparatus, aiming apparatus).

Munitions (cartridges, shells, bombs loaded or unloaded, stocks of exlosives or material for their manufacture).

Instruments for use on aircraft.

Wireless apparatus and photographic or cinematograph apparatus for use on aircraft.

Component parts of any of the items under the preceding heads.

The material referred to above shall not be removed without special permission from the Allied Governments.

The Versailles Treaty did not exactly encourage the existing German aircraft companies; and these latter examined the situation and came to the logical conclusion that the boom was over.

Many of them decided to quit aviation. In spite of their engineers, who had new and good ideas which they wanted to try out for peaceful purposes, in spite of frantic requests from the General Staff whose members were already thinking in terms of the next war, they decided that for at least ten or fifteen years there would be no money in aviation—and that was that.

Out went the big aviation department of the AEG—the General Electric of Berlin—which had built a fine single-engined reconnaissance plane and had done a first-class job on twin-engined night bombers. Out went the Gotha and the Friedrichshafen Aircraft Companies, which had manufactured wonderful twin-engined night bombers in wood. Out went the D.F.W. (German Aircraft Works) in Leipzig, the Pfalz Works in Speyer, the Fokker Works in Schwerin, the Zeppelin Aircraft Works in Lindau and Staaken, the Siemens-Schuckert Aircraft Company in Berlin.

A few carried on. Those which did were not motivated by calculations of immediate profit. The men who decided to carry on were more or less idealistic individuals who believed in their ability to create something so good and so new that it was bound to succeed even in troubled times, but especially in the better world which they intended to help create. These men knew very well that the path before them would be a stony one, but they continued anyhow.

The Versailles Treaty had stated that Germany had to deliver all military and naval aeronautical material to the Allies and associated powers, and that the delivery must be effected and completed within three months after the Treaty's coming into force.

The Treaty came into force on January 10, 1920. And, therefore, the whole transaction should have been completed by April 10. German experts, even before the Treaty was signed, had declared that this would be impossible. It was impossible on account of the almost total collapse of German railroad traffic. Another difficulty arose from the fact that German industry didn't want to destroy its aeronautical stocks, which represented enormous investments, before the government had decided how much in the way of indemnity it would or could pay. As it happened, the delivery and destruction of the aviation material was by no means carried out in three months, not even in six months.

I mention six months specifically because, according to the Treaty, Germany had the right to begin manufacturing aeronautical material after a lapse of six months from the day the Treaty went into effect, which would have meant July 10, 1920. Now the Allies decided—in the conference at Boulogne on June 22, 1920—that Germany could not begin to build any aeronautical material at all till three months after the day all the material to be delivered or destroyed had been delivered or destroyed.

The gravest consequence of this change was of an indirect nature. German aviation circles naturally felt that everything was unsettled, that nothing was definite, that there was no security whatsoever and no certain future. Some people thought that perhaps the building of commercial planes was permissible, others thought it was not permissible. The Inter-Allied Control Commission contributed to the general confusion by setting free 150 obsolete warplanes for the air traffic and then confiscating these very planes when they appeared in Riga and Vienna. Even the planes built by Junkers for the United States were confiscated, though only for a short time. At this time occurred the confiscation and dismantling of a Junkers four-engined passenger plane and of Rohrbach's passenger plane in Staaken.

In the meantime, the French and English aviation press announced that Germany had delivered everything. Indeed, by the end of 1920, 14,000 planes had been surrendered or destroyed and 27,000 engines.

Then the high council of the Allies in a conference on January 31, 1921, demanded something entirely new. It demanded recognition by Germany of "definitions"—to be worked out by the Allies to distinguish civil aircraft from military aircraft. Germany also had to agree that Allied commissions would supervise the carrying out of these definitions.

The German government on May 10, 1921, agreed to all this. The nationalists in Germany howled. So did we fliers, who felt that this was really too much. We who did not think of war recognized that the Allies now had a definite chance to frustrate all attempts to build up a German air traffic by creating definitions which would simply make such an air traffic impossible. The men who dreamed of the next war and who hoped that civil aviation in one way or another would help prepare military aviation were also, of course, averse to having civil aviation handicapped in any way.

The regulations for German civil aircraft—those long awaited definitions—were finally released in the "Nine Rules" formulated by the Conference of Ambassadors on April 14, 1922. German civil aircraft were restricted to a maximum speed of 170 kilometers (105 miles) per hour, a useful load of 600 kilograms (about 1,300 lbs.), and a ceiling of 4,000 m. (13,000 feet). It was agreed that these definitions should be revised every two years. But there was no revision whatsoever before June 1925, when the Conference of Ambassadors insisted that the Inter-Allied Control Commission should have the right to fix the number of civil airplanes, engines, pilots, and trainees. In exchange, the Commission would permit a maximum speed of 180 kilometers (112 miles), a useful load of 900 kilograms (about 2,000 lbs.). But the ceiling was to be kept at 4,000 m. (13,000 feet).

The German government never answered that note.

Thus it was not until May 1926, that a new agreement was reached between the German government and the Conference of Ambassadors. Germany was to be free of all aviation fetters, except, of course, that no armed or armored planes were to be built. The supervision was to be in the hands of the League of Nations. By September 1926, the Inter-Allied Control Commission had withdrawn and things began to look brighter.

All this was not achieved without some clever planning and a lot of tricks on the part of certain German politicians, and also not without pressure from certain interested circles outside of Germany—the French and English airlines. Since, in my opinion, this meant a great step forward in the direction of the rebuilding of a German air force, I shall have to go into all this further a few pages hence.

It is important to keep the date in mind: By 1926 there was no international control over German doings in the air. Those who looked upon aviation as a part of the armed forces began to breathe easier. They could begin to act more openly.

They did act more openly.

But before I discuss at greater length the rearmament which started then, I want to dwell a little longer on the Versailles Treaty.

A cry of rage had resounded through German aviation circles when the Treaty was signed, what with the indignity of Control Commissions, what with the destruction of all flying material as well as manufacturing facilities and raw materials in stock.

Little did anybody comprehend then that all this drastic destruction was to prove a blessing in disguise.

Germany had intended—as all the other countries had intended and, indeed, as they did—to use the enormous quantities of existing planes, engines, etc., after the war for airline services, with perhaps only slight alterations that might be necessary for the safety of the passengers and the mail.

If a plant is geared for mass production it has invested in it so much money, work, and skill that it cannot suddenly switch to something entirely different and expect to survive financially. That is the reason why in aviation as well as in motor car construction, for instance, the improvement of the product on the market is a much slower process than it would be if it depended only on the progress of scientific research. When jigs, machine tools, installation methods, etc., are all worked out and more or less frozen, when the personnel is adapted to building let us say a wooden bi-plane, it is simply not possible to manufacture with the same equipment, tools, and procedures, or with the same supervisors and workers, an all-metal monoplane. That is a hard fact which had to be learned all over the world by would-be manufacturers of mass-produced articles especially when they went into the airplane business, or the motor car business, for that matter. And that is one of the reasons why, from the point of view of recent scientific knowledge, modern aircraft as well as motor cars are already obsolete when the first one begins to roll off the production line.

Versailles meant that the Germans had to begin all over again. The Allies were able to go on where they had left off. The Allies were burdened with their old warplanes and installations; but the Germans had to start from scratch.

Since all German aircraft facilities had been destroyed, we had to invent something new. Since the peace treaty permitted only minimum horsepower engines, we engineers had to develop great resourcefulness in constructing planes capable of maximum performances with low horsepower motors. Since little money was available, we had to build sturdier planes.

It was thus that while the Allies were still flying their old crates of braced bi-planes in wood and fabric, Junkers had already designed and built his famous all-metal transport plane F 13. In other words, he was roughly ten years ahead of aircraft development in other countries.

And here, parenthetically, is an interesting parallel with the motor car industry of today and tomorrow in the United States. When motor car building was stopped for the duration, the tools and jigs and machines necessary for the production of the existing models were dismantled and used as scrap. That will make it possible, even necessary, for our motor car industry to build cars after the war which will not trail behind new ideas and new scientific developments, as the motor car industry all over the world has done for so many years.

The question will be raised how it was possible for the aircraft industry to go on at all after Versailles. I have already said that a great number of companies decided not to go on. The others managed to struggle along for a time on the great profits they had made in the war. But those means lasted only a short time, and then came the inflation which melted away all the money that man or company possessed.

The financing of the new aircraft industry was truly a problem. Not only was there relatively little money in Germany after the war, but also most of the financing had to be done secretly—that is, without the knowledge of the Allies. Large amounts of money were given officially only by the Ministry of Transport—especially to Dornier and to Junkers, who, officially, built only commercial transport planes. Then there were the subsidies given by the government for so-called "orders of development"—moneys used for experimental purposes in the construction of new models—always for the development of commercial air transport, of course.

Foreign countries, too, provided a great deal of money. Almost immediately after the end of the war, German industry started exporting again. As I have mentioned, General Billy Mitchell ordered the first Junkers planes even before America was officially at peace with Germany.

The German Defense Ministry—that is, the army—became interested in new planes immediately after the Versailles Treaty had been signed—I might say even before it had been signed. Since, under the Treaty, they were somewhat restricted, certain officers suggested that the industry design commercial planes that could easily be converted into military planes. Such amateurish suggestions were followed for quite a while, but eventually it became clear that neither good commercial planes nor good military planes could be built in this fashion.

It didn't take the army long to see the light. In 1924, it began to disregard the Versailles Treaty completely and to build military planes in secret and ship them abroad. There—that is, in factories which German aircraft men had built in other countries—these planes were put into what seemed then to be mass production—ten to twenty of a type was a series. The training of German military fliers, too, was partly accomplished abroad, at least during the first years. Later, especially after the conclusion of the Treaty of Locarno and Germany's entry into the League of Nations—the aforementioned date of 1926—training went on inside Germany and without much attempt at concealment.

Looking back over those first years of the rebuilding of German aviation, it seems to me they resemble nothing so much as an old-fashioned mystery story. The period was full of intrigues, secrets, mysteries; there was no sensible over-all plan whatsoever. Many different plants were working and producing in a haphazard manner. None of them was quite sure of its own goals—to say nothing of what was being attempted in other plants. Sometimes the army and the Ministry of Transport would work together—indeed, many military models were constructed on orders from the Ministry of Transport—but just as often they worked separately and even against each other. The illegal business had to be kept secret, not only from the Allies but also from the democrats and the socialists in the Reichstag. These latter were trying to live up to the Versailles Treaty, and many of them hoped—as it turned out, not without reason—that it might be possible to change particularly onerous conditions of the Treaty by way of negotiation. The situation being what it was, many murders were committed with the sole purpose of keeping secrets of the airplane industry.

Sometimes the business of financing became dramatically involved. In at least one case certain army officers speculated on the stock market in an attempt to increase the meager funds allotted to the building of airplanes. The outcome was that all the funds involved were lost. And that precipitated an enormous scandal which, in turn, led to a socialist protest in the Reichstag. But finally, as so often—as too often—in Germany, everything was hushed up.

All this was bound to have a psychological effect on the men working in the aircraft industry. It made for a certain unity between the workers and management of the plants. A sort of conspiratorial atmosphere developed. Managers, designers, workers made common cause in deceiving the Inter-Allied Control Commissions. Models that should not have been built were built and hidden—in woods, on meadows, in stables—till the Control Commissions had left. Everybody concerned felt that this was only right. The Commissions—why, they were the enemy.

Not for a moment did it occur to any of these people that there happened to exist a state of affairs called peace. But peace was what we had, and it was because of that peace we were able to expend so much energy and try out so many ideas to build up civilian air transport and air traffic.

The original idea that there would be possibilities for civilian air traffic enterprise goes back to the middle of the war. As early at 1917 the AEG (General Electric of Berlin) had formed the *Deutsche Luftreederei*, which was to start air transport after the war, thus creating a market for the AEG's excellent twin-engined bomber in peacetime. In 1919, this company started some traffic between Berlin and Weimar, and Berlin and Hamburg, transporting 10,000 passengers and 10 tons of mail. In 1920, it obtained subsidies from the German government and also concluded some international arrangements. The Malmoe-Kopenhagen-Hamburg-Amsterdam line was started first. The newly created organization was called International Air Traffic Association or, for short, IATA.

At the same time, several other companies were formed in Germany. There was a general gross misjudgment of the economic possibilities involved. But these new companies obtained important airline concessions from the German government and also from governments of countries around Germany. In the spring of 1923 most of the German airline companies consolidated within the framework of two newly formed companies. One was the Deutscher Aero-Lloyd (DAL), the second was the traffic division of the Junkers works, Junkers Airline Company.

The man who was the driving power behind the Junkers traffic division—and who really created it—was Gotthard Sachsenberg, the famous leader of the Marine Corps fighter squadron. If Hugo Junkers was the most eminent of the German aviation pioneers, Gotthard Sachsenberg certainly was the most brilliant. He was an average-sized young man, with steel-blue eyes, good-looking, very fascinating, a born leader, who could inspire those who believed in him to great sacrifice and hardship and work. Like most of the German war fliers, he had a burning desire at the end of the war to do something constructive. Since he didn't know exactly how to use his energies, he kept his fighter squadron together and led them to the Baltic States for the purpose of conquering settlement land for themselves. When he was finally called back to Germany, he and his men took possession of an old airport near Koenigsberg, and there they started their settlement experience. While most of his men began to till the soil, Sachsenberg bought up at a bargain price a few of the planes he had flown back, and somehow obtained the concession to fly passengers between Berlin and Koenigsberg. He built roofs over the passengers' seats and sold tickets to passengers. But the business did not last very long because the passengers, who were cooped up in those coffin-like quarters and almost died of fright or suffocation, never came back for more.

It was then that Sachsenberg got together with Junkers. Junkers had not been interested in air traffic—it meant too much mass production, too much routine. Sachsenberg convinced him. Junkers, he said, would perish if there was no market for planes. A market could be created only if Germany—if, indeed, the world—were to see that air traffic worked. The world had to be shown.

Junkers was soon convinced. He was always the man to do something new, something out of the ordinary. The air traffic division was founded. Sachsenberg began to make himself at home in Dessau. A lot of his strange and adventure-loving friends came to Dessau, too. But the old Professor didn't mind. Anyhow, the air traffic division grew by leaps and bounds. Sachsenberg not only put his own concession into the newly created business, but also a lot of other part concessions—concessions to fly between certain German cities—through the simple device of bringing the men who owned the concessions but had no planes to make use of them into the business.

That is how it happened that a young officer who had in his possession one obsolete plane and the concession to fly between Danzig and Warsaw found his way to Dessau. This young man, whose name was to become prominent in connection with German aviation, was Erhard Milch.

The new Junkers venture was the first combination of building and operating in aviation. It was a form of trust, to be sure, and later on Junkers was severely attacked for having formed a monopoly. But his ideas were far from commercial.

He and Sachsenberg understood that Germany's craving for *"Lebensraum"* was an atavistic throwback to an agricultural or nomadic period when prosperity depended on the possession of large agricultural and grazing areas. In our times such a struggle for new *Lebensraum* would lead not to prosperity but again and again to wars against the whole world. Germany's highly industrialized population, therefore, had either to emigrate or to concentrate on producing within Germany and selling abroad. This meant that Germany depended on the good will of the rest of the world, a good will that could be brought about by creating speedy planes and high-speed communications with proof of intent of peaceful commercial exchange with the whole world.

Private airlines were the answer—private, not state-controlled enterprises.

It was important, it was absolutely necessary, to keep an airline enterprise away from politics. That meant that

it had to be kept independent of government or large industrial subsidies. That is, it had to be financed privately and
only by people whose peaceful long-range ideas were
known to the world.

That is where Hugo Junkers came in. He was a man
who could be trusted. He could be depended upon to steer
clear of military interference. And once his airlines were a
success, it would prove that airlines were necessary all
over the world, thus creating inexhaustible markets for
aircraft production and making it possible for Junkers
himself to make enough money to support his own airlines.

But there was still another reason why Junkers went into
the airline business. He had always preached and stressed
the necessity of developing a product according to the
changing requirements of the market. He believed that
such development and improvement could only be based
on intimate interrelations between customers and producers. The Junkers airlines were the perfect set-up for
Junkers: they supplied him with a kind of research organization and an opportunity for plenty of experience.

That is why he went into the airline business.

The rival organization, the Aero-Lloyd, had no inten-
tention of going in for any idealistic nonsense. It was
financed by the Deutsche Bank, shipping companies, and
private industries, and from the beginning it counted heavily on subsidies. The president of the Deutsche Bank, Emil
von Stauss, had some excellent connections. He knew influ-
ential people in the army, and he pulled every string to
convince those men that his company would serve best as a
front behind which to rebuild the German air force.

Herr von Stauss also knew people in the Postal Ministry.
That was important because this authority had a lot of

money to give away. But most important was the fact that Herr von Stauss was in close contact with one of the seemingly lesser members of the Ministry of Transport, a man named Ernst Brandenburg, who had been famous as a commander of a German bomber squadron in World War I.

The men who got behind Herr von Stauss did not do so because they were eager to help him, but because they wanted to promote his company. From the beginning, it was a fight not for von Stauss but against Junkers. How could the army make use of a man who had the crazy idea "to make the airplane a tool of a happy humanity"? Something had to be done about that old crackpot, Junkers, and it had to be done fast—or it would be too late.

For, from the very beginning, the Junkers airlines had encouraged the formation of foreign co-operating companies with a close technical, commercial, and operational relationship and no secrets from one another. This at a time when the army wanted to use German aviation to rearm!

Indeed, the circle around Junkers and Sachsenberg became more and more international. At the favorite hangout of young Junkers engineers, the little inn of Papa Rossow in Ziebigk, surburb of Dessau, were often to be found Karl and Adrian Florman, the directors of the great Swedish airline company, charming Herr Deutelmoser, of the Austrian airlines, the Wygard brothers from Warsaw, Renato Morandi, of the Italian company, Señor Moreno from the Union Aerea Espagnola in Madrid, the Swiss flier Walther Mittelholzer, and General Kuksin, of the Red air fleet. Yes, and Erhard Milch, too, who somehow did not seem to fit in very well with this mixed company.

The airline companies represented by these men were soon organized into two big "unions." There were the

"Trans-Europa Union" and the "North-Europa Union," respectively covering air traffic from Zurich, Munich, Vienna, down to the Balkans, and Denmark, Sweden, Finland, and the Baltic border states.

By 1925 the two unions were ready to merge into an "Europa-Union."

It seemed as though the Aero-Lloyd was beaten. It seemed as though the men behind the Aero-Lloyd would have to stand by powerless and watch German aviation, which they had hoped to make the backbone of German rearmament, become the backbone of international understanding.

It was then that Ernst Brandenburg spoke up—for the first time. It was only a warning of the campaign against Junkers which was in the offing—or shall I say of the trap which the army was about to spring?

It happened in Munich in the Aula Maxima of the university. During the annual meeting of the German Scientific Society for Aviation, Herr Ministerialrat Brandenburg gave a lecture about the development and progress of German civil aviation during the last five years (1920-1925). Junkers, Sachsenberg, I, and a lot of our friends were sitting in the second row.

With a hint of mockery in his voice, Brandenburg praised the ideals, the devotion, and the work of the Junkers companies but added that the German government, which he represented, could not back a development which—if left to itself—"will be marked by later historians as the first outstanding step on the road to the United States of Europe." Then he made a little pause and added, with a malicious smile and a glance toward where we were sitting, "under German hegemony."

Thus, the official representative of the German Republic

publicly discredited a movement that had steered clear of political and military entanglements by charging its founders with the very aspirations for power which he and his friends in the army nursed.

We around Junkers did not heed these warnings. We were busy building up the net which spread over Europe. New airlines, subsidiary companies in Hungary, Poland, Greece, Turkey, Italy.

But Sachsenberg and Junkers wanted more. A whole world was to be conquered, or, to be precise, a whole world was to be connected and brought closer together by means of airplanes and airlines. We had no intention or ambition to run all these airlines by ourselves. What we wanted was to build the bridges connecting the different parts of the world with each other and to leave the construction of the local airlines to the people who were living and working in the various countries.

It is difficult—even within the space of a book—to give more than an idea of the huge span of our projects. Russia figured prominently in them; there was a line from Moscow to Turkestan and plans for lines radiating from Moscow to Russian border areas. There was the Sweden-Persia project which was to lead from Stockholm via Moscow, Rostov, Baku, and Teheran. We worked on an air bridge to China, and there was South America, which Junkers and Sachsenberg decided could be reached by plane directly from Europe.

All of these ideas were tackled and many of the preparations progressed with such enormous speed that in only a few months' time certain sections of the lines could be opened at least for irregular service, though some of the projects never got beyond the planning stage.

In the meantime a real airline boom started in Germany. In 1925 the mayors of practically all the towns of Germany visited Dessau and waited in line to see Sachsenberg. They all brought money along and insisted that Sachsenberg take it and put their town on the airline map. Sachsenberg took their money. Then on a Sunday a few months later a Junkers three-engined passenger plane would appear at the newly built airport of the town and be duly baptized. The following Sunday our plane would appear at another new airport and again be baptized. I suppose that the populations of those towns always thought it was "their" plane—and had a lot of fun. The entire development inside of Germany was somewhat unsound, to say the least, and had all the earmarks of a gold rush. But I am sure that if Junkers had been given a few years' time, something permanent would have come out of it. Something which the world had never before seen—an airline system independent of state subsidies and therefore independent of power politics.

But Junkers was not given any more time. Those who considered him dangerous prepared to strike against him. And the blow was to fall where he expected it least.

5. *The Fifth Columnist*

In the last chapter I mentioned a young officer who, because he controlled a certain airline concession, joined the Junkers airline company at about the same time as Sachsenberg. We must now take a closer look at Erhard Milch.

Milch was a good-looking fellow. He was of medium height, but carried himself erectly and was well enough proportioned to look taller than he was. He looked younger, too, on account of his rosy-cheeked baby face. His baby face and his military carriage and his cold, impersonal, cutting voice were in strange contrast. When you got to know him, as I indeed did, you soon discovered that his way of talking was an affectation; he wanted to look and act like his great ideal, a Prussian officer.

Milch was a hard worker. He would stay at his desk for hours on end. He was intelligent, but he was not and never will be what Nazi legend has made out of him—a mental giant. In fact, when issues or problems become too complicated for him, he becomes uneasy. He has a cute trick which has helped him out of lots of such difficult situations. He merely oversimplifies the problem to be solved; he just divides the problem into two alternatives—yes or no, black or white.

Looking back over those years when I worked with him at Junkers', I think we all felt that he was an opportunist, and we were all a bit unsure of him. Somehow he simply did not belong in the Junkers company nor did he fit in with us, Junkers' collaborators and friends. But there was nothing at that time that I can put my finger on now. Of course, there was the rather strange fact that he never made a friend among us. He always seemed alone. Curiously enough, in spite of the fantastic career he had ten years later, he has never made a friend yet. He is on excellent terms with Goering, and the Fuehrer is supposed to like him. But that is all.

That the Fuehrer does like him is rather amazing. Because Milch, as far as can be ascertained, is a Jew. Born in 1893, the son of a Jewish pharmacist and his Christian wife, he was educated in a Berlin high school and then joined the army. By 1912 he was a lieutenant, and he went into active service the very day war was declared. Later he joined the air force. He was promoted to a captaincy and flew as an observer, first with a reconnaissance squadron on the Western front and later with a pursuit group.

After the war he returned to the Reich and then went on east along with his comrades of the air corps. He joined the police and had some function or other with the "Eastern Border Protection," which was formed then in order to "defend" Germany against Poland. Later he became chief of an air squadron in the Prussian air police. In 1920 he joined the first East Prussian airline company formed by Gotthard Sachsenberg, only to leave it a few weeks later. He had been able to buy himself one airplane, and he was also able, as has been mentioned, to secure the concession to fly the Danzig-Warsaw route. In 1923 he finally came over to Junkers.

This is what I knew about him then, and this is what everybody knew. It was later, much later, that we found out that even then Milch was by no means a lone wolf. His attempts to keep in touch with flying after the war was over and his persistent efforts to get into the mushrooming airline business were by no means only on his own initiative. Milch was probably already at that time an agent of the Reichswehr, had never ceased to be an agent of the army. He was representing the army when he joined the Eastern Border Protection. It was the army which gave him the little money necessary to buy his one plane and to obtain the Danzig-Warsaw license. It was the army which prompted him to join Junkers.

It is understandable that the army wanted a man of its own in the rapidly developing private airline industry. After all, here was a possibility for a later switch to something more military. It is also pretty clear that the army, interested from the very beginning in Aero-Lloyd, soon began to have misgivings as to whether Aero-Lloyd would be able to justify its hopes and confidence—as, indeed, Aero-Lloyd did prove itself unable. It was therefore only logical that the army should want to have an agent inside the other airline organization, within the "pacifistic" Junkers-Sachsenberg group, which it had never trusted anyway.

The army.... I think this is the place to bring in some discussion of the men behind Milch, the men who, after their defeat in 1918, never ceased to think of new ways and means to rebuild Germany's military machine for the purpose of starting a new war as soon as possible.

We are, of course, not interested here in a general exposé of these activities; we are interested mainly in the aviation angle.

As has already been mentioned, the army first wanted the aircraft industry to design and build civil planes which could be quickly converted into military planes, but these amateurish ideas were soon recognized as worthless and discarded. The German officers were the first to recognize the error of such a procedure. Many military experts in other countries fell victim to the same illusion and they remained so much longer than the Germans. For instance, the French General Requin, in a book entitled *How Will the Next War Look*, said that passenger planes could easily be converted into night bombers and that, therefore, the civil plane would be of definite military value in the next war. A Japanese expert, Hosono, was very much of the same opinion. Only in England the experts never fell for this nonsense.

Looking back today, it still seems to me amazing how the army and the illegal general staff went ahead with the secret rearmament in the air without anybody's knowing anything about it. How organizations were founded by fliers who were interested in flying purely as a sport. How whole units of fliers were trained at secret bases in the state of Wuerttemberg and in the *Lueneburger Heide* in Northern Germany. For many, many years military planes did not exist—officially. During maneuvers the army would rent a few obsolete private planes and have them circle above the sham battles, just to give an idea of what it would do if it had any real military planes. Present at such maneuvers, of course, were the military attachés of all the great powers, who were amused by such childish exhibitions in the air, and who probably felt very secure because Germany was not armed in the air. If they only had known how amused the heads of the army must have been by them. . . .

Two men were largely responsible for the secret armament of Germany in the air. One was General Wilberg.

Wilberg had been my higher aviation commander of the Fourth Army in the battle of Flanders in 1917. He had been one of Germany's few pre-war fliers, and during the war he proved to be a most brilliant aviation commander. After Versailles he was made head of the secret aviation division (*Fliegerzentrale*) in the German Defense Ministry, where he directed the entire German aviation rearmament program. He was the man chosen by the generals to be the head of the coming Luftwaffe. He would have been a very able chief, no doubt about it, but he never liked the Nazis and he particularly disliked Goering for his corruptness. It is easy to understand why, after 1933, he never had much of a career.

The other man who was responsible for the rearmament in the air was Ernst Brandenburg, who was in charge of civil aviation in the Transport Ministry. He directed the rearmament plan according to the wishes and ideas of Wilberg.

One of Brandenburg's first and most important jobs was to get rid of the restrictions of the Versailles Treaty. As I pointed out in another chapter, there was, in addition to the articles dealing with what Germany would and would not be allowed to build (articles 198-202), a set of articles having to do with aerial navigation. These articles, 313 to 320, laid down the rules for passenger traffic and international passenger traffic, and made sure that the Allied Powers would enjoy the same rights as German aviation over German territory or German territorial waters.

Article 313: "...Allied aircraft shall enjoy the same privileges as German aircraft..."

Article 314: "...Any regulations which may be made by Germany...shall be applicable equally to the aircraft of Germany and to those of the Allied and Associated countries."

Article 315: "... Aircraft of the Allied and Associated Powers ... shall be treated on a footing of equality with German aircraft. ..."

Brandenburg said: Fine. We are going to treat you on a footing of equality. Since we are restricted in our speed, in our ceiling, etc., etc.—he was referring to those definitions created by the Conference of Ambassadors—you will be restricted, too, as long as you fly over Germany. French and British airlines were forced to use planes of reduced speed and ceiling when they flew over Germany. That crippled their service to the east and southeast. Thus, Brandenburg acquired valuable allies in British and French civil aviation, who did their best to have the regulations changed. So finally the "definitions" were officially tossed out. The Control Commission left Germany. The biggest handicap to German rearmament had been removed.

The army found helpers everywhere for the task of air rearmament. Ground organizations had to be organized. They were organized and subsidized with municipal and state contributions, under the guise of air police, groups which ostensibly were not of military character.

Fliers had to be trained. They were trained in numerous air sports organizations which were subsidized by moneys from the education budget or by private contributions. Also there were certain clandestine military organizations, such as the Black Reichswehr.

And there was industry, which did a lot for the army in the way of subsidies. Industrial engineers designed military planes in Germany which could be built, as has already been mentioned, in a number of factories outside of Germany that were built by German industrialists for that very purpose. Dornier, Heinkel, Rohrbach, and even Junkers had plants outside of Germany. There was also the very important task of watching developments in military aviation abroad and of collecting intelligence—a task that in the beginning was almost entirely handled by industry.

Commercial air traffic could have been most important of all, perhaps, in furthering the army's plans to rearm Germany in the air; and, later on, it actually was of great importance. Air traffic could be subsidized without running afoul of the Versailles Treaty. Air traffic lines could train pilots without arousing suspicion, since they needed pilots. Through the channel of the airlines large amounts of money could go to industry without arousing suspicion. Airline companies could build transport planes (then still considered easily convertible into bombers), and could fly them at night—a procedure that would amount to training pilots as night bombers. In a word, airlines would be the perfect camouflaged set-up for secret air rearmament.

That is why General Wilberg and Ernst Brandenburg were so interested in the Aero-Lloyd, and that was why they, and, indeed, all the key men in the army, had to concentrate on Junkers when it turned out that the Aero-Lloyd was a flop.

But Junkers was just the man they could not work with. Junkers was the contrary of militaristic. Junkers did not want Germany to rearm in the air. Therefore, the army had to get rid of Junkers.

Ironically enough, Soviet Russia presented an ideal opportunity to the army for getting rid of Junkers.

The German army had been in close contact with Soviet Russia ever since the Polish war of 1920-21 and had even built up the Luftwaffe partly on Russian soil. A German air base was established somewhere in Turkestan. A factory for the manufacture of poison gas was built there also, and experiments with poison gases and with tanks were conducted.

Then one day Ernst Brandenburg sent for Junkers. The army, he explained, was proposing an interesting business deal to him. How would he like to build an aircraft plant in Fili, near Moscow? The army wanted planes built there, and it would also be necessary for Junkers to manufacture certain airplane parts in Dessau and ship them to the Russian plant where they would be assembled. The Russian government, Brandenburg said, was interested in this deal because Russian workers and engineers would be trained there. The Russian government had been promised an option to buy the factory at a later date. That proposal was made to Junkers in 1922.

Junkers had many talks with General von Hasse and Oskar von Niedermeyer of the Defense Ministry. They told him that naturally they could not sign a contract, since the whole business was a military secret involving a third power. Junkers protested that he did not want to have anything to do with military aviation. In vain the others told him that the entire enterprise was a purely defensive one. However, they were able to interest Junkers when they told him the Russians would, in return for his building a plant for them, give him a concession to organize civilian airlines all over Russia. This, indeed, meant a lot to the Professor. It would connect the German airlines with the Middle East. As far as the military part of the deal went, he was finally convinced that it did not concern Germany, but only Russia, and was, therefore, none of his business.

Finally it was agreed that Junkers would be paid certain sums after the plant was finished, and that he was 'also to get orders for two hundred planes from the Ministry of Transport.

Junkers spent many millions in building up the Russian plant and in manufacturing and sending plane parts there. In fact, he invested all of his own money. The airline company, too, cost a lot of money, and Sachsenberg mortgaged many of the planes in order to keep the airlines going.

That is why Junkers was eager to get his money back when the Russian job was done. But when he went to Berlin, Generals von Hasse and von Niedermeyer told him bluntly that they could not pay him—because they did not have any money. When he asked for the order for two hundred planes which had been promised to him, they said they could not give him this order. It turned out that the two gentlemen had speculated on the stock exchange in order to increase the funds at their disposal and had lost all their money.

Junkers had no written contract. When he threatened to sue anyhow, the army men became very nervous. They hinted that Junkers might find himself dead one morning. They also suggested that if he sued, he would be accused of high treason. Junkers was furious. He hired some of the best lawyers in Germany, and a scandal threatened. In the meantime General von Hasse shot himself.

That was the moment when Ernst Brandenburg came on the scene.

Up to that point Junkers and all of us around him thought that the whole thing was a mess but that the fault lay really in those two officers who had speculated. But it later turned out that while the two officers had lost the money for the order of two hundred planes, they had not lost nor even speculated with the money that was to be paid to Junkers for the factory in Russia. The simple fact was that no money had ever been allotted for such a purpose.

Junkers had been led to make an outlay of five to six million marks though the army had never had any intention of paying Junkers that amount. Junkers had been led into a trap. And now Ernst Brandenburg closed the trap.

Brandenburg's proposal was simple. Either Junkers would be forced into bankruptcy or he had to hand over his airline company. The Junkers airlines concern was to be amalgamated with the Aero-Lloyd into a new company, to be called *Deutsche Lufthansa* (German Air Hansa). The Lufthansa would be under the financial control of certain banks and financial institutions which directed the Aero-Lloyd.

As a kind of compensation, Junkers would be allowed to sell his Moscow plant to the Russians. Also Junkers would be allowed to keep most of his airlines abroad, especially in Persia. In addition, there was to be a cash settlement—but it was not anywhere near the real value of the Junkers airlines.

Professor Junkers had no choice. If he had said no, all his other companies would have been endangered and his life's work would have been ruined. So he said yes.

But we, the young men around Junkers, the representatives of the German war youth who had not wanted to give up the dream of flying, we did not say yes. We were angry. We were furious at the treatment accorded our Professor by what we then believed to be the banks behind the Aero-Lloyd. We held a solemn meeting in Dessau and decided that none of us would accept a job with the Lufthansa. We pledged our word of honor not to do so—not under any condition.

That seemed only right to us. After all, Professor Junkers had been our teacher, our benefactor; we owed everything to him.

Everyone pledged his word not to desert Junkers. Only one of us broke his word—Erhard Milch.

As soon as he got an offer from the Lufthansa, he walked right out on Junkers. At first he was only a third director under Otto Merkel and Martin Wronsky, both of whom had proved their inefficiency as managers of the Aero-Lloyd. But Milch was soon able to kick Merkel out and relegate Wronsky to an insignificant role. Given the great powers behind Merkel and Wronsky, this could not have been done just by muscling in. It was done only because Milch had even greater powers behind him than Merkel and Wronsky. He had, indeed; Brandenburg and the army were stronger than anybody or anything in Germany.

It is symbolic that the Lufthansa started functioning in the year 1926. That was the year when, as a result of Brandenburg's clever manipulating, the last fetters which the Versailles Treaty had fastened on German civil aviation were broken. That was the year when the last Allied Control Commission left Germany. There was no reason for secrecy any more.

From 1926 on, Lufthansa pilot-training schools sprang up everywhere in Germany, and Lufthansa's inventory of planes increased rapidly. A great number of planes were used for training purposes, on night routes, for airmail transport from Berlin to London, from Berlin to Koenigsberg to Scandinavia.

From 1926 on, one finds even in such widely publicized, internationally known surveys as *Jane's All the World's Aircraft* certain purely military types designed and built by German engineers, which up to then had been listed under Denmark or Sweden or Switzerland or Holland, listed under Germany.

There was no need for secrecy any more, and the men who continued to direct the air rearmament were almost cynical about it.

Everything was done so openly that even the German Reichstag, which hardly ever found out anything, learned in 1929 about the central role the so-called civil Lufthansa was playing in the air rearmament, and the misuse of Lufthansa funds. Indeed, the Reichstag cut the Lufthansa subsidies from 68 million marks to 28 million marks. But General Wilberg and Ernst Brandenburg arranged for loans and there was, of course, always Herr von Stauss and his Deutsche Bank to fall back upon for ample credit.

In July 1932, when I returned to Berlin from one of my many trips abroad in the interest of the Junkers company, I went to the central office of the Lufthansa to see Erhard Milch on some business. I was shown into a sumptuous office where Milch was dictating to one of his secretaries. He dismissed her and was friendly enough to me, but he appeared to be nervous. He seemed to be expecting something.

Every other minute he would inquire over the telephone whether there was any news from Danzig. Since there wasn't any, he became even more nervous.

Finally a call came through from Danzig. As he took it, I started to go out of the room, but he beckoned me to stay. Then he listened, and when he hung up a smile broke over his troubled face.

"Thank God," he murmured and wiped his brow. Then he explained. "Hitler has arrived safely at Danzig."

I didn't understand and said so. I knew, of course, who

Hitler was. But I didn't know why his traveling across Germany was any of Milch's concern.

"You don't understand. Hitler and a lot of his friends use Lufthansa planes for their trips around Germany. You know, that way they save time and can make more speeches." Since I still didn't understand, he went on. "The plane which he chartered to fly to Danzig was overdue. I was afraid there might have been an accident."

"Surely the Lufthansa carries insurance."

Milch laughed. "Of course, of course. But you see, I let Hitler use those planes for nothing. If an accident should occur, plenty of questions would be asked. The Reichstag would stick its nose in. It wouldn't look good."

It did not, indeed, look too good to me. So Milch was on friendly terms with the Nazis? Did he hope that they would eventually take over power in Germany? But he couldn't hope that. He couldn't be a Nazi. After all, he was a Jew, at least a half Jew.

But, then, Milch had always been an opportunist. And he always had a good nose for what was likely to succeed. He probably had very early recognized the Nazi party as a potential power. And then immediately had started cultivating men like Goering and Hess. Putting Hansa airplanes at their disposal was a simple enough way to ingratiate himself with them and with the Fuehrer.

That such transactions constituted, to put it mildly, a gross mishandling of his duties as manager of the Lufthansa apparently did not dusturb Milch very much. Naturally, anybody including Herr Hitler could charter an airplane from the Lufthansa—but not without paying.

The irony of the situation was that the Lufthansa was owned and heavily subsidized by the German Republic, precisely the Republic which Hitler attacked so sweepingly in all his speeches—of which, in turn, he could make so many only because he made use gratis of Hansa airplanes.

And Hitler took full advantage of Milch's offer. In the year 1932 alone he and other leading Nazis traveled more than 35,000 kilometers (23,000 miles) by air without paying a cent.

I have often wondered whether Milch's friends in the German army knew about his relations with the Nazis and whether they approved of them. Or did Milch perhaps betray the generals for Hitler, as he had betrayed Junkers for the generals? I think everything indicates that he did betray the army and decided at an early stage to pool his forces with the Nazi party. And he was most certainly on the side of the Nazis in the struggle between the party and the army over which was going to control the German Luftwaffe—a struggle that was to break out almost immediately after Hitler came to power.

But then again, Milch may have been even cleverer than that. He may have made his swing over to the Nazi party in his old role of agent for the army, as a fifth columnist of the army. He may have become second man in the Nazi Luftwaffe with not only the approval of but very definite orders from the army. He may have known all the time that no matter how strong the grip of the party over the Luftwaffe might appear in the beginning, the army would assert itself in the end again—as indeed the army did.

Milch was by no means the only one connected with the German army who felt that the Nazis were about to take power. One can see in the old army lists that many officers who had been in charge of aviation left the army rather suddenly in that summer of 1932. Many of the men who later became leading officers in the German Luftwaffe—

Kaupisch, Wachenfeld, Halm, and Zander. Evidently, they began with the preliminary work of establishing cadres of the Luftwaffe under the camouflage of working at private jobs. Maybe they, too, were instructed to act as army fifth columnists inside the Luftwaffe-to-be.

When the Nazis came to power in 1933, they did not, as they later claimed for propaganda purposes, have to build German aviation from scratch. On the contrary, Germany at that time was in possession of a well-balanced aviation system which was among the best and the most modern in the world. A civil aviation, of course. It is true that, as far as military aviation goes, only the groundwork had been laid. But preparations in that direction had been carried on for a long time.

There existed at the time in Germany ground organizations of more than a hundred airports and a large number of landing fields connected with each other by an excellent communication system which included wireless and other facilities for the dissemination of meteorological and other reports, direction finding, etc. There was also a communication system between airdromes and flying planes.

The Lufthansa had an enormous network both inside and outside of Germany, and in addition there was the Junkers company. All in all, there were about sixty-five national and international lines that ran as far as Moscow, London, Barcelona, and Athens, and the Lufthansa was ready to open transatlantic services to South America. In 1932 the Lufthansa had covered no less than 6,500,000 miles in scheduled service, with a regularity of 93 per cent and with a safety factor of one passenger injured per 1,750,000 miles. Lufthansa planes flew, on a daily average, 30,000 miles.

Germany's training facilities were better than those of any other country at that time. The German School for Airline Pilots (*Deutsche Verkehrsflieger Schule*), too, trained air captains (and bomber pilots) in a carefully planned course of three years. Private flying schools sprang up all over Germany. And in 1932 the Air Sport Association (*Deutsche Luftfahrtverband*)—with its 52,000 members—trained 1,500 pilots in its schools and had under training 3,000 motor pilots and 15,000 glider pilots....

I don't have to enlarge here upon the resources and facilities of German industry, which was then one of the most powerful and most progressive in the world.

By 1933 Heinkel had developed his famous He 70, which was to be the forerunner of the modern military Heinkel planes, and he had a number of other models ready for military and naval use. Heinkel's "Kadett" and the Focke-Wulf "Stieglitz"—which also was in production—became the elementary training planes for the Luftwaffe. Messerschmitt, too, was ready, and so was Dornier.

Eight German engine works were in operation then. They became and still are the backbone of the Luftwaffe—among them Daimler-Benz, Bayrische Motorenwerke, Junkers, and Siemens—and all of them had 800-horsepower engines in production or ready for production.

All in all, the German aircraft industry in 1933 was in a position to build without any effort twenty planes a month and had a capacity for building at least fifty, including all necessary engines. This does not seem a big output in comparison with today's production figures, but the point is that German industry contained all the elements necessary for the purely quantitative expansion which the Nazis carried through during the next few years and for which they were so much admired by themselves and the rest of the world.

The tremendous impression which the Nazi aviation industry made upon foreign visitors from 1936 on was due mainly to the head start and the time advantage they had been allowed to secure.

At the time the Nazis came to power, Professor Hugo Junkers was no longer the manager of the Junkers company. He had to leave this post early in 1932.

Even before that, Junkers had recovered financially from the terrific blow the army had struck him in 1925. By the end of 1931, however, the army—or better, the men behind the rearmament idea—prepared to strike another blow. This time Erhard Milch came out in the open against his former chief. As managing director of the Lufthansa, he was able to block all orders which had been promised to Junkers, who had made considerable financial commitments in preparing for just such orders. When Junkers inquired why the Lufthansa was going back on its word, Milch let it be known that Junkers could not expect any business unless he ousted from his board of directors his old, loyal collaborators who were as pacifistic and as anti-militaristic as the Professor himself.

When Junkers inquired whom he should put in charge, Milch suggested Junkers' own son Klaus.

Junkers thought it over for a time and in the end complied. Klaus was only twenty-four years old and he was sure he could control him. However, it turned out that he could not. Klaus did not know very much about producing airplanes. He had worked for a year at one of the Ford plants in Detroit, but that was about all his industrial experience. Upon his return to Germany he joined the

Black Reichswehr, and later, probably without his father's knowledge, he became a storm trooper. From the very first he was but an obedient tool in the hands of the Nazi party. At the party's request, he immediately threw out of his father's company all "pacifists, internationalists, and Jews." He also re-engaged a little accountant who had been dismissed by his father as a rabble-rouser—a fierce Nazi—and placed him in charge of all labor relations.

I never had an opportunity to talk to the Professor in those days because I did not happen to be in Germany. Somehow, I am glad I did not see him then. It must have broken his heart to witness the collapse of everything he had built up in a lifetime.

Though no longer active in his old company, Junkers was still living in Dessau when the Nazis came. The Nazis— when they took over—put a stop to this. They forced him to leave Dessau. Actually, they exiled him, under the pretext that he had to leave town within a few days' time "for reasons of safety of the state." Milch was the man behind that. There was some talk about high treason which the Professor was supposed to have committed by selling a certain license abroad.

Junkers went to Munich. By that time he was well over seventy. But still he wasn't broken. Against hopeless odds he tried to start all over again. He devoted himself to the completion of his revolutionary free-piston engine. There was still life in him.

Gotthard Sachsenberg, too, suffered from Nazi persecution. He had left Junkers after the fusion of the airlines with Aero-Lloyd in 1926. He wanted to continue the fight for an independent civil aviation and decided to go into politics the better to carry on the fight. He became a member of the Reichstag, where he clashed with the Nazis on many occasions.

Once he could have made his peace with the Nazis, when Goering came to him and suggested a political deal of questionable character. Sachsenberg threw him out and made him his deadly enemy.

Sachsenberg's experiences were interesting enough. His close friend Gottfried Treviranus was Minister of Transportation and should have been able to help him in his fight for an independent aviation. But Treviranus proved powerless against the men in his own ministry, especially Ernst Brandenburg.

In 1932 Sachsenberg, foreseeing the doom of the German Republic, left politics in disgust and once more went into business. He built pontoons for float planes. Milch, who liked him, directed a few orders his way before the Nazis came to power and even afterward.

But Goering did not like him, and it was probably he who put his name on the black list of people who were to be purged in June of 1934. Treviranus, too, was on that list, but he escaped in a sensational flight to England. Sachsenberg was arrested, put on a truck, and was well on his way to Lichterfelde to be shot when suddenly the truck was stopped and he was forced down and put into a prison. Thus he survived the purge. For those who were not killed right away were allowed to go free a few weeks afterward.

I doubt whether it was all a mistake. Somebody had decided to save Sachsenberg. Perhaps Milch, or maybe even Goering. In any case Sachsenberg had learned his lesson. From that time on he behaved. He knew that the others were stronger.

While Junkers was forced out of Dessau, while Sachsenberg was almost put to death, their former employee,
Erhard Milch, was continuing his career and even starting
on a more sensational career. Less than two months after
the Nazis came to power and the Air Ministry under
Goering was organized, he was made Goering's right-hand
man. Later, when the Luftwaffe came out into the open,
he advanced rapidly from lieutenant-general to general to
colonel-general and finally to field marshal. (He had been a
captain when the first world war was over.)

All this was a sensational achievement for a man who
was a half Jew. However, Goering had declared him an
honorary "Aryan." Milch had helped by forcing his aged
Gentile mother to swear that he was not the son of her
Jewish husband, but instead the fruit of a love affair which
the old lady pretended she had had with an "Aryan" the
year preceding Milch's birth. Perhaps it was really so—
which does not render Milch's part in exposing his mother's
past any more chivalrous.

Incidentally, when the Nazis came to power Milch finally
decided that he would have to learn to fly. Yes, this man
who had been an observer in World War I, who had been
at the head of the Lufthansa for many years, could not
fly. Now he began taking lessons from the famous flier,
Ernst Udet.

Udet quite openly told anybody who wanted to listen
that Milch was not a good flier and would never become
a good flier. Milch never forgave him this.

Old Professor Junkers was persecuted by the Nazis to
the very end. His son Klaus—who, incidentally, a short
time later was kicked out of his father's company—did
everything he could to make the old man's life miserable.

Junkers died in Munich in February 1935 on his seventy-sixth birthday. The services took place in extreme privacy. The Nazis saw to that. Only Junkers' best friends came to Munich to be present. In Dessau the death was not even made known till a few days afterward. In Munich in the little factory that Junkers had created during the last two years of his life, a few workers stood for three minutes in silence to honor him. The German people in general scarcely noticed the passing of the man who had tried harder and more consistently than anybody else to help them and to build a future for them.

The day after the cremation the Nazis started to build up a new Junkers legend. The man whom they had fought without mercy, whom they had hunted to his grave—now that he was dead—they claimed for themselves. They began to rewrite his history so that in the future their version would become the accepted one.

How the old man would have hated it! How he would have protested and shown his contempt for those unscrupulous liars!

PART II: THE LUFTWAFFE IS BORN

6.   Goering in the Limelight

The Nazis have a hard time proving that the Germans are a master race. But they try hard. It is a favorite trick of theirs to prove that all great inventions have originated with the Germans. That goes particularly for the great inventions in aviation. You may point out to them that as far as is known the airplane was invented by two American brothers by the name of Wright. Well, not even the Nazis can deny that. But they have discovered that the Wrights were really German because they had a German grandfather, Johann G. Koerner, who emigrated from Germany to Virginia.

The Nazis claimed, too, that it was they who built the Luftwaffe. Unfortunately, the world believed them, though there is just about as much truth in this statement as in the one about the Wright brothers.

I have written at such length about the rebirth of German aviation after Versailles in order to debunk the Nazi legend that it was they who saved and rebuilt German aviation. I have pointed out that no Nazi had a hand in the constructive expansion of German aviation which, apart from its politically sinister background, was quite an achievement from the point of view of technique and organization.

None of the men who were responsible for that expansion were Nazis. Neither Erhard Milch nor his right-hand man in the Lufthansa, Freiherr von Gablenz, neither Brandenburg nor Colonel Alfred Keller, the head of the *Deutsche Verkehrsfliegerschule* (German School for Training Airline Pilots). There was no Hitler, no Goering, no Hess anywhere around, either in the airlines or in the industry.

Much has been made of the fact that Rudolf Hess was a flier in World War I, or rather, toward the end of the war. Well, he was. But once the war was over, he was not interested in flying any more. He was interested only in politics.

Much has been made of the fact that Ernst Roehm, later to be murdered by Hitler, created—in 1930—organizations of flying squadrons among the storm troopers and the elite guards. But nothing much came out of that whole business up to September 1932, that is, four months before Hitler came to power. And even then, only flying units of the SA were ordered set up by Roehm and an elementary organization to teach flying storm troopers how to fly in squadron formation.

At about the same time, Hess organized some sports flying groups, also with the idea of training them in military flying or, at least, preparing them for such training later on. Hess was also interested in the glider movement and it was mostly due to him that the Nazis arranged for glider competitions, gave prizes for the best models and the best exhibitions.

But even all that put together didn't amount to very much. The whole Nazi party scarcely did as much for German aviation in all the years before it came to power as Professor Junkers did on any one day of the year, in any year.

Some may contradict me and put forward the argument that a great many of the German pilots—and by far the majority of them—were Nazis, even before Hitler came to power. This is true, but it was not on account of anything the Nazis had done for aviation. It had to do with their psychology. A great part of German youth at that time was embittered and despairing of the future. The young men were willing to believe anybody who promised to change the dark outlook. Young people, especially pilots, who have to do with aviation are, according to all experiences, more daring and, therefore, more disposed to a radical solution then others. Thus, it was only natural and understandable that a great number of pilots should go Nazi as soon as there was a Nazi party. Also, there is no doubt that the whole rhythm of the Nazi party, the "dynamic" of the party—which they, of course, could not recognize as a phony dynamism—appealed strongly to the men of aviation.

This is the reason, too, why it became relatively easy for the Nazis to make the Luftwaffe a real party weapon and why the Nazi fliers to this day are the most loyal of Nazis on whom Hitler can depend—even more than his army or his navy.

I have waited till now for a detailed discussion of Hermann Goering. Two days after Hitler came to power he made Goering Reichs Commissar for Aviation. A few weeks later—on April 29, 1933—a Reichs Air Ministry was established and Goering was appointed its minister.

Nazi legend has it that the man who was later to direct the Luftwaffe had a decisive part in the rebuilding of German aviation. I have reviewed the rebuilding of German aviation and I think I have not once had to mention Goering as a factor of any importance. And this for the simple reason that Goering had nothing to do with the whole business—absolutely nothing. When he took over the Air Ministry, he found more or less a made bed. All I can say is that what he did during the first two years of his leadership amounted to unmaking that made bed. And that in spite of his many glowing speeches during those and later years.

Nobody can deny that the young Goering was one of the best fliers of World War I. He was distinguished by the highest German order, the *Pour le merite*. He was the last chief of the famous Richthofen squadron after Richthofen himself was killed.

Goering, unlike most other Nazis, comes from a family of officers. His father served in the German Colonial Office, first in Germany, then in German South West Africa, and later on in Haiti. Hermann Goering was educated at the Cadet School in Karlsruhe and became a lieutenant in 1912. He went to the French front in 1914 and soon afterward joined the air corps. For more than a year he flew as an observer; then in 1916 he got his pilot's license. During the war he shot down thirty-six enemy aircraft, quite an achievement for that time.

On November 11, 1918, instead of surrendering the planes of his squadron to the Americans as was stipulated in the Armistice conditions, he flew back to Germany with his squadron and landed with most of them at Darmstadt. A few of his pilots had to make forced landings at the airdrome of Mannheim, where they were immediately arrested for disobedience. (There was a revolution going on in Germany at that time, and the police forces were on the side of the revolutionary masses.) Goering very typically sent out an ultimatum that either his pilots would be allowed to take off or he would bomb the airport and the city of Mannheim. The authorities of Mannheim decided to release the pilots.

At Aschaffenburg, a small town on the Main, the squadron finally disbanded. There was a little celebration at the Stiftskeller restaurant, and Goering made a speech. He said:

"We are proud of what we have accomplished together. And we will hold together. I will never relax, comrades, till our squadron and German aviation are reborn."

That, at least, is how Goering's biographers have quoted him. It is entirely possible that Goering, who was given to theatrical flourishes, uttered just such words. Then, again, it may be just a story. In any case, though I have known a number of men from the old Richthofen squadron, I have never met one who was present at that famous scene in Aschaffenburg.

If Goering did swear such an oath, he perjured himself. Because immediately after the little dinner in Aschaffenberg was over, he lost all interest in German aviation. And some years elapsed before he thought of it again.

Of course, he had to make a living. First he went to Sweden, where he tried his hand at many an odd job and for some time even became the pilot of the small air charter company. During one of his flights he made a crash landing on a big estate where he met the beautiful Karin von Fock, the wife of a Swedish officer, who fell in love with Goering, divorced her husband, and married him. Later Goering went to Munich, supposedly to study history and economics, but nobody ever saw him inside the university, and he never took any of the examinations. At that time he made a living, or at least tried to make a living, as a dealer in secondhand motor cars. He drank a lot.

In 1922 he met Hitler, and from then on his life had a new meaning. He immediately began to play a big part in the struggling little party, and became the first Chief of the Storm Troopers (before Ernst Roehm). He was involved and wounded in Hitler's famous beer cellar putsch of November 1923 and had to flee Germany. He spent the next years partly in Italy, partly in Sweden. Most of the time he was in sanatoriums for drug-addiction cures. He took morphine. Later, after a political amnesty had been granted, he returned to Germany. It was then that he remembered German aviation.

By that time he was again looking for a way to make a living, especially since his wife's funds were exhausted and his wife's family did not seem to want to advance any more. He was often in the company of one Theo Koerner and one Fritz Siebel, with whom he drank and quarreled a lot. The three of them decided that with German aviation on the upgrade there had to be a chance for them to make a living without actually working.

Thus, they hit upon the splendid idea of selling parachutes to companies that manufactured airplanes. But, as it turned out, the idea wasn't so good. Even if there had been a law requiring one or more parachutes in each plane manufactured at that time in Germany, there would hardly have been a living in it for three men, especially since they did not manufacture the parachutes themselves but only acted as salesmen for a little factory. Also, there were other parachute factories and the market was more or less covered.

But Goering was not one to be easily discouraged. He did not consider it beneath his dignity to resort to blackmail to get orders. If the head of an airplane factory declined to buy his parachutes, Goering told him that he would have him shot as soon as the Nazis came to power. I know of a number of actual cases of such attempts at blackmail on Goering's part. I know also that Goering became very successful in selling parachutes in this original way, though the moneys he derived did not cover his enormous personal expenses. He also obtained some small sums from Heinkel and from the later Messerschmitt factory. How he was able to get more money, how he was able to get the enormous credit he did during the next years, until Hitler was finally installed into power, is another story. . . .

In any case, the parachute business was the whole of Goering's contribution to German aviation from the day of the Armistice to the day he became Air Minister. At that time many people wondered why Hitler appointed him to that post. Everybody expected General Wilberg to get the assignment. Indeed, Wilberg would have been the logical man.

But, then, Wilberg was not a Nazi, and he was much too closely aligned with the army for Hitler's comfort. The fact that he disliked Goering thoroughly and never tried to hide his contempt was probably the reason Wilberg never had much of a career inside the Luftwaffe.

Hitler had many reasons for appointing Goering.

One undoubtedly was that Goering had been a famous flier during World War I. Another one was that he undoubtedly understood something about airplanes, something that could not be said of any other prominent Nazi at that time. Equally important was the fact that Goering was the only "gentleman" among the higher-ups in the Nazi party, a man of good family, and one at least who could hold his own at the many conferences to come with the "big shots" of the aircraft industry and with officers of the army.

By that time Hermann Goering was already quite fat. Nobody who had known the slender, good-looking *Oberleutnant* of 1918 would have recognized him. His fatness was somewhat symbolic. Goering, who even in his youth had the manners of a feudal lord, now could follow his incredibly expensive inclinations which, for one reason or another, impressed many people inside Germany and also many distinguished foreigners, among them the British Ambassador in Berlin, Sir Nevile Henderson. The world knows, of course, all about his love for uniforms; his acquisitiveness in regard to castles, houses, and estates; his admiration for old masters, which he stole from museums; his famous lion cubs, which played around him; the incredibly tasteless ceremony that took place when he brought the body of his late wife Karin from Sweden to his estate in the Schorfheide—Karin whom he had left to die alone.

All this spelled bad taste and a pathologic vanity. Goering had become extremely rich and powerful, and he could not refrain from showing off. I mention all this because it is in such contrast to the very spirit of aviation, military or civil. It is the very opposite of the spirit of young fliers who are hard and tough and who don't care for luxury, but only for hard work and adventure. Scarcely a man could have been found who represented less the spirit of the young German flier than the Goering of these years.

But he had become Air Minister. And then he constructed an immense building for the Air Ministry, something unheard of as to size and modern devices, and very impressive and very beautiful.

And then a lot of things began to happen.

7.   *Business Not as Usual*

On January 30, 1933, Hitler became Chancellor. By the middle of March of the same year, Hermann Goering had been made Germany's first Air Minister. Exactly two years later, on March 10, 1935, Goering asked the air attachés of France and England to call upon him at his Air Ministry.

The gentlemen arrived. Goering told them that Germany had decided to rearm in the air. He told them that decision had not been made that day or the day before or the week before. It had been made a long, long time ago. In fact, he told them, Germany had already rearmed in the air.

As though to give point to his words, there was a mighty roar outside. The attachés went to the window. The sky was covered with planes. Four hundred of them circling over Berlin. Had the attachés looked closer, they wouldn't have been so terrified as they were. For most of the planes were really nothing but converted transport planes, good old Ju 52's, painted dark gray and dark green, to make them look like mighty bombers.

The very same day Goering had an interview with the *Daily Mail's* correspondent, Ward Price, who was used often by the Nazis to make public their opinion and their decisions. It was through this interview of Ward Price's that the world learned in the next few days that Hitler had rearmed in the air. The world learned it and was thunderstruck. The world believed that Hitler was already invincible in the air.

Erhard Milch later said—in articles, in speeches, in interviews—that the building of the Luftwaffe had been achieved speedily, easily, and without any great difficulty. Nothing is further from the truth, however. Nothing was achieved speedily, easily, and without difficulty.

When, after Hitler's coming to power, it was decided to build up a Luftwaffe, all did not go smoothly. On the contrary. During the first years there was little but disorder and disorganization. Milch, who was immediately called upon by Goering to direct the production, understood something about air traffic but little or nothing about production problems. He had a vague notion that first of all it would be necessary to enlarge the existing plants, and then that it would be necessary to build plants. But he had, for instance, no clear idea that before production on a large scale could be started it would be necessary to organize the influx of raw material and then to reorganize on a more comprehensive scale the industries that manufacture the parts and the accessories necessary in the construction of aircraft.

There was no real master plan in the beginning. It was only during the course of the years, in the course of the expanding production, that bottlenecks were encountered and fundamental errors were discovered and removed.

There were, for instance, not enough officers and not enough flight instructors. There was not a big enough reservoir of trained personnel to man the growing apparatus, there weren't sufficient airports nor hangars. Milch never even tried to organize all this in a methodical and planned way. That would have meant too much loss of time. And there was no time. Goering was impatient

because Hitler was impatient. Hitler wanted "to see results." Hitler wanted and demanded in the shortest possible
time and in no uncertain terms an air force impressive
enough to be used as a political weapon, not to defeat
another air force.

It seems to me, as I look back at those first years of the
Luftwaffe, that this idea of Hitler's to use it as a political
weapon influenced the very way the Luftwaffe was built.
In other words, that building process was not a planned
affair but a political maneuver. There was a lot of fighting
and agitation and jockeying for position around the Air
Ministry during these years. There was not much planning.

Perhaps this had also to do with the fact that Goering
was not so sure that the German people really wanted a
Luftwaffe at that time. After all, it was then the Nazis were
talking about peace and peaceful work. So Goering decided
on a trial balloon. On June 24, 1933, all German newspapers carried an article that stated that foreign aircraft
of an unknown type had appeared over Berlin and had
managed to get away unrecognized. They had dropped
leaflets that were insulting to the new government. Unfortunately, those planes could not be intercepted because
the air police force had no planes of its own, and the planes
available at the airports were too inferior in speed.

This incident, the German papers explained, demonstrated clearly that Germany was defenseless against attacks from the air, that things could not go on as they had
gone on. Today it was leaflets, tomorrow it might be
poison gas.

It was all very disturbing. But the trouble was that
nobody in Germany had actually seen any of those mysterious foreign airplanes, and neither had anybody seen any
of the leaflets. The text of those leaflets was not published

anywhere. And with good reason. Because there had been no foreign planes. In a way, one may term this whole incident the "Reichstag's fire" of German aviation. It gave Goering an excuse at least to ask for police planes or, as he called them "defense planes." To increase the general agitation created by the phony foreign planes, Goering immediately introduced the *Luftschutz*—a compulsory air raid precautions organization—as though an enemy attack was to be expected at any moment.

Slowly the building up process began, slowly it continued. There was nothing speedy about any of it. The rebuilding in 1919 and 1920, after the Versailles Treaty, had been much faster, though, or perhaps because, there was less rhetoric. It took the Nazis much longer than they had expected to build up the Luftwaffe, and it certainly took them more time than the world thought afterward.

When Goering started his Ministry, a number of military experts assembled themselves around him. There was a Major Bodenschatz, who became his adjutant, there were the Colonels von der Hagen and Quade. There was, of course, Milch, and General Wever, who was later to become the first chief of the general staff of the air. There was Captain Loerzer, who became chief of the German Air Sports Association; Major Kesselring; Colonel Christiansen, a famous navy flier in World War I; and von Gronau, later air attaché in Tokyo, just to name a few.

But among them all were only a very few men of real ability. These men could not be compared, for instance, with the extremely intelligent officers who had revamped the German army after Versailles—von Seeckt, von Fritsch, Ludwig Beck, etc. There were—all Nazi propaganda talk notwithstanding—no real leaders among them.

Real leaders would have striven toward a powerful Luft-waffe for strategic air warfare. Goering and Milch, and all their friends, fumbled the issue. They insisted on self-contained, autonomous units, organized and administered as army units, to be mobilized in air fleets. But there ended their imagination and their understanding of air strategy.

Goering talked a lot. He was very happy about the unity of the air command. He said, for instance:

"Everything will be in the hands of one responsible individual, and this will greatly help to promote all technical developments. The whole industry will become the instrument of a leader who knows from his own practical experiences what we need most. Technical centralization of air development will help the army and the navy. Even though at first there might be some interdepartmental difficulties."

There were, indeed, plenty of interdepartmental difficulties in the beginning. There were many fights with the army. One of the fights was over who should get the command of the anti-aircraft units. Goering finally won. There was another struggle about who should get the command of the aircraft units to be used in co-operation with the army and navy. Again the decision was in favor of Goering (while, for instance, the Royal Air Force has no control over the army or navy auxiliary planes). Goering was insatiable. He wanted and finally got the searchlight units, the groups operating the listening devices, the parachutists. For good measure he also incorporated into the Luftwaffe the Hermann Goering Regiment, which really belongs in the army, if it belongs anywhere at all.

The Air Ministry from the very beginning was a department where secrets were closely guarded. It must be recalled that for a very long time the Air Ministry was supposed to be interested only in civil aviation, in airlines, and to some degree in aviation as a sport. Actually, however, the departments of the Air Ministry were interested only in military aviation. In Department I, technical specifications for military planes were fixed and revised from the point of view of war technique. Department II, called Arms and Equipment, was divided into subdivisions which had to do with machine guns, bombs, instruments, bomb sights, gas, and photographic apparatus, respectively. Only Department III had anything to do with setting standards for and inspection of planes and engines—which, indeed, would have been enough for a Ministry devoted only to the building of a civil aviation.

Immediately after Goering took over, Bruno Loerzer was asked to reorganize the *Luftsportverband* (Air Sports Association). Decrees were issued to incorporate all clubs, associations, and groups which had to do with aviation in the *Luftsportverband*. Thus, the association, which had consisted of about 300 clubs before Hitler came to power, soon comprised about 2,500 clubs. These 2,500 clubs were reorganized and rebaptized. The sports association suddenly became very military—it was still called so—and the clubs were called *Landesgruppen* (regional groups). The membership was raised from 60,000 to 500,000 by means of an enormous promotion program. Immediately, a full-fledged training program disguised as many different sports activities was instituted. There were officers, uniforms, titles, and what not. When Loerzer did not prove himself efficient enough in the administration of the association, Goering took the job away from him. Finally, in 1935, the whole Air Sports Association was incorporated into the Luftwaffe proper.

But in spite of this apparent organization there was no real organization.

From the very beginning the Luftwaffe consisted of the flying units, the engineer corps, the anti-aircraft artillery, the air force communications service (which also should have been under army command), and the aforementioned Hermann Goering Regiment, which consisted of one detachment of engineers, one infantry battalion to fight parachute attacks, three anti-aircraft battalions that were supposed to guard Goering's personal headquarters, and one searchlight battalion.

All this was ready by 1935. But in 1938, when Der Tag had come nearer, the set-up of the organization was changed radically, and again in the spring of 1939 fundamental organizational changes were made. (By organization, I mean the regional units of the Luftwaffe set-up which were to be changed over in time of war to tactical units.)

One of the most interesting sections of the Luftwaffe was its engineer corps. It is to me more than anything else convincing proof of the shortcomings of both Goering and Milch. Neither one liked technical problems. They did not understand technical problems and, therefore, did not want to have anything to do with them. So they created the engineer corps—and thought that would settle the matter. But they were unable to understand the enormous importance of engineering in aviation. Milch expressed it once when he said to me, "After all, engineers are only plumbers of a kind, in white shirts. Plumbing is useful and unavoidable. But all the same no officer would dream of having social intercourse with a plumber, or would he?"

Thus, an engineer corps was created under a diploma engineer, Guenther Bock. But it was made clear from the beginning that members of this corps were not to be officers. They were to be *Militaerbeamte* (military servants as against civil servants). Bock, on the other hand, wanted to be something important and wanted his engineer corps to be something important. He, therefore, created military ranks corresponding to the different officers' titles in the medical corps. But the air officers themselves felt as Goering and Milch did, and never accepted the engineers as their equals or even as people they could talk to.

The consequence was what anybody with any sense could have foreseen. No intelligent young man with any kind of ambition wanted to join the engineer corps of the Luftwaffe. If they wanted to join the Luftwaffe they wanted to become pilots and eventually officers. Thus, Bock only got what was left over—which was not much.

All this is more important than it seems at first glance. Bock, who was no great shakes himself, and the men around him proved utterly unable to solve the enormous technical problems involved in the building up process of a large modern air force. The inferiority of the engineer corps finally became such a scandal that something had to be done about it. But by then it was too late. By the beginning of May 1942, fresh entries in the existing engineer corps were no longer accepted and the corps was slowly disbanded. Engineer officers were finally given official recognition as Luftwaffe officers, and were treated accordingly—this in order to get the best technical brains into the Luftwaffe. Even Goering and Milch by that time had learned that "plumbing" in aviation was something extremely important. (Incidentally, by that time, the incompetent Bock had been replaced by the extremely competent Ernst Udet.)

When in 1935 Goering let the world in on his secret

that Germany had rearmed in the air, he also boasted that he had solved all the production problems. That was pure and simple bluff. When the Nazis came to power there were no plans available to start production of military aircraft on a large scale. After they had been in power a year, there were still no plans.

I said before that Milch understood something of air traffic, but nothing of the production angle. He had a hazy idea that the plants should produce more, but he did not know that the first thing to do was to arrange for the necessary raw material and for the necessary accessories—which means that all the subsidiary industries had to be built up beforehand. Therefore, the beginning of the building up process of the Luftwaffe was marked by the existence of a great number of bottlenecks, and furthermore it would have been even worse if Milch had started right in producing new types—as Goering wanted the world to believe Germany was doing—instead of going ahead and producing obsolete planes. And this is exactly what it did. For some time no plant brought out a new model. Every plant was too busy turning out old models that had been in existence before the Nazis came to power. Because the Fuehrer wanted results—and fast.

The two outstanding raw materials necessary for construction and operation of airplanes are aluminum and oil. Aluminum could be derived only from bauxite, which does not exist in Germany. There are deposits of it, however, in Hungary and in Yugoslavia. It was for the sake of the Luftwaffe that Hitler always tried to remain on good terms with Hungary and Yugoslavia—and imported enormous amounts of bauxite from them.

The oil problem was, of course, the most urgent one from the very start.

In 1938, I talked to one of the closest collaborators of Milch and Goering—for private reasons I cannot give his name. This man told me that even in the event of war, the fuel needed for the Luftwaffe and the mechanized army units could be produced synthetically in Germany. Under one condition, however, which was that there would not be a long war but only a blitzkrieg or perhaps a succession of blitz campaigns with enough time in between to create new synthetic gasoline reserves. Otherwise Germany would have to conquer oil fields.

However, nobody at that time was very pleased with synthetic lubricants. They had not proved satisfactory, my informant told me. Therefore, it would be necessary to have an understanding with Russia—in spite of all the anti-Bolshevistic propaganda—and to get oil from Baku and Grozny.

Before the war, or shortly after the outbreak of war, Germany had at its disposal synthetic oil, oil imported from Russia and Rumania, oil from Poland, and a small quantity from Germany itself.

How much did the Luftwaffe need?

The average oil consumption (fuel and lubricants) for all types of aircraft under conditions of intensive warfare—and all calculations had to be made on the basis of such conditions—is estimated at two tons a day per plane. Planes in battle do not themselves use so much. This figure takes into consideration the fuel used in transport and training planes, in test flights, and losses through spillage and evaporation.

Let us take, for example, an air force of 6,000 planes. About one-third, or 2,000 planes, are involved in actual battle or used at the front. That calls for 4,000 tons of oil a day or, allowing 500 additional tons of oil a day for

Luftwaffe ground vehicles, about 4,500 tons for all air force requirements. In a year, this would amount to approximately 1.6 million tons.

Many attempts were made to reduce the consumption of oil. Diesel-motors which operated on much less were introduced. On the other hand, enormous reserves were accumulated underground and under water. According to good authority, up to the time of the outbreak of the war, 35 to 40 million barrels had been accumulated—roughly six months' supply.

There was a lot of talk on the part of Goering, Milch, and all the others designed to point out the superiority of German invention, of German construction, of German methods of production, of German labor, of German everything. But, underneath, the men in the Luftwaffe who knew something about aircraft, from Milch down, not to speak of Ernst Udet, were perfectly well aware all the time that English aircraft, at least, was in many instances superior as to quality, and that plenty of models were being produced in other countries which Germany could not yet produce.

Ernst Udet visited the United States and bought two Curtiss Hawk military aircraft—for private purposes, as he said. He was a sportsman, flying only for the sake of the sport. At any rate, by 1938 the Nazis were building nine different types of war aircraft fitted with engines built with American licenses.

At the time of Udet's purchases in the United States— 1934—the British sold eighty-five engines to the Lufthansa. The French government protested, and Prime Minister Baldwin had to calm the French as well as his own parliament.

On one of his many visits to England, Udet saw the "shadow works," which are plants that were erected for the mass production of models developed in other factories. They were built with government funds. Udet and even Milch were able to visit these shadow works as late as 1937. They were both very much impressed, and there can be no doubt that the ideas they got there helped a lot to accelerate German production.

Goering and Milch received regular reports about the latest developments in the airplane industry from their air attaché in London. Many licenses were bought from England. Finally Germany suggested to English industry that it create a patent pool to sell to Germany so that not every single license would have to be bought. Heinkel paid 40,000 pounds sterling for a license, but he never started to build the planes themselves. Later I learned that in this particular case Milch had never intended to have the planes built. The 40,000 pounds which had been paid over by the Reich was considered the price for good will.

The Nazis went far in their attempts to create good will. The British Armstrong-Siddeley concern had a representative in Berlin, a Mr. Reney, who was married to the sister of the late Dietrich Eckart, the closest friend Hitler ever had, the man who had started him in the Nazi movement. Mrs. Reney, who, of course, could talk to Hitler any day, suggested to him that it might be possible to win the good will and the co-operation of Sir John Siddeley, the owner of the Armstrong-Siddeley concern. And with Sir John, Hitler would have the whole Cliveden set.

Hitler immediately invited Sir John to Germany and gave him an order for eighty-five aircraft engines, quite a big order at that time. This was done by the Fuehrer personally, without the knowledge, let alone the approval, of the technical department of the Air Ministry. It was all very amateurish; no specifications were given. Therefore, when the engines arrived, they could not be used for any German plane.

Later, in the middle of 1938, when Hitler no longer considered the good will of Sir John Siddeley too important, the Air Ministry tried to give back the engines or to sell them somewhere else. I don't know whether it succeeded.

In short, Germany tried to buy everything concerning aircraft which could be bought abroad. On the other hand, the Nazis themselves sold a few licenses. They also sold a great number of obsolescent planes to the Balkan countries, to South America, to China—planes that had already been discarded by the Luftwaffe for its own use. But from 1936 on, they did not sell anything new, neither aircraft nor patents and licenses. In fact, while they were still very busy looking around abroad and purchasing abroad, everything that was being developed in Germany was considered a military secret.

One of the most pertinent problems to present itself during the building of the Luftwaffe was the organizing of manpower to produce aircraft and to keep it in fighting condition, repair it, service it, and so on. Since the Luftwaffe was built for war purposes and had to be maintained during a war, I insert here a calculation of how many men are needed for a Luftwaffe of 6,000 aircraft during a war. Not considered in this calculation are the men employed in anti-aircraft service, whose number is around 1,500,000 today.

According to all experience, 30 per cent of an air force is first-line force while the rest is stationed behind the front.

For planning, the losses of the first-line force have to be calculated as 50 per cent per month, the losses of the rest as 25 per cent.

That means a yearly loss of 11,000 first-line aircraft and a loss of 12,500 other aircraft—or together 23,500. The relation of losses of aircraft to losses of engines is two to three, which means roughly a loss of 35,000 engines.

An all-metal single-seater fighter represents between 14,000 to 18,000 working hours or 5.5 to 6.5 workers a year.

An engine of 1,000 to 1,200 horsepower represents 8,000 to 9,000 working hours, or 3.0 to 3.5 workers a year.

Now figure that out for 23,500 aircraft:

	Men
To build 23,500 aircraft proper (23,500 × 6)	140,000
Supply industry (33⅓ per cent)	47,000
To build 35,000 engines (35,000 × 3)	105,000
Supply industry (66⅔ per cent)	70,000
Accessory industries	30,000
Repair, overhaul, development in industry	80,000
Plane crews	60,000
Ground crew (4 men per flier)	240,000
Auxiliary personnel	720,000
	1,492,000

The leaders of the Luftwaffe were able to find and organize and get those original 1,500,000 men started—which perhaps constitutes their most important and astonishing achievement. But they never got around to the tactical schooling of the personnel. Their training in operative air warfare was very sketchy. (In England this was

the most important item in the whole business of preparation.)

There were some half-hearted attempts in Germany to
do what England did. Already in 1935 the *Hoehere Luft-
waffenschule* (School for training of Air Force Commanders) was established in Gatow near Berlin, for the
purpose of training men who, in turn, would train the
millions. But the school never functioned well, and had
great difficulties in the beginning. There were no teaching
tools, no textbooks, no curriculum. And, above all, there
was no conception of strategy or tactics as a basis to start
on.

There were other negligences. There was never a fully
developed military air transport system. A squadron of
fifteen active aircraft needs the actual presence of at least
150 to 200 men or else it cannot function. These men in
turn need an enormous apparatus of repair shops, tools,
kitchens, etc, which have always to be where the aircraft
are. Only if everything is assembled at the base can the
squadron function. But Milch never thought of organizing
transport facilities from one airport to another. It was only
after the war in Spain that something was done about this.
And it was done only because a great number of Ju 52
transport planes, which had been tried out unsuccessfully
as bombers, could now be used in transport—for which
they had been designed anyhow.

The greatest deficiency—which, in my personal opinion, is one of the main reasons for the collapse of the Luftwaffe—was Milch's unwillingness to busy himself with the
organization of repair facilities and the production and
transport organization of spare parts. I shall go into the
matter at greater length when I have progressed in my
story to the time when this deficiency made itself felt.

What did the Luftwaffe actually build in those years before the war? There has been much speculation about the matter, and there is every reason to suspect that the actual figures were never published. I have talked to many men in the Luftwaffe about this, and I have received many different answers. As far as I could make out, and as far as I was able to calculate German output according to what I know of the facilities of German aircraft industry, the figures are somewhat as follows:

Goering wanted to have, by the end of 1935, roughly 100 first-line squadrons (15 planes each), or 1,500 planes. But by that time only 1,000 planes were ready, 50 per cent of them bombers, 25 per cent reconnaissance craft, and 25 per cent pursuit planes.

By October 1936, 2,000 machines were supposed to be ready, and by the end of 1937, 3,000 planes. The fact is, however, that these 3,000 planes were not ready until the end of 1938, or anyhow not before the Munich agreement (end of September 1938). By March 1939, however (when Hitler marched into Prague), German production finally was running in high gear. By that time there were 6,000 first-line planes, exclusive of army auxiliary planes, and also exclusive of second- and third-line aircraft—which then amounted to 60 or 70 per cent of the first-line aircraft.

But the figures don't tell the whole story.

By starting really big production from scratch, the Nazis could lay out plants and equipment according to the latest ideas in mass production as well as according to the latest ideas about protection against air raids (workshops underground, etc.). But time was pressing. It was too pressing for experiments and it was too pressing to consider everything before making decisions that would influence the production of many years to come.

The consequence was that the standard of scientific research declined steadily. Another consequence was that, in general, the existing models were frozen for mass production at too early a stage.

A third, and perhaps the gravest, consequence was that no heavy bombers were built.

It is a moot question whether heavy bombers would have been built in Germany even if there had been more time. For the men in charge did not like heavy bombers.

Since we know today that it was probably the lack of German heavy bombers more than anything else that decided the battle of England—and thus the war—I think I should explain that the reason for this neglect was by no means only lack of time. There was a psychological reason, too. Goering, Milch, and even Ernst Udet were against building heavy bombers. They had a notion that the Luftwaffe should be extremely fast. Heavy bombers, in their minds, were slow and ponderous, something they could not reconcile with their idea of attack, blitzkrieg, heroism. One may say that heavy bombers were not glamorous enough to please them or, in general, to please the Nazi mind. As I set this down, I realize that it sounds thin and unconvincing. However, all I can say is that I have talked about this very subject with Milch and Udet and a number of other leading men of the Luftwaffe, and I learned that they simply didn't like heavy bombers. They wanted to rely on their fighters and on the speed of their light and medium bombers. Perhaps the fact that Goering and Udet and other leading men in the Luftwaffe had been fighter pilots in World War I led them to see in the Luftwaffe, perhaps unconsciously, a kind of successor to their squadrons of World War I.

In any case no heavy bombers were built. Goering,

Milch, and Udet relied on sleek, medium-sized, two-engined bombers, which were fast, but without heavy defensive armament. And on the converted transport planes, Ju 52's.

And always there was the question of time. Heavy bombers would have taken so much more time. And there was no time. The Fuehrer wanted "results." The Fuehrer wanted to use the Luftwaffe as a political weapon long before it was ready as a tactical one.

The lack of time led to a somewhat unconventional development of production. The idea was unusual but not bad. Goering and Milch decided early, long before there was any kind of definite war program, that it was most important to build as many planes as possible. Superiority of number. The quantity counted—not the quality. What was being built didn't interest them so much. Milch finally arrived at a kind of program that was divided into three phases.

The first phase was to be devoted entirely to the mass production of partly dated models. It was to be followed by a phase in which new models, designed in the meantime, would be put into mass production. Milch hoped—and he said to me that he was sure—that during the second phase the standard of development in other countries (especially the English and American standard, which during the first years was still superior as far as military value went) would be equaled in Germany.

The third phase was to bring about the mass production of still more highly developed models and, as Milch hoped sincerely, models that would be superior to anything the other countries had at that time. This third phase was scheduled for around the end of 1937. I am quite sure that

Milch did not reach this objective until the latter part of 1938, and even then not with the entire capacity of production, but only with certain parts of the production.

Milch's many attempts to buy licenses and patents abroad are strong indications that he never deluded himself about the fact that certain British models were superior in quality to German models. Goering quite openly and cynically admitted to some of his friends as late as the middle of 1935—that is, after German rearmament had become official—that he would not mind if the entire production of 1933, 1934, and 1935 were to be tossed on the scrap-heap later on. The most important thing was that there would be enough planes to train fliers, that enough planes would be constructed to make it necessary for the industry to expand, and, last but not least, that enough planes would be assembled to make an impression on Hitler and to allow him, in turn, to make an impression on the world.

I have tried to show in this chapter that not everything went smoothly during the first years of the building up of the Luftwaffe, that there was a great deal of chaos and disorder, and that many errors were committed, some of which were to prove fatal later on. But there is no use denying that after the first handicaps were overcome, many things were done and done well. The achievement as a whole is worthy of superlatives. It was, indeed, *"kolossal."*

In 1933, the Junkers works could not have built more than sixty Ju 52's during the whole year, and even that could have been done only if there had been no other jobs, no repairs, no overhauling, etc. In 1933, the entire German aircraft industry—including the auxiliary industries—had a pay roll of not more than 3,500 men.

In 1935, Junkers built 600 airplanes.

The pace in other plants was similar. This miraculous achievement was not the doing of the Nazis in charge of the Luftwaffe. It was made possible through the genius and the work of industrial leaders like Koppenberg, Mader, Tiedemann (in charge of Junkers) and of men like Dornier, Heinkel, Messerschmitt, and their staffs.

But one thing the Air Ministry did achieve. It got the necessary manpower into aviation. It got millions into the aviation industry. It organized schools and shops all over Germany, and in those schools and shops unskilled labor was trained for skilled aircraft work. Former barbers, bakers, tailors, and miners became qualified specialists.

The Air Ministry founded flying schools by the hundreds. It trained German youth to become sports fliers, and glider pilots. Students and workers learned to fly not just one particular type of craft but every sort. A great number of soldiers was trained in ground crew work.

In short, the Air Ministry made flying a mass movement.

But again and again it must be stressed that none of this would have been possible, that the problem as such could not even have been approached, let alone solved, without the work that had been done before the Nazis came to power. Without the work on the one hand of men like General Wilberg and Ernst Brandenburg, and on the other hand that of Professor Junkers and his staff of brilliant young men who dreamed of aviation as a means of assuring eternal peace.

Also it would not have been possible without the help of practically every flier of World War I who was still alive. As I have said before, in describing how we young German fliers felt at the time of the Armistice, none of us wanted to give up the dream of flying. Some of us had to in order to make a living, in order to eat.

But now everyone who had ever flown came back. Not only the famous fliers but the rank and file. The pilots, the observers, the navy fliers, the staff officers, including old, very old men. Many of them had become officers in the army and they, in turn, brought along their friends, other officers who didn't know how to fly. Others who had gone into business or had become salesmen or teachers now returned. Many had emigrated to find a new way of life in other countries, and they now came back. Many had become commercial pilots in the Lufthansa or in airlines abroad.

They all came back.

I think a lot of them knew exactly what they were doing. They must have realized that a weapon was being forged, a weapon that would one day avenge the defeat of 1918. But I think the great majority did not know then what they had let themselves in for. They just wanted to fly again or, at least, they wanted to be connected with aviation again. They had never really given up the dream of flying.

8. Secrecy and Bluff

How much did the world know about German rearmament in the air? Perhaps the question should be put differently—How much did the Nazis wish the world to know about it?

There are three periods of changing Nazi tactics as to what they wanted the world to know. During the first period, from 1933 to March 1935, they denied everything. From March 1935 to the middle of 1938 (second period) they admitted that they had rearmed and that they were very strong; but they still shrouded themselves with deep secrecy. During the third period they gave ample proof of their rearmament in the air. Up to the outbreak of the war they were willing, only too willing, to show anybody and everybody who wanted to see that they could not be beaten in the air.

The first period was characterized by a great number of speeches, declarations, and interviews of Hermann Goering. Whenever he opened his mouth, he said that Germany was not rearmed or rearming in the air. There was, for instance, the famous interview with Ward Price of the *Daily Mail* in February 1934, in which he said that the entire German aviation set-up consisted of not more than 300 planes, including obsolete types, and that there was not a single aircraft that could be used for military purposes. He also gave assurances that the German aviation industry was in a weak condition (!) and could not be compared to that industry in other countries. He said it would take at least two years to reorganize the industry, and not before then could he start building an air force which, he asserted solemnly, would be purely defensive.

Only a few weeks later, on April 11, the British Ambassador in Berlin protested against Germany's apparent intention to create a military air force. This protest was countered by a protest from the Nazi government that whatever Germany had done to build up aviation had been undertaken with the idea of creating a "passive air protection"—that is, Germany now admitted the existence of something that Goering had said could not be started for at least another two years.

Again, in December 1934, Goering explained to a Reuters correspondent that all he was interested in was passive air protection. Even as late as May 1935—that is, after he had made German air rearmament official—he took the attitude that Germany had to be protected against air aggression from other countries. This time he used the London *News Chronicle* as his loudspeaker. He denied that Germany had 3,000 military planes and he indicated that he was ready to sign a pact limiting rearmament in the air, but that first France and Russia had to disarm in the air since their planes constituted a danger to Germany.

Goering was able to make such statements because he had taken every precaution to eliminate leaks of information as to what was going on in Germany and in the German aviation industry.

All workers in airplane plants, also those who designed and actually constructed airfields and hangars—as well as the members of the Luftwaffe itself—were told that if they even breathed a word of what went on it would mean high treason. In many plants the workers had to sign a written declaration that they would not talk; in other plants they had to swear an oath; in still other plants the workers were guarded by soldiers during the working hours and at home by the Gestapo.

In any case, high treason meant the death penalty. A great number of executions took place in connection with the building of the Luftwaffe. Even greater was the number of those who were executed without the benefit of trial, murdered by storm troopers or Gestapo men—or those who just disappeared.

Then there was the censorship, which was handled more or less by Dr. Goebbels. Goebbels from the very birth of the third Reich had told newspapers and magazines what to print and what not to print. In matters of aviation he became especially severe. Everything was a military secret: the number of workers in a particular plant, the number or location of hangars and airports, not to speak of the funds invested—statistics of any kind which might lead to some small idea as to what was going on in aviation. Every word about German aviation was *verboten*.

Occasionally the Goebbels censorship became too severe even for the Air Ministry, and there were some conflicts between Goebbels and Goering on this score. I could tell any number of stories about news items which the Air Ministry wanted to have published—after all, Goering was always a publicity seeker—and which Goebbels did not allow to pass.

There is, for instance, the amusing anecdote about the editor of the aviation magazine *Luftwacht*, who published the story of the flight of Russian pilots from Moscow over the North Pole to California. The editor commented on the flight in very laudatory terms. Goebbels was beside himself with rage and immediately suppressed the magazine. The editor, however, was able to prove not only that

he had obtained his material from Goering, but also that
the Air Ministry had even ordered him to comment in a
positive and praising way. Why Goering wanted this has
never been explained. Perhaps already at that time he had
certain ideas of his own as far as the Russians were concerned. In any case the *Luftwacht* was allowed to continue publication and the editor heard no more about the
affair.

Of course, neither Goering's lies not Goebbels' censorship would have successfully kept the world in ignorance
if it had not been for camouflage on a national scale.
Subterranean gasoline storage tanks and underground
hangars were constructed; the grounds around airports
were disguised in such a way that even from short distances and especially from the air they could not be recognized as flying fields. Artificial trees which could be removed within a few minutes were set about new air fields,
and many devices were employed to create shadows that
would wipe out the contours created by buildings and
aircraft. Along both sides of railway lines near airfields
or air plants, hills were built so that it was impossible for
the passengers in passing trains to see what was beyond
those hills. Other railway lines and especially air lines were
routed in such a way that certain areas in Germany were
almost completely cut off from the rest of the world—
islands on which many things could happen without anybody on the outside knowing about them.

In spite of all these precautions, leaks did occur. The
British Intelligence Service, of course, knew what was
going on and informed, among others, Winston Churchill.
Churchill started back in 1934 to point his finger warningly
to Hitler's air force. He never relented, but for years on
end nobody listened to him. Neither did anyone in the
United States listen to General Billy Mitchell, who started

early to predict that Germany would be a formidable opponent in the air and that the air would be the most important theater of the next war.

There were others who issued warnings. Some of them exaggerated grossly—for instance, Wickham Steed, who in May 1934 not only accused the German army of preparing gas and bacillus warfare to start in the Paris and London subways, but also gave somewhat fantastic figures as to the strength of the Luftwaffe.

In France Lieutenant Colonel Reboul wrote also in 1934 that by the first of January 1935, the Reich would be able to put into action within three or four days not less than 80 heavy bombers, 180 medium bombers, 250 reconnaissance aircraft, etc. According to him, by the end of 1935 Germany could put into action 300 Ju 52's as daylight bombers, 300 Do X 1's or 2's as night bombers, etc., etc.

All such revelations excited and angered Goering. But what made him and Milch perhaps most furious—and I have this from one of their closest collaborators—was the fact that certain anti-Nazi emigrés published articles and books in 1934 and 1935 pointing out how Germany was preparing for air warfare. Those men were in possession of much more accurate figures than anybody else, with the exception of the British Secret Service and Winston Churchill. They knew enough about Germany and they had enough connections with Germany to give very precise figures as to the number of plants, the number of workers, and so on. Reading again what they wrote during those first years, I am amazed at how sound their judgment and their figures were. However, nobody wanted to listen or to believe. When they charged Hitler with his crimes, they were accused of personal resentment and their lives were made miserable by the authorities, especially in France, where it was insisted that "they endangered the friendly relations

existing between other countries and Germany." If only
the world had listened to them!

If only British Prime Minister Stanley Baldwin had listened to them or even to his own Secret Service and to
Churchill. But Baldwin was only intent on calming his
Parliament and making speeches to the effect that there was
no reason to get nervous about German air rearmament.
As late as November 25, 1934, he declared that Germany
could not achieve air equality with England in the near
future and, furthermore, that by the end of 1935 England
would still have a 50 per cent margin of superiority. By
March 1935, however, the undersecretary in the British
Air Ministry, Sir Philip Sassoon, was forced to admit that
the situation had changed unfavorably for England and
that by the end of 1935 England would not have a large
superiority. Again a few weeks later, on April 3, 1935, Sir
John Simon had to tell the same House of Commons that
during his recent visit in Berlin, Hitler had informed him
that he had achieved air equality with England.

During all this time and for much longer, Mr. C. G.
Grey, editor of the *Aeroplane*, continued to tell the English and the world that Germany was not rearming in the
air, that if Germany were rearming he would know about
it since he traveled often and extensively in Germany. Indeed, Mr. Grey did travel a lot in Germany. He liked the
Nazis and the Nazis liked him.

In any case the Baldwin government could not get very
worked up about Germany's rearmament in the air, just
as Baldwin's successor, Neville Chamberlain, could not get
very worked up about whatever Hitler did.

There is no doubt that this indifference greatly helped
the Nazis, that it enabled them to pass through the danger
zone of the beginning of rearmament in general and of
the rearmament in the air in particular.

The complete secrecy was somewhat lifted in 1935, when Goering conceded the existence of a Luftwaffe—a defensive Luftwaffe, of course. Up to that time, the Nazis had denied having an air force. Now they not only admitted it but they admitted to having much more than they actually had. In other words, after having put the world to sleep they now tried to shock the world awake.

They not only admitted that they were rearming. They declared boldly that they were in possession of the greatest and best air force on the globe, that no country anywhere would be able to contest German air supremacy.

On the surface it seems illogical that at first they tried to keep everything secret and that later they told more than there was to be told. But there is no real contradiction in this. Through both seemingly paradoxical devices, the Nazis tried to keep the other countries from rearming in the air. First because there was no need to rearm, and second, because it was too late to rearm. In both they succeeded admirably.

Today, experts realize how exaggerated the Nazi claims were in those years, especially during the last months before Munich. But only a few who know the inside story of the Luftwaffe have an accurate idea to what extent all this was bluff and how little of the information concerning the strength of the Luftwaffe which was publicized up to the very eve of the war had any real basis in fact.

As I said before, for some time the Nazis only talked about their strength without showing it. Afterward they invited inspection—but those tours of inspection were very carefully arranged beforehand.

The means by which this gigantic publicity trick was carried out were manifold. The very fact that Hitler, Goering, and all the others cynically admitted that they had not told the truth, that they had lied to the world about German rearmament, disturbed and confused the world to such a degree that it immediately decided that the Nazis again were lying—which they were. But the world thought the Nazis were understating their case, that rearmament had progressed much further than it actually had. This impression was strengthened by many speeches made by Goering and Milch in which they boasted about the enormous achievement of the Luftwaffe and in which they asserted that nobody could attack Germany and escape annihilation.

Then Goebbels organized a whispering campaign that started in Stockholm and Zurich, or at least it seemed to originate in those places. In reality, it started in the Wilhelmstrasse. In that whispering campaign fantastic figures were quoted, secret weapons were mentioned. Goebbels, furthermore, was able to arrange for a number of false documents revealing German strength to be "smuggled" out of Germany into the hands of French, English, and American journalists.

Then came the period of invitations. At first the invited ones were not allowed to see very much. Afterward, they were shown so much that they were overwhelmed.

Among those who did not get to see very much was, for instance, the English engineer, Major Mayo, who had designed a composite aircraft—a large four-engined plane—that could take off with a little plane on its back, which in turn could be launched into the air and thus carry a much heavier load.

Mayo and his staff were invited to Berlin, where they were put up at the Hotel Adlon. A high SS officer, a count, put a car and two SS men at their disposal. They were free, he explained, to go anywhere. But, naturally, the SS chauffeurs took care to take them only where they should go. And only by prescribed routes.

Major Mayo and his staff were invited to the Air Ministry, where they were received by Milch, who had become a general by that time, and a large staff of engineers and officers. They were invited to the House of Fliers, they were wined and dined every evening for about four or five days. They were even taken to view the airports of Tempelhof and Staaken. When they returned to England they were enchanted. It took them a few days to find out that they had really seen nothing, that they had done no business.

The same thing happened to the French air general, Veuillemet, when he visited Berlin. There were great receptions and many scenes of fraternization. But the good Frenchman saw exactly nothing.

Later foreign visitors were shown around, but there was always some good, sound reason for showing them around. And the reason was never that the foreign visitors should learn anything about German air rearmament, but that they should be impressed with German strength without learning too many details. A number of English officers were shown around extensively in 1938. They visited the Junkers works at Dessau and the Heinkel works in Oranienburg. They inspected subterranean canteens, workshops, a subterranean telephone system that proved to them that German aircraft production, in case of war, would be able to go on just the same.

Shortly after Munich the American, Lawrence D. Bell, was shown around by the Nazis who asked him not to reveal in Paris or in London anything he had seen. Bell promised, but added that he would have to tell his own government in Washington—which the German officers assured him smilingly was quite all right. Bell was especially impressed by the Messerschmitt plant.

According to Marc A. Rose, who published his findings in the American magazine *Forum* in March 1939, experts had not believed rumors that Germany had 10,000 war planes at the time of Munich (September 1938). In reality Germany had 12,000 planes then, and now, in March 1939, they possessed 16,000 to 18,000. Rose thought that Germany had three times as many planes as England at the time of the Czechoslovakian crisis, ten times as many as France, and that Italy possessed as many as England and France together.

Another expert who was impressed by what the Nazis had achieved was Igor Sikorski, and still another one was Glenn L. Martin.

Still another visitor whom the Nazis impressed enormously was Oswald Garrison Villard, the well-known publicist, who has been both pacifist and isolationist. Since he is no expert on airplane production, the Nazis let him go wherever he wanted. He did exactly what they hoped he would do. He went to England and told the English the fantastic figures he had learned in Berlin.

The Luftwaffe's prize publicity agent turned out to be Charles A. Lindbergh. He visited Germany in 1936, 1937, and 1938. He was first invited through the intermediary, Major Truman Smith, then military attaché at the United States Embassy in Berlin.

I will not discuss in this book Lindbergh's political leanings. But I must say that there can be no doubt whatsoever about his sympathy for Nazis or Fascism, at least at the time of his visits. And there can be no doubt that his sympathy toward the political philosophy of the Hitler regime influenced him in his judgment of the Luftwaffe.

I am sure he meant well. I am sure that he really wanted
to find facts and thought he had found them. He was given
more freedom than anybody else in his tours of inspection.
He was allowed to choose his own routes. He saw factories, airports, hangars which no other foreigner had seen.

He reported what he had seen to Major Truman Smith;
he told it in Washington and to the American Ambassador
in London, Joseph P. Kennedy. What he said was that the
Luftwaffe was superior in quality and in quantity to anything he had seen in Europe. He thought that German
aircraft production, if need be, could be raised to 5,000 a
month (which never happened).

On the other hand, he was very much disappointed in
the Russian air force and aircraft production. He had been
in Russia in 1931 and in 1933, but he went there again in
1938 for the specific purpose of learning about the Red
air fleet. He decided that the Russians had imitated—especially they had imitated the Germans—and had done so
badly. He admitted that the Russians had great quantities
of aircraft, but he said they would not tell him how much.
He thought that organization and maintenance were on a
low level in Russia. The machines, he felt, were in poor
condition. He never for one moment suspected that the
Russians, mistrustful as a matter of principle and doubly
mistrustful of a man who was on good terms with Goering
and the other Nazis, had seen no reason whatever to show
Lindbergh their cards.

During the winter of 1938-39 Lindbergh inspected the
French air rearmament, which he found deplorable. Again
his political leanings played a part in his conclusions. He did
not blame the French military leaders. He blamed the inner
political difficulties of France (statistics, which were available to Lindbergh but which he apparently did not study,

showed that industrial production during the time of Léon Blum's Popular Front government and its "new deal" reached an all-time high).

English aviation, even Lindbergh admitted, was in better shape than French. Production was inferior to German production in quantity and partly in quality, too. Lindbergh thought that the English produced too many different types. . . .

Lindbergh was then, as he is today, a private citizen with a right to his private personal opinion. He was free to believe, as he unquestionably did, that the German Luftwaffe could not be beaten. It was his privilege to express such an opinion publicly; and we know that never for a moment till America's entry into the war did he cease expressing that opinion publicly and declaring that the R.A.F. was waging a hopeless war against Hitler.

But if Lindbergh had actually been just a private citizen, Goering would scarcely have made so much fuss about him, would hardly have decorated him, would hardly have shown him around in such an extensive way. Goering did all this because Lindbergh was more than just a private citizen. He was supposed to be a great expert on problems pertaining to aviation. He was considered an expert by Neville Chamberlain and his government; and the late British Prime Minister could construct for himself at least a moral right for what he did in Munich by referring to what Lindbergh had told him. And the American people who joined Lindbergh in his "Keep America out of the War" movement had every right in the world to believe that what he told them was the truth and nothing but the truth.

They could not know, nor could Mr. Chamberlain know, that certain men in Berlin enjoyed Lindbergh's private and public utterances enormously, and that there was much chuckling in the inner circles of the Luftwaffe about how easy it had been to fool him. Because fooled he had been, consistently and easily. After all, a man can be an excellent flier and still not have any deep understanding of production problems, let alone problems of air strategy.

Another man, who may also be considered a famous flier, Alexander P. de Seversky, was not fooled so easily. In fact, he was never fooled at all. In 1939 he spent seven months in Europe, part of that time in Germany. He studied German aviation, and he saw exactly how things were. He was impressed by German production and he was not at all impressed by the quality of German aircraft. He never doubted England's potential supremacy in production. He fought Lindbergh and Lindbergh's thesis tooth and nail, especially Lindbergh's assertion that England could not win the war, not even with American help, and that America could become impregnable to attack from the air and, therefore, should stay out of the war. Today, of course, we know the facts. But at the time when Seversky came out with his attacks against Lindbergh, he really went out on a limb. I think that if Seversky had never done anything else or written anything else this nation should be grateful to him; in fact, the Allied nations should be grateful to him for his courageous stand against Lindbergh.

Another American observer who proved to be correct was T. P. Wright, then vice-president of Curtiss-Wright, who is the leading aviation expert today on the War Production Board. The calculations and specifications at which he arrived after his inspection of the German aviation industry were entirely correct.

Aside from the wish to impress—and terrify—the world, there was perhaps another reason for the German policy under Dr. Goebbels to invite inspection of aircraft on such a large scale. I think it was a political reason. I think, and many conversations I had with the Nazis in those years prove my point, that Goebbels wanted to underline, to point up the contrast between Germany and Soviet Russia.

The Russians, as we have seen, were by no means eager to give out valuable information as to how their aviation stood. They were hiding developments behind a thick veil of secrecy. In contrast to this, the Nazis appeared to be acting especially openly. No, they had no secrets. Anybody who wanted could see for himself. And everybody could see that the Luftwaffe was, indeed, something wonderful, terrific, colossal, invincible.

The Russians, on the other hand, were sly. Goebbels used every trick at his disposal to prove it. As far as Goebbels was concerned, and that meant as far as the German press and radio were concerned, the Russian air force was nothing but a Jewish-Bolshevistic hoax.

I know that at least one man in the Propaganda Ministry was assigned to the task of inventing stories from time to time of aviation catastrophes, crashes, and explosions supposed to have taken place in Soviet Russia.

This was, of course, in line with the general anti-Soviet policy of Hitler Germany. But Goebbels hoped, and I think rightly so, that at least some of this adverse criticism of the Russian air force would find its way beyond Germany to the world at large. After all, the world believed almost everything he said about the Luftwaffe. By the beginning of 1939 Dr. Goebbels must have felt that you could make the world believe anything—anything at all.

9. Air Strategy

After World War I ended with the collapse of Germany, many Germans asked: "How did it happen? For four years German armies smashed through from victory to victory. German fliers had complete air superiority. German U-boats brought England to the verge of starvation. German troops stood everywhere in enemy territory, from France to the Suez Canal, from Palestine to the Taurus, from Finland to Iraq, from the Don to the Caucasus. How and why did we lose?"

Numerous commissions and inquiry boards were set up in an attempt to find an answer. The German General Staff, then existing only *sub rosa*, also asked questions. And in true German fashion it immediately embarked on an objective study of the real causes of defeat. It finally came to the conclusion that in similar circumstances, Germany would lose every war. These circumstances were:

1. If the war lasted too long and, therefore, led to exhaustion.

2. If Germany had to face a coalition of powers and had to fight on several fronts simultaneously.

3. If German troops were spread over wide fronts, and forced to fight far from the homeland.

The obvious conclusion had to be, and indeed was, that the next war, and, indeed, any war waged by Germany in the future, would have to be a blitzkrieg. By 1920 the General Staff had decided on a blitzkrieg, and everything that was done to rebuild the German army was geared for a blitzkrieg.

When the first plans for the Luftwaffe were framed, they had to be fitted into this general over-all plan for blitzkrieg warfare. This was no hardship for the men who were to devise an air strategy. On the contrary. The very idea of air warfare suggests blitzkrieg, lightning strokes, aggressiveness. Even if there had been no German army in 1933, that is, if the Luftwaffe had been chosen as the pre-liminary instrument for leading the next war, the blitzkrieg solution would have been the only possible solution. It must be remembered that a war of exhaustion, a stalemate, had to be prevented at any cost. And how could such a stalemate be prevented more easily or more radically than by making war by means of a few thousand planes, a million men—or, if you counted the workers in all the sub-sidiary industries and in anti-aircraft defense, about two to three million men? Only a blitzkrieg would not seriously disturb the economy of the country, and only a blitzkrieg by air would reduce the cost in human lives.

Indeed, German rearmament in the air had to have as its goal a blitzkrieg, whether the air weapon was considered as auxiliary to the other armed forces or whether it was considered a separate arm, a strategic weapon in itself, operating according to its own laws and necessities, and able to fight and win a war.

Operative air warfare was born in the fall of 1917, when German night bombers began a series of attacks. Up to that date, in World War I as well as in the Balkan Wars, aircraft played only an auxiliary and co-operative role.

How should aviation be used—as a strategic weapon or

as an auxiliary weapon? The strategy for military use of planes varies in the application of these two principles.

There are adherents of the doctrine that airplanes should be used only as an auxiliary and supporting weapon in co-operation with surface forces. According to this theory, airplanes should take over certain duties that other auxiliaries of the army and the navy have fulfilled in the past. Because of their technical possibilities, airplanes will fulfill those duties better. Reconnaissance, tactical as well as strategical, constitutes one of the most important duties. Airplanes, further, should act as concentrated artillery (short and long range), but mainly on the battlefield to prepare for assaults and victories on the part of the army and the navy. They should transport supplies as well as troops, ammunition, and all kinds of provisions. They should act as a means of communication between the front and staffs behind the lines. And lastly, they should provide the commanders of surface formations, and especially of spearheads, with the means to guide those formations to the battlefield and direct them in the battle area itself.

The other extreme is represented by the school of thought that advocates autonomous air forces as the exclusive means to win a war, that is, to destroy the enemy's will and power to resist. Theories based on this principle admit usefulness of surface forces, if at all, only as accessories to air power, especially for mopping up and police activities after the enemy has been crushed—the best example being the British when they controlled Iraq after 1918 from the air and then sent in troops under R.A.F. command.

Between these two extremes there exist any number of combinations and compromises. The German General Staff before entering World War II, for instance, was all for some sort of compromise, so that the Luftwaffe could act as the spearhead of an invasion into other countries but not destroy these countries or their industries because Germany wanted to use their production facilities after the conquest.

Another compromise theory, nearer the second extreme, has been presented by Major Alexander P. de Seversky and William B. Ziff in this country. But all these theories have been formulated and published only recently. They could not and did not have any influence on the development of the Luftwaffe's strategy.

However, the classical theory of General Giulio Douhet—tending to the extreme of employing an air force as the only operative weapon—had great influence on the development of the Luftwaffe.

Douhet was commander of the Italian airship battalion during World War I. During the hostilities he sent to the war minister an exposé in which he severely criticized Italy's conduct of the war. He was court-martialed and sentenced to one year in prison. But in 1917, when Italy all but collapsed, it was recognized that it was exactly the defects that Douhet had picked out to criticize which had led to disaster. Whereupon he was reinstated. Shortly before the war ended he became commander of the air force, and after the Armistice he was made a general. Soon afterward he retired to devote himself entirely to his strategic theories of air warfare. But it must be kept in mind that Douhet's basic ideas were already formulated as far back as 1909, and that the book in which he presented them in a comprehensive and more popular way was published in 1921.

Douhet contended that modern warfare between industrially developed nations—because of the time it consumes and the number of men withdrawn from their jobs and, in general, because of the dislocation of the entire economic structure—is nearly as disastrous for the winning as for the defeated nation.

But, says Douhet, the airplane is the only weapon that can finish a war or nullify the enemy's will to resist in a much shorter time without dislocation of great armies of men and without disruption of the entire economy. The airplane can strike at the heart of the enemy instead of fighting only at its *glacis*. An airplane attack possesses the elements of speed and surprise.

Therefore, big heavily armed bombers used in large formations, able to force their way to targets deep inside the enemy's country, should be the only means of offensive warfare. The surface services, then, should be used for mopping up operations and occupation.

Douhet further taught that the first objective of this autonomous air warfare must be to gain mastery of the air. Such mastery can be achieved only temporarily by means of battles between airplanes. But by destroying the enemy air power on the ground and also destroying his ground facilities and aircraft industries, it can be achieved once and for all.

Once air supremacy is gained, the air forces can be used to break down the material and moral resistance of the enemy by destroying factories, power plants, railways, towns—in brief, to strike at the heart of the enemy.

Douhet expressly excluded the use of air power as an auxiliary weapon even on a small scale because that would involve splitting up the operative efforts.

Douhet insisted that the enemy should be surprised, that he should be attacked without a declaration of war. That hostilities once commenced should be sustained and concluded with the greatest energy and utmost speed. That to concentrate on any other object than mastery of the air would mean playing the enemy's game.

In order to put such a theory into practice the fields of organization and of technical equipment would have to undergo a thoroughgoing revolution. Of main importance would be the construction of heavily armed bombers, battle planes able to transport heavy loads of bombs and fight their way to the target. (Very heavy losses, up to 50 per cent during the first assaults, were anticipated and discounted in advance by Douhet.) Douhet came to the conclusion that civil transport planes had practically the same specifications as these big battle planes—which was later proved wrong.

Douhet's theses had a tremendous influence on the thinkink of air strategists everywhere in the world. But the theory was never applied a hundred per cent in reality—not even by the Nazis.

There were men whose theories, however, were used as the working basis for building up air forces. There was a French commandant, M. Jauneaud, and the former Czarist Lieutenant-General N. N. Golovine, then living in England, who is supposed, at least in Germany, to have formulated the official theory on which the Royal Air Force strategy is based. Then there was the British Air Marshal, Ernest Leslie Gossage, who had ideas similar to the Golovine version of the Douhet theory.

Gossage was an air attaché in Berlin before the Nazis came into power. He was very much interested in our civil aviation and its developments, and I met him a few times in Berlin in 1930. I was greatly impressed by his personality and by the amazing logic and clarity of his thinking. Incidentally, General Wilberg and Ernst Brandenburg were equally impressed and said so.

It is no exaggeration to say that apart from Douhet and Golovine no living person has had so much influence on the ideas underlying the Luftwaffe as Gossage. It is one of those strange ironies of history.

Aside from Douhet and the two Englishmen, it was perhaps the American, General Billy Mitchell, who influenced German air strategists most. His bombing experiments immediately after World War I, which demonstrated that a plane could sink a battleship, figured again and again in German publications concerning air warfare. Just as Charles de Gaulle's theories of tank warfare were studied and accepted in Germany while he was laughed at in France, Billy Mitchell's teachings were believed in Germany at a time when he was being court-martialed in America.

Billy Mitchell. . . . Isn't it strange that he should have had the same fate as Giulio Douhet? With the exception that his "reinstatement" came only after his death. But today it has come. I am quite sure that most Americans feel it might have been better to listen to Billy Mitchell before Hitler demonstrated how right the American was.

The Douhet-Golovine-Gossage theory of air warfare was accepted by the men who were at the helm of the Luftwaffe, even before they had started to build the Luftwaffe. There are numerous German publications to prove that. I quote an excerpt from Captain A. D. Thelen's article in the *Militaerwochenblatt* of May 11, 1934:

Operative air war tends to fulfill two tasks.
1. Destruction of the enemy's air force.
2. Decisive influence on the entire war on land and on sea

by directing the home air force against targets on enemy soil. The first task cannot be fulfilled by means of a victorious air battle alone. Even driving the opponent into the defensive, or a local air superiority do not suffice. The destruction of the enemy's air force must go hand in hand with the complete destruction of the production plants of his aircraft industry in order to prevent forever a rebirth of the opponent in the air. . . .

Hitler and Goering definitely wanted an independent air force that would win the war speedily and without disrupting the economic life. They also wanted this for political reasons. They wanted the Nazis to win the war—not the army. The Luftwaffe is their weapon. The army is a weapon that was in existence long before anybody heard of Hitler.

Hitler and Goering had heard something about air strategies and also about Douhet, and they wanted "something like Douhet."

But although a modification of the Douhet plan was adopted by the Nazis, somehow his fundamental ideas and directives as to how his theories should be put into practice were never followed up. In only one case did the Nazis follow Douhet implicitly. And in that one case Douhet was wrong. I am referring, of course, to the Italian's deduction that civil planes could be converted into heavy battle planes to crush the enemy's material and moral resistance from the air. The Nazis believed they could use or convert the excellent transport plane, Ju 52, into a heavy bomber.

But they never succeeded in fulfilling Douhet's postulate that among the three services the operative air force had to dominate. On the contrary. The Nazis had their hands full trying to keep the all-powerful army from taking over the air force and using it as an auxiliary weapon.

But most important of all, the *pièce de resistance* of Douhet's theory, the almighty heavy bomber, the bomber that could get through to its goal in the heart of the enemy's country—this weapon without which the whole Douhet theory disintegrates into thin air—this heavy bomber was never built.

To come back to the army and the General Staff:

We have seen how the General Staff after its investigation of the causes of the defeat of 1918 came to the conclusion that blitzkrieg was the only possible way to wage the next war or wars. In order to make such a blitzkrieg possible, certain political conditions had to be fulfilled. There had to be secret rearmament in order to make a surprise attack possible. This meant suppression of the parliament, of the freedom of the press, indeed, the introduction of dictatorship in one way or another. In order to avoid wars on many fronts or against a world coalition, it was necessary to sign many treaties, to divide the world into many camps, and then to destroy one country after another through separate blitzkriegs or campaigns. Such a scheme would make it possible for the German armies and all the armed forces to have a rest after a relatively short war, to recuperate and to start all over again. Thus a war of attrition, dreaded by the General Staff because it was one of the reasons for the defeat of 1918, would be avoided.

A blitzkrieg, furthermore, needed certain psychological prerequisites, as far as the human material was concerned. It needed aggressive men who were willing to stake everything on one card, to fight at least for some time against overwhelming odds—panzer spearheads.

If one considers carefully all the requirements needed for the blitzkrieg which the army wanted, it is easy to understand why the generals called Hitler into power. Hitler meant no parliament, no criticism, no freedom of the press. Hitler meant fanatics, die-hards, daredevils.

So far so good. But the generals hardly expected that Hitler also meant a *separate* air force.

In World War I the air force was not a separate unit but a part of the army. The leading men of the army during the twenties had a pretty good idea as to the role airplanes should play in the next war. In a blitzkrieg, military planes should play the part of an advance thrust, should be a preparing weapon, should constitute the first line of assault. In other words, airplanes should be definitely an auxiliary weapon.

But the German generals were very shrewd. General Hans von Seeckt, the man who above all was responsible for the rebirth of the German army, was very definitely open-minded as to the possibilities of an autonomous air force. According to his own writings, he thought simultaneous offensives by a highly trained professional army with self-contained tank and motorized spearheads and, in addition, by an autonomous air force would be entirely possible. But Seeckt, as well as the generals who came after him, thought that the army would control any air force, auxiliary or autonomous.

When the Nazis reached power, and when they decided to build up the Luftwaffe and to make it their own weapon —a very definite Nazi weapon as distinguished from the rest of the armed forces—difficulties began to break out between the Nazis and the army. At that time General von Fritsch was in command of the army. He was a strong opponent of Nazi infiltration into the army, and therefore he could not but loathe the idea of the air force becoming an exclusive Nazi weapon. It will perhaps never be established definitely whether Fritsch and the other generals were, as they seemed to be, against a separate, autonomous Luftwaffe for strategic and formal reasons or for anti-Nazi reasons. Probably they had both reasons. Anyhow there was a long duel between Goering and Fritsch, and the duel was finally won by Goering. Of course, the Nazi had to make certain concessions. He could never achieve recognition as a military leader from the generals. In vain did Hitler promote Goering overnight and bestow on him the rank of a general. The real generals never forgot that Goering had been discharged as a captain at the close of World War 1—and that was that. As for Erhard Milch, the generals regarded it as a joke that he was made a general and even a field marshal. There was a saying in higher military circles: "Milch may be an able general manager, but he will never be a general."

As far as the Nazi party was concerned, it really accepted the army's idea of the coming blitzkrieg. But Goering, and probably Hitler, too, went beyond the army's conception. Why should the blitzkrieg of the future not be a total war carried out by an autonomous air force? Why should it not be led and won by the Luftwaffe, that is, by the Nazi weapon par excellence? After all, there was Douhet who had provided the recipe. Uncompromising destruction from the air of the enemy's war potential and destruction of his morale and his will to resistance. No ground operations.

And then the Nazis would have won the war.

That is exactly what the Nazis decided upon. And that decision was made without Douhet's famous heavy bombers, the only means of winning a war à la Douhet.

As I have said already there were two reasons for not constructing heavy bombers, one was that the very idea of heavy bombers did not appeal to Nazi psychology, the other that there was no time. Hitler needed something to show off by 1935, and heavy bombers could not be designed and built in large numbers in two years. That would have necessitated at least four to five years, and being a tremendous technical problem, it would have delayed production in general and the handling of other important technical problems.

In the last analysis, the reason for this compromise—which from a strictly military point of view was not a compromise at all but something utterly impossible, something that sooner or later was to lead to a catastrophe—is the fact that the two men in charge of the Luftwaffe, Goering and Milch, were not strategists. The men of the General Staff were probably more right than they thought. Goering had been a good pilot; Milch had been a good airline manager. Neither one knew anything about strategy; neither one knew anything about how to conduct a war.

But there it was. Goering and Milch wanted to win the war because the Nazis had to win the war. They wanted a plan "something like Douhet's."

But that wasn't enough. Wars aren't won that easily.

10. *Toward War*

Since the leading men of the army did not consider any of the top men of the Luftwaffe military experts, and since these top men had no very definite ideas as to the strategy of the future wars—or at least could not decide on a definite strategy nor on the necessary preparations for the building of certain types—the army took over the general staff of the Luftwaffe or, as it was called, the *Luftwaffe-Kommandoamt*. Any number of fights took place backstage, since the Nazis did not want to give the army control of such a key situation, but the army won. In 1935, the chief of the army, General von Fritsch, succeeded in getting his close friend, Lieutenant General Max Wever, appointed head of the *Luftwaffe-Kommandoamt*. That meant, at least for the time being, the closest collaboration in all strategic problems of both general staffs. It also meant that the viewpoint of the army had won, at least temporarily, and that the Luftwaffe was to be considered an auxiliary weapon.

It was an important victory for the army.

General Wever was not a flier, and had only learned flying when appointed to the Luftwaffe. He was a young staff officer during World War I, and continued as a staff officer after the war. He was sound and dependable without being brilliant. He knew that he had to consider himself only a representative of the army and the strategic ideas of the army in the Luftwaffe.

Unfortunately for the army, he did not stay very long

in this post. Early in 1936 he crashed with his own private plane near Dresden and was killed instantly.

After Wever's death the Luftwaffe again became purely a party weapon in direct and deliberate opposition to the politically neutral army. All the key positions—especially in the general staff—were filled with reliable party members.

Albert Kesselring became head of the general staff.

He was a close friend of Goering's. He was an officer in World War I. Then—after the war—he took to morphine, exactly as Goering himself did, and spent a lot of time in sanitariums. When Goering formed the Luftwaffe he immediately called on Kesselring. Kesselring soon came out for the tactical principle of continuous mass air attack. He was the man who innovated the "rolling attack." The principle was based on large formations operating as units.

Kesselring had a hard row to hoe when he tried to put his ideas into practice. Even in the Luftwaffe itself. The fliers of the good old days did not take to the notion of giving up their independence in the air and becoming members of a big anonymous mass. I should rather say: they did not want to give up the independence of their formation or squadron. In World War I all of these squadrons had names, special uniforms which they sometimes devised themselves, significant marks of identification.

So strong was the opposition against Kesselring that as early as 1937 he had to leave his post in the General Staff. This was perhaps the reason why the Luftwaffe units that took part in the Spanish Civil War did not yet employ the "rolling attack," indeed, used no mass actions. And this in turn led observers of the Spanish war, especially experts from neutral countries, to believe that air war was still an individualistic type of action.

That is what made the Polish war the great surprise it was to all the experts. It was only then they realized no lone wolf in the air, no matter how fast and courageous, could fight against continuous mass operations.

Needless to say, Kesselring was a follower of the Douhet idea. Every word he ever said or wrote gives proof of this. Let us just quote from his speech of March 1940 to pilots who had just completed their training.

When we circle over cities and fields of the enemy, we must choke any sentimental feeling. These people, every one of us must say to himself, are not human beings like the Germans. An enemy of Germany is inhuman. There do not exist any so-called civil objectives for the Luftwaffe nor emotional considerations. The countries of the enemy must be razed, all resistance must be broken.

After Kesselring's step backward, Hans Juergen Stumpff took over the General Staff. He came from the army, had been an officer in World War I, and on the staff of the army after Versailles. Still, he was not at all—like Wever— the puppet of the generals. He was, rather, a compromise between Hermann Goering on the one side and the generals on the other side. He had no outstanding strategic ideas of his own, and I think that is one of the reasons why the Civil War in Spain did not indicate anything decisive so far as the Luftwaffe or the strategic conception of the Luftwaffe was concerned.

He was followed in February 1939 by Colonel Jeschonnek. He had been a flier in World War I, after which he became air staff officer. About a year before Hitler took power, Jeschonnek suddenly reappeared as chief of the transport pilots' schools, in which capacity he helped to train the men that Goering needed. He was with Goering from the first day, and by 1939 had become the oldest member of the general staff of the Luftwaffe.

It is interesting to note that Jeschonnek was appointed at a moment when the last preparations for a war which could not be delayed much longer had been made. Hitler and Goering felt that it was good to have a man at the helm who knew, from many years' experience, the intricate business of strategic planning and the intricate set-up of the Luftwaffe. It is also interesting that they selected a man—and kept him at least up to this writing—who was definitely not brilliant, who did not bring along any new and revolutionary conceptions, but who could be depended upon in difficult times.

Such a man was Jeschonnek. If proof were needed, could any be found more convincing than the fact that this man who, thus far in World War II, has been the brains of the Luftwaffe, is still all but unknown to the world at large?

In addition to Kesselring, the Luftwaffe possessed at least one genius. I refer to Ernst Udet. In 1936 Ernst Udet was called in, when Milch and Goering finally got rid of Herr Bock, who was such a dismal failure as chief engineer.

Udet was by no means a Nazi. The world-famous flier who had achieved such spectacular successes during World War I wasn't in the least interested in politics. He loved to fly and to have a good time. But Goering was in dire need of a technical expert. When he asked Udet to join the Luftwaffe, he really let him choose between the Luftwaffe and a concentration camp. This doesn't mean that Udet became the chief technician and finally the quartermaster-general of the Luftwaffe because he was afraid for his life. Things were much more complicated than that.

In the first place Udet was one of the few men who very definitely was not afraid for his life. He was one of the few men whom I would unhesitatingly call a hero.

I think his descriptions of his dog fights during World War I are still among the most heartening proofs of how real heroes act in time of danger. I refer here to the original book he wrote, not to the one the Nazis re-edited. I remember his description of a jump with a parachute that didn't open. During those awful seconds many thoughts flashed through the mind of the young Udet. He thought of a girl. He thought, with regret, of the new uniform he had ordered which now would not be necessary. He didn't pretend to have had any heroic thoughts. I am sure very few heroes ever have, particularly in such moments. The parachute, however, did open about 300 feet above the ground, and Udet escaped with a few minor bruises, though he landed in the very midst of a battle.

No, Udet was not afraid for his life. He proved it a thousand times, after World War I, when he became the world's No. 1 stunt flier, a profession which even under the most favorable circumstances has never been recognized by life insurance companies as being without hazard.

I said he was not a Nazi. When he met Hitler in 1927, the Fuehrer did not make a favorable impression upon him. To his friends, Udet quite openly said that he thought Hitler was a crazy man. That was perhaps indiscreet in 1927; in 1937 such a statement meant taking your life into your own hands. Well, Udet never made a secret of what he thought of the Fuehrer and of most of the men around him, with the exception of Goering, whom he liked personally. He made caricatures of the leading Nazis. He told jokes about them. An excellent shot, he was fond of using a picture of Hitler as a target—and this in a Berlin apartment to which many people came.

He had many Jewish friends. While he was a stunt flier, he also made a few movies, and he belonged to Berlin's café society, of which Jews formed a large part. He knew any number of Jewish writers, moving-picture producers, actors, journalists, etc. After Hitler's rise to power, when some of them had to get out rather hastily to save their lives, Udet helped them generously. I know of at least two instances when he, all by himself, flew Jewish people who were in danger across the frontier—a terrible risk which he took without a moment's deliberation.

No, you cannot explain Udet's joining the Luftwaffe on the grounds that he feared for his life. It can better be explained by his love for flying and for aviation in general. He must have been tempted by the idea that unlimited funds would be at his disposal for the purpose of developing and improving the technical side of an air force. If he had not been seriously interested, he would not have been able to do for the Luftwaffe what he did. After all, you can force a genius to take a job, but you cannot force him to have ideas. In a word, nobody could have forced Udet to become what he did become, the technical brains of the Luftwaffe.

I think in the final analysis Ernst Udet didn't take the Nazis very seriously. Like many of us, he probably did not imagine that they could stay in power for very long. And I like to think that he must have hoped that somehow the instrument which he helped build up would never be tried out in a war.

A foreign journalist once called the new men assembled around Goering and Milch who have played the most im-

portant parts inside the Luftwaffe, "a bunch of first lieutenants and captains who became generals." Indeed, one
can hardly describe them better. Naturally, every general
must have been at one time or another a first lieutenant or
a captain. But there are first lieutenants and captains whom
one may call eternal first lieutenants or eternal captains,
because, under normal circumstances, they can never become generals—should never become generals. That Hitler
and Goering made generals of them is symptomatic—or
perhaps the cause—of the dilettantism that ruled the Luftwaffe.

Of course, many of these new men, who incidentally
were almost all not new men but participants in World
World I, had their merits. Some of them were even very
talented. But they were not what the Luftwaffe really
needed—military leaders.

There was Friedrich Bodenschatz, an adjutant of Goering's during World War I, who in the years after the war
prepared air rearmament in the Defense Ministry under
General Wilberg. When Goering created the Air Ministry,
he became his adjutant. He still is his adjutant and his close
friend.

There is Wimmer, flier and air staff officer in World
War I, who officially retired from aviation after the war
but came back to the staff of the Luftwaffe in 1934 and
took over the Department of Operations. Later he became
commanding general with his own air corps.

There was Kaupisch, a captain in the Greater General
Staff during World War I, a member of the Bavarian Artillery during the Weimar Republic, then one of the leading
aviation generals under Goering, up to March 1938, when
in the course of the famous purge of the generals he disappeared. Incidentally, he was one of those aforementioned

army officers who during the winter of 1932 to 1933 rather suddenly left the army in order to prepare, as "private citizens," the rearmament in the air before Hitler came to power.

Much more important was and still is Hugo Sperrle, one of the famous "three dimensionalists," that is, one of the officers who had served in the army, in the navy, and in the air force.

Son of a Wuerttembergian brewer, he was an infantry lieutenant in World War I, then became a pilot, and finally the commander of the air corps of the Seventh Army. He was involved in the rightist Kapp Putsch in 1920, and then was given a job in the Defense Ministry. Here he experimented for many years with electromagnetic rays with which he tried to stop airplane engines and cause airplanes to crash. His "death rays," however, never amounted to very much and were never effective at a distance exceeding twenty yards. By 1928 he was working in the Navy Ministry. Three years later he returned to the army. In 1934, he was transferred from the army to the Luftwaffe, where he made a rapid career. He was a leader of the Condor Legion in the Spanish Civil War, and one of his most important achievements was the destruction of Guernica. Today he is one of the air field marshals.

Theo Osterkamp was a pilot in World War I, too, and was well known for his daring and for his insubordination. After the war he became a member of the Free Corps and later of the navy, taking part in the illegal building up of naval aviation. In 1926 he retired from the navy, took various jobs with private airlines, and made himself a name as a sports flier. He immediately joined Goering in the Luftwaffe and had quite a career. His last job, at this writing, was commander of the fliers under Rommel in

Africa. He was recalled when the African adventure turned out a disaster.

There was Wolfram von Richthofen, in World War I a pilot in the wing of his famous cousin, later during peacetime an officer in the German army, since 1933 member of the Luftwaffe, in 1937 Chief of Staff of the Condor Legion in Spain, then its commander, and in World War II commander of the Eighth Air Corps in Belgium, France, the Balkans, Crete, and Russia.

Felmy was one of the outstanding World War I pilots, afterward became director of a pilot school in Luebeck, joined the Luftwaffe in 1933, and in 1939 became a general and the commander of Air Fleet II.

Alexander Loehr was a member of the Austrian flying corps up to the Anschluss and later organized the Luftwaffe in Austria. He turned out to be one of the few military brains inside the Luftwaffe. He was also a master of intrigue and an early Nazi.

Albert Keller is called "Iron Keller" and also "Bomb Keller." (*Keller* is the German for cellar.)

He was the first man to fly over Paris in World War I, when in October 1914 he bombed the Gare du Nord. Later he directed the training of pilots in Montmedy; among his pupils was Richthofen. From 1917 on, he was the daring chief of Bombing Wing I. After the war he went into civil air traffic training pilots. He joined the Luftwaffe in 1933, rose swiftly, and today is one of the outstanding flying generals.

Friedrich Christiansen comes from old seafaring stock. His father was a captain, and young Friedrich joined the German navy early. He learned how to fly before the outbreak of World War I, and was one of Germany's outstanding navy fliers during the war.

He was not only a good flier but also a good sportsman. Whenever he shot down an opponent over the Channel, he tried to save him. The British were full of praise for him. After the war he went into civil aviation and made himself a name as the captain of the famous Do X, when it visited North and South America.

I think it must have been about this time that something happened to Christiansen. It is well known that he suddenly folded up while the Do X was lying at anchor in Long Island Sound and could hardly bring himself to fly the ship back to Germany. He joined the Nazis early and became a prominent man in the Luftwaffe, finally advancing to air general in January 1939. While he had been an extremely gallant and fair-minded man up to 1930 or thereabouts, he then became a vicious and extremely hateful person, a bad comrade, a man who would knife anybody in the back if it helped his career. He has created an especially bad name for himself since the time he was named Governor of the Netherlands by the Fuehrer.

He is today easily one of the most unpopular members of the Luftwaffe, and is, in my opinion, a typical example of the maxim that you cannot collaborate with the Nazis without danger to your own character.

Last of all, I want to set down some things about Bruno Loerzer, who not only proved himself a brilliant and romantic flier during World War I, but also is one of the few who had his own ideas about air tactics, about co-operation between air force and infantry, and about fighting in wing formation.

One of the first fliers of World War I, he induced his friend, Hermann Goering, then wounded, to become a pilot, too. He took him from the hospital to the front as his observer, which was gross insubordination and a glaring breach of discipline. When his colonel wanted to ship Goering back because there were already too many observers around, Lieutenant Loerzer declared that he would not fly without "his" observer. That was Goering's start in the air.

Loerzer made a rapid career during World War I, forming the famous "Black and White" wing, taking part in the Battle of Flanders of 1917 under Wilberg, who was then a captain. It was, incidentally, then and there that Wilberg created new air tactics. He had his fliers attack enemy infantry marching to the front, also infantry in reserve positions, and thus helped his own infantry. Loerzer was in command of the wing entrusted with this task. Later, especially during the first week of September 1918, Loerzer used the same tactics on his own initiative, first attacking the enemy fliers and then when they were out of the air the enemy's infantry reserves and even tanks.

Loerzer was a good leader. He did not like his pilots to take unnecessary risks; he did not like individualistic exhibitions; he wanted not heroic duels but battles in wing formation.

After the war Loerzer became a cigar salesman. He still continued as a sports flier. Goering called upon him to join the Luftwaffe immediately in 1933, where he started to reorganize the *Luftsportverband*—with results not too much to the liking of Goering. Loerzer continued his career in the Air Ministry and was made commander of an air division and finally of an air corps, but never was given command of a whole fleet. He is known as "Lazy Bruno."

He is one of the few men in the Luftwaffe who never at any time had any connection with the army General Staff or with the army at all.

In the middle of 1938 the French Air Minister, Pierre Cot, made an interesting statement. He admitted that Germany and Italy were producing more in the way of aircraft than France, England, and Czechoslovakia together. The Russian air force he judged "immense," and he also thought that Russian productive capacity was very great. But his chief point was—and he was practically the only man who ever made this point—that strategically, that is, air strategically, the position of Germany was hopeless. The Czechoslovakian air bases on the one side and the French air bases on the other side were so close to German industrial regions that the Germans could not make a move without risking a bombing of these regions.

I think that this precarious situation was really one of the reasons why Hitler had to get Czechoslovakia out of the picture before he could think of starting a war. Even if there had been no Munich, he couldn't have started anything because of his immense vulnerability from the air.

We have examined in past chapters the building of the German air force and the development of a strategic idea for the Luftwaffe—or, rather, the reasons why no such basic idea was formulated and followed up. Before I go on to describe how Hitler tried out his weapon and then, with a few last-minute changes, employed it in actual war, it might clarify the picture to examine the other side. That is, we should glance at the strategic ideas and the production and production capacity both of the British and Russian air forces.

The British were the first nation to adopt early the principle of an independent operative air weapon, which had already been formed in the last war. The Royal Air Force and its strategists studied and put into practice the requirements of an independent air force. Such eminent strategists as Golovine and Lord Hugh Trenchard adapted Douhet's teachings to special British requirements, and saw to it that every air marshal and every formation leader—indeed, every flier down to the last pilot—was trained in the fundamentals and tactics of real, independent air warfare.

In Germany, military circles watched with great interest the first British experiment of this kind, namely, the policing of Iraq entirely by the Royal Air Force. The British commander in chief was an air officer, and all ground forces and facilities were under his command. The scheme proved highly efficient and inexpensive in a relatively wide area which had previously not yielded to ground occupation.

This early success of the R.A.F. and similar successes in other British territories greatly encouraged Great Britain to continue with its independent Royal Air Force.

I believe that the Royal Air Force had a plan to destroy German synthetic fuel plants and other industrial and ground facilities of the Luftwaffe immediately upon the outbreak of the war with Germany. That would truly have been operative air warfare. In my opinion the British would have succeeded while the Luftwaffe was busy in Poland. But, of course, Mr. Chamberlain would not hear of any such thing. All the R.A.F. was allowed to drop over Germany was leaflets, which did not prove quite as effective as bombs might have.

While the English conception of air warfare was far in the vanguard, English production trailed German production considerably, as soon as Goering got going. At the beginning of 1935 the English still had air superiority with their 2,800 military planes. They did not believe Goering's assurance that he was as strong as the English.

In September 1938, the British possessed roughly 4,000 military planes of the first line. From that time on, of course, they started producing on a much bigger scale and at a much faster rate.

These figures, by the way, were taken from authoritative British publications. The British played with their cards on the table as long as possible. The Russians never did, and I think they were perfectly right not to.

Like the British, the Russians at an early date had very clear ideas about operative air warfare. They started building heavy bombers—four-, five-, and six-engined machines—before all the intricate technical problems were effectively solved. They also recognized early the value of parachutists and the necessity of transporting large formations of infantry by air. They started to make the Russian people air-minded—through their far-reaching organization *Ossoaviachim*—at least ten years before Goering proclaimed that "Germany must become a nation of fliers." But, the basic strategic conception of an aggressive operative air warfare was bound to become more and more handicapped by the basic defensive conception of Russian policy.

It was, however, very difficult to learn anything definite about Russian air strategy. But when I first went to Moscow in 1923 in connection with the construction of the Junkers aircraft factory in Fili, I got the impression that the Russians had a very definite strategic line. There was an administrative council for the Red air fleet, and a chief of military aviation, General Alksnis, a former Czarist officer. The air fleet was divided into brigades, comprising many different types of aircraft, at least till 1930. Later, this was to be changed. (The brigade is a peace unit; in the event of war they were to be divided into air divisions and air corps.)

As I have already mentioned, there was a fatal tendency all over the world to underestimate Russian air strength, her production capacity, the quality of her models. It seems to me that the Russians didn't mind being underestimated. Statements like the one by Stalin in March 1939 —"We need at least ten more years to reach and pass the standard of capitalistic technique"—were designed for just such a purpose.

Reading back over what was written during the twenties and thirties about Russian aviation, I find it really incredible. A serious newspaper like the *Journal de Genève* as late as 1940 was of the opinion that the Red air fleet was negligible in comparison with the Luftwaffe. That newspaper traced the history of aviation in Russia, came to the conclusion that it was only during the first five-year plan (1928 to 1932) that there had been any aircraft production at all, and that not until the next few years did the production really get going. In 1940, the paper asserted, the Russians had finally achieved a production of 1,000 planes a month. There had been no new types since 1939. (It was claimed that the purges had done away with all the able technicians.) There was much deprecation of the fact— and not only in the Geneva paper—that the Russian engine industry was concentrated near Kharkov and thus was vulnerable to enemy bombing.

On the other hand, some estimations of Russian aviation strength deliberately enlarged the figures. Almost all these judgments originated in Germany, where the impression was created that Russia was able and, indeed, intent on attacking Germany at any moment. Herr von Buelow wrote in 1936 in the *Militaerwissenschaftliche Rundschau* that the Russians had 4,700 first line aircraft, the biggest air fleet in the world. He also said that the Russians were producing mostly heavy bombers and were powerful enough to attack any other country in the neighborhood.

He thought that they had at their disposal 1,400 heavy bombers and 1,700 light bombers. He also said that the Russians had 28 aircraft factories, 14 engine factories, and 32 factories for accessories. He estimated that there were 250,000 men working in those factories. And, lastly, Herr von Buelow was quite sure that Russian production capacity in 1936 was three to seven times as great as that of any other country.

Italian appraisal of Soviet air strength was exaggerated. The leading aviation magazine, in the middle of 1941, pretended that the Russians had fifty air divisions ready, each consisting of from three to five air regiments, or a total of 15,000 first-line planes. This source thought that 45 per cent of the entire figure was composed of heavy and light bombers—an estimate which not even the Italians could have taken seriously and which evidently was made up in order to prove the "aggressive" intentions of the bad Bolsheviks.

The estimate that perhaps came nearest to the truth was made by the *Deutsche Wehr* of July 1939, which stated that the Russian air fleet consisted of 5,000 aircraft, of which 3,000 were fighters and only 500 were heavy bombers. It also thought that the Russians had 5,000 machines in reserve which could be considered obsolete.

This estimate was perhaps even an underestimate. The relation between bombers and fighters was, as the war has proved, approximately correct. The war has proved also that all the talk about Russia's intention of waging an offensive air war was simply a web of falsehood. The air fleet was created and built up as a defensive weapon. Hence the predominance of fighters, which are a defensive weapon.

Beginning in 1938, the Russians speeded up airplane production, introduced new working methods, imported tools and machinery, built new plants and factories, and enlarged the old ones. At the same time the decentralization of production began, and many plants that were situated in vulnerable regions were shifted beyond the Volga and even behind the Urals. Still, when the war broke out, almost 80 per cent of the aircraft industry was still in European Russia.

The alleged inferiority of Russian models, Russian workers, and Russian pilots I shall discuss in greater detail in the chapter devoted to the Russian war. Just now, it suffices to say that:

1. Nobody on the outside knew exactly the strength of the Russian air fleet before the war.

2. The picture was confused through the unwillingness of the Russians to release any definite figures and also by the propaganda maneuvers of the Germans and the Italians, who pictured Russia as a potential aggressor and a great danger to Europe in general and to Germany in particular.

The Luftwaffe was built for war. One of the most vital means of preparation for war is espionage. And plenty of espionage activity went on in connection with the growth of the Luftwaffe. This one subject alone, if all the incidents and the stories could be told, would make a book by itself. I can, of course, give only an indication of what was going on.

Aircraft was, as far as Germany was concerned, an object of espionage as well as a means of espionage.

The work of German spies in aircraft companies in this country is, of course, a matter of public record. There was, for instance, the case of Wilhelm Lonkowski, alias William Schneider, alias Willie Meller, alias William Sexton, alias William Lonkis, which came out during the spy trial in New York in September 1938. This Lonkowski had made it his business to work in numerous airplane factories and had been able to smuggle blueprints out of his workshop—not, however, out of the country.

In California dozens of workers of German descent and Nazi sympathies worked in important aircraft factories, and it was a well-known fact that whenever a German ship arrived at a near-by port they would go on board and visit the captain or some other officer. All this has been written up too often in American publications to merit further discussion here.

German espionage undertook some daring ventures in an effort to find out what other countries were producing.

I know that Goering spent a lot of money trying to find out about Russian production, but with much less success. The Russians had a way of locating foreign agents and seeing to it that they would never talk. Ironically enough, the other country in which espionage in the field of aviation came to naught was Japan. The air attaché in Tokyo, Herr von Gronau, could sing quite a song about what he and his agents tried to find out and how they did not succeed. The Japanese were always very polite, but able to guard their secrets well.

Aircraft was not only an object of espionage, but also a means of espionage. Ever since Hitler became Chancellor and even before, numerous scientific expeditions have been undertaken by air, not so much for scientific purposes as for the purpose of photographing from the air areas in which the High Command had an interest of one kind or another. There were also a number of airplane expeditions for the purpose of taking moving pictures, and which ended without a moving picture ever being produced but with a lot of photos being filed away in the intelligence departments of the German army and navy.

The Lufthansa sometimes sent planes to England which did not have any passengers in them and which made certain detours over parts of the British Isles that were not on the direct route between Berlin and Croydon. I understand that it finally became so bad and so obvious that the British government protested to Berlin.

The most transparent case of espionage by means of aircraft was South America. After the last war, many former German officers and pilots went to South America to help establish airlines. By 1927 the Condor system was set up, which alone covered 4,000 miles along the Pacific coast. The Lufthansa built up a great network, too, and expanded all the time, though most of the lines cost a lot of money and could never hope to be self-supporting. In the end, there were nine different German lines, more or less covering the whole of South America. Hundreds of German pilots flew all over South America familiarizing themselves with the lay of the land, taking pictures, and sending them to Germany. Many airfields with uncommonly long runways were built by the Germans, even long enough for heavy bombers to take off. The Panama Canal and adjoining territories were flown over, even at a time when regulations were enacted against this very thing. Before the United States stepped in, the Germans controlled 21,762 miles of air routes, averaging (in the last year before the war) 3,700,000 flying miles.

This does not mean that the many German airlines in South America were established and run for the sole purpose of espionage. There were many other reasons, especially in the minds of the men who were the pioneers and who, in the early twenties, built the first airlines. But when

Hitler was preparing for war, all these airlines proved to be admirable instruments for espionage.

The Luftwaffe prepared for war. It built as many war planes as it could. It was being organized according to military principles, but it had not yet a basic strategic idea. And its leaders had not yet definitely decided on many questions of tactics.

What the Germans needed was a maneuver or a series of maneuvers in order to settle these questions without any important risk. Better even, an actual war, if such a war did not mean too great a risk.

II. *Dress Rehearsal*

On February 20, 1937, Dr. Goebbels made the following remarkable statement:

"By order of the Fuehrer and by law it is forbidden for Germans to take part in the Spanish war. It is needless to say more than this when answering the malicious lying propaganda abroad concerning German participation."

The facts were a bit different. In spite of the law there were "volunteers." Incidentally, those first "volunteers"— that is, men from the Luftwaffe—were bona fide volunteers. When the men of the Luftwaffe were informed that eighty-five men were needed to go to Spain, eighty-five of the men immediately stepped forward.

That was in the first week of July 1936. On July 31, General Wilberg made a little farewell speech in Doeberitz to those eighty-five. He talked about the Fuehrer's decision to aid people in an emergency, and to help save them from Bolshevism. Since for reasons of international law help could not be provided openly, the thing would have to be done with the utmost secrecy.

Then the eighty-five men of the Luftwaffe under the leadership of Lieutenant-Colonel von Scheele, sailed on the *Usaramo* from Hamburg to Cadiz. They had formed a "pleasure trip group," they had a good time on board lying on deck eating, drinking, relaxing. All that changed in Cadiz when their trunks were unloaded. Among their baggage were bombs, two flak guns, half a dozen He 51's and

spare parts for three-engined Ju 52's. The Ju 52's themselves were flown to Spain.

The Franco revolt had succeeded only in Morocco. In
Spain proper there had been scattered uprisings, especially
in larger cities. But the Republican government speedily
took care of most of them. Only two regions were in the
hands of Franco: in the north the territory around Sara-
gossa, Pamplona, Valadolid, where General Mola and his
troops were situated, and in the south the territory around
Cadiz, Seville, Granada, where General Queipo de Llano
was situated.

The bulk of the Morrocan troops was in Tetuan, in
North Africa, and they could not get to Spain because
the Republican government had mastery of the sea. That's
where the Luftwaffe came in. First it had to do the job of
transportation. The "pleasure trip group" was organized
into something called "Hisma"—a company for troop transport. Forty Ju 52's shuttled the 20,000 Morrocans from
Tetuan to Seville. Each plane packed in forty men, all of
whom were very uneasy about it since they had never
flown before and prayed loudly during the whole trip.

Only after this transportation problem was taken care of
did the Luftwaffe start to do something about the war
itself. There were bombings of the ports of Bilbao, San-
tander, Gijon. More important, perhaps, though less impressive was the task of getting supplies to the Francoists
enclosed in the Alcazar.

There is a school of thought which believes that Hitler
and Mussolini actually engineered the Franco revolt. In
view of the wars that Hitler was planning for the near
future, there is ample reason for such a belief. To establish
a friendly Fascist regime in Spain would have meant—and

actually did mean—the outflanking of France politically and militarily. There was also good reason to promote the Spanish Civil War from a purely political point of view. It would force—and, indeed, did force—the democracies to show their cards and to go on record as to just what extent they would become involved.

I personally do not think that Hitler and Mussolini actually started the thing, though I think they grasped eagerly at the unique opportunity. In order to start it they would have had to anticipate the abominable game to which the British and French governments lent their hands when they started the so-called non-intervention policy. A friend of mine, a German diplomat who was then attached to the German Embassy in London and represented Germany in the Non-Intervention Committee often told me about the sickening hypocrisy of the French and British representatives. Among other things they charged German and Italian warships with the task of preventing "pirate" submarines from sinking British boats in the Mediterranean. As it was, those Axis warships formed relays announcing the approach of British ships, which then were attacked by Italian U-boats or by German and Italian aircraft based in Spain. Even to this day it is not generally known that about one hundred British ships were sunk during the Spanish Civil War by German and Italian aircraft.

But no matter whether Hitler promoted the Spanish Civil War or only used it, no matter how many military and political reasons he had for doing the one or the other, the Luftwaffe certainly had every reason in the world to welcome its outbreak. In 1936 things were still in a muddle, as far as the Luftwaffe was concerned. True enough, the Nazis had sent observers to Manchuria and to Abyssinia for the purpose of learning something about air warfare. But I happen to know that the experience thus acquired was by no means considered conclusive in the Air Ministry or in the air general staff. Those experiences were, indeed, not conclusive because neither the Japanese nor the Italians had encountered any opposition in the air.

The Spanish Civil War, however, presented an ideal opportunity and a wonderful laboratory for trying out the German Luftwaffe. Since the Douhet theory had not been accepted in its entirety, it was so much the more important to formulate a new theory or even to formulate very definite tactical plans as to how to use the Luftwaffe in actual combat. And obviously this could best be done in a war that did not involve too big an investment for the Germans and no risk whatsoever.

There were, of course, the experiences of World War I. But they were considered obsolete. Not only had the new models to be tested—this was still the second period of the Milch plan in which no model had yet been "frozen"—but also the ground equipment had to be tested. Tactical experience had to be collected to find out, for instance, what was most important for bombers: loading capacity, speed, or defensive armament.

It had to be found out in which order maneuverability, speed, fire power, armor, and climbing speed were important for the fighters; whether fighters could really attack in formation; whether bomber formations had to be escorted; what was the effect of aircraft co-operation with infantry on the actual battlefield.

Most important to ascertain was which would be more effective—autonomous air operation or co-operation with ground troops.

Aside from that, it was necessary to provide actual combat experience for the personnel. Experience in the last war had proved beyond doubt that an old experienced fighter had an enormous advantage over a greenhorn in the first clashes. This was especially pertinent since the Nazis intended to fight their future wars as blitzkriegs.

That is why Spain became a laboratory for the Luftwaffe. And in view of the glaring defects of the Luftwaffe which showed up during those years in Spain and the many changes that were made consequently, I can only say that this Spanish experience was extremely necessary. If it had not been for the lessons learned in Spain, the Luftwaffe would have been beaten to a standstill during the Battle of Britain and would never have been heard of afterward.

A detailed account of the Spanish war is unnecessary here. I need only mention the role of the Luftwaffe. It was mostly thanks to the Luftwaffe—which transported Morrocans from the south to the north and to the Portuguese frontier—that Franco by August 1936 was able to establish a connection between the northern and the southern "fronts." In September 1936, more pursuit planes were shipped from Germany with a whole squadron of reconnaissance planes, heavy anti-aircraft guns, and two motorized companies. Again in November more reinforcements were sent. A whole group of bombers arrived in Spain and a whole group of pursuit planes (a group had three squadrons, a squadron nine planes). There was also a squadron of reconnaissance planes for sea and land, another anti-aircraft unit, and an air communication detachment.

The Luftwaffe bombed the ports of Malaga, Alicante, Cartagena, the munitions industries of Albacete, the power works at Rio Segre.

But the most important role of the Luftwaffe was not

bombing. In spite of Guernica, which had no strategic importance whatsoever.

More important, aside from transport flying, were its low-flying attacks against infantry. It functioned, therefore—a tactical novelty—as an *ersatz* artillery. Positions which in former times would have been softened up by heavy artillery now were softened up by attacks from the air. Of course, this had only local importance. It was only necessary and indeed only possible because neither of the two sides had any heavy artillery to speak of, nor could they use it in this war of movement.

German anti-aircraft fire, the flak, also played an interesting part. It was able to bring down quite a number of enemy planes. In some cases it even helped soften up enemy positions before the infantry made an assault.

Again something which could never have been done in a real full-dress war, without the rehearsal.

In November 1938, the fiercest battle of the whole war took place around the Ebro. It was here that the Luftwaffe, which by that time had learned a great deal, helped by bombing Republican positions and again was used as artillery when strafing Republican troops on the march to the front.

The Nazis learned a lot in Spain. They learned in Guernica that bombs could really raze a defenseless town or city. They also learned that the single-seater fighters and the army auxiliary planes as well as the light bombers proved to be efficient for the functions for which they were designed. On the other hand the "heavy" bombers—converted Ju 52's—did not come up to expectations. Battle tactics still were amateurish and had to be developed and expanded. Also the co-ordination between land armies and the air arm still left much to be desired.

A great deal was learned about flying in formation and in which cases such flying was impossible. It was found out that the defensive armament of the planes would have to be strengthened. The first reliable figures and statistics as to how many incendiary bombs were needed to destroy a certain area were compiled.

When I say that Spain was a laboratory, I mean it literally. Day after day, month after month, technical, military experiences and experiences in the field of organization were sent to the "Special Department for Own War Experience" (*Sonderstelle fuer eigene Luftkriegserfahrung*) in the form of reports. There were also the personal interviews with squadron leaders, pilots, engineers, and members of the ground crews. Every member of the Condor Legion, when on leave in Germany, had to appear at the Air Ministry to be questioned. The reports were sent to the General Staff and to the technical department, where they were broken down, and the new findings were immediately incorporated into the plans of production and of strategy. It can be truthfully said that the Spanish experience was not wasted.

Of the enormous amount of experience thus derived, I shall mention only a few high lights. I have already pointed out that the "heavy" bombers were a disappointment. It was also found that the standard of accuracy of the bombing itself was very low; even well-trained crews had not been able to achieve any very accurate bombing scores and, with minor exceptions, the aiming was poor. Day bombing in long forays also proved difficult. The ammunition was soon exhausted and so was the personnel.

The transport plane, Ju 52, converted into a bomber,

proved utterly inadequate. There were too many blind spots. The speed was not sufficient. Ju 52 was also much too vulnerable to fighter attack. So the Luftwaffe switched to the smaller, high-speed twin-engined Ju 88 with a crew of three, and the corresponding He 111.

Reconnaissance was unsatisfactory. Though the Germans had a number of long-range reconnaissance craft, they were unable to search out enemy troop concentration and deployment, and were thus unable to predict coming enemy offensives, even large-scale offensives. (I never found out why.)

While the flak had scored some striking successes, the Germans realized that this was mostly due to the mediocre quality of the aircraft on the Loyalist side. It was found out—as, indeed, every flier of World War I knew already—that anti-aircraft can only serve to keep enemy planes higher up and thus make it more difficult for the bombers to aim. In Spain it was proved that if enemy planes stayed above 20,000 feet, the flak could do nothing.

On the other hand, the aircraft cannon had proved very efficient against planes, ripping up even metal-clad wings and destroying the aero-dynamic efficiency. The machine guns had proved disappointing, being effective only within 100 yards. The outstanding feat of the Luftwaffe was the development of active co-operation on the battlefield itself —especially ground attacks on marching troops, which also had a great demoralizing effect. It was devastating when enough planes were used. Troops could be attacked with most telling effect when caught by surprise, but it was found out that if they were properly led they could not be routed on the march.

It was in this theater that the Stukas made their first appearance in modern warfare; and so successful were the dive-bombers that the men at the head of the Luftwaffe decided to build them in maximum quantities.

Aside from co-operating with ground troops, the Luftwaffe was extremely valuable as a means of transport and as a means of supplying troops who were surrounded.

And, too, Spain provided extremely interesting observations to the pilots themselves. It was established that aggressive spirit was essential. That any slackening of an attack proved fatal. That, with the enormous speeds involved, a split second could be of the utmost importance and could decide the outcome of an air battle.

As to the tactical experiences, it was found out that bombers had to be escorted by fighters, that Stukas could be used to bomb airfields or troops, that fighters could not do combat in strict formation.

But as to the strategy—the main and central problem— nothing much could be decided after Spain.

The air war there was on too limited a scale for that. Franco had only 500 planes, the Loyalists 300 planes, with an approximate 20 to 30 per cent loss per month (many of the losses caused not in actual air combat but through emergency landings and landings on poor fields). There had been no decisive operational activities in the air, aside from the use of aircraft as artillery. Douhet's theory, far from being tested and proved, had not even been put into practice, since Germany's "heavy" bombers were much too vulnerable to be left to themselves. Even Spain, where relatively little resistance was met, proved that an escort of fighters was essential.

The fact of close co-operation between the air force and the ground troops in itself meant that the Luftwaffe as an operative weapon was through before it even began to be one. But perhaps this last and more decisive result of the

Spanish experiences could only be recognized for what it was after a certain time had elapsed. I don't remember that any of the leading men of the Luftwaffe at that time realized that the Luftwaffe was destined to be what Hitler, Goering, and Milch had not wanted it to be—an auxiliary weapon.

The destruction of Guernica through merciless bombing—which rightly horrified the world—had no strategic importance at all. It simply proved to the Luftwaffe the extent to which any given town or city could be pounded, if there were no defenses. It was, of course, of no concern at all to the Nazis that they destroyed a great number of human lives, that they killed women, children, innocent people. The old Imperial army and even the new army up to 1938 would never have dreamed of doing such a thing. The generals of the old school were hard men, but they abhorred unnecessary cruelty. In fact, Warsaw was bombed only on direct orders from Hitler and over the protests of all the old-line generals.

But Hitler did not feel the same way about Germany. It has always been a phobia with him that one day Germany might be bombed and a lot of damage might be done. He knew, of course, that all the boasts of Goering that no foreign aircraft would ever cross the frontier were just so much bunk. It was for this reason that he tried early in his regime to bring about an international understanding to rule out heavy bombers and to outlaw the bombing of cities.

Now, early in 1938, with the dress rehearsal under way and the all-out war just around the corner, the Nazis began to get very nervous about what reprisals such a war might bring to Germany. In the spring of 1938, for instance,

German air intelligence learned that the R.A.F. was conducting experiments of a highly interesting nature. It was attempting to find out whether, with the help of copper cables hanging down from low-flying planes and coming in contact with high-tension conduits, it would be possible to create short circuits. Since the high-tension grid system spread all over Germany, a grave disturbance of German war industry might result. The Air Ministry was alarmed, fearing that this might handicap airplane production. There was a meeting, under the chairmanship of Major-General Thomas of the *Wehrwirtschaftsamt*, to discuss the problem. A commission was created to work out ways and means to counteract such a move on the part of the British. The committee met in June in Berlin. There were a lot of important men present from the *Wehrwirtschaftsamt*, from the War Ministry, and from industry. The air people considered the danger a grave one since enemy airplanes could not be prevented from flying over uninhabited and thus unprotected territory over which such high tension conduits were strung. The English might also operate with small bombs, and if they succeeded it would take a long time to make the necessary repairs. Indeed, in such an eventuality, Germany's power lines might prove to be a fatal bottleneck—not only for industry and transportation, but especially in connection with the manufacture of aluminum.

The only safe thing, the experts insisted, was to transfer the conduits underground. Major General von Hanneken declared confidentially that there would be no time for such a move. It would take five to ten years. And that fall, at the latest, Germany would start the campaign against Czechoslovakia, and in another year the campaign against Poland.

A lengthy discussion ensued, and committees were formed to study all the questions involved and to find a way out. In the end, nothing much was done, and very little could have been done anyhow. But the R.A.F. did not go into Germany to destroy those wires because it was contrary to Mr. Chamberlain's idea of warfare. By the time Mr. Chamberlain was out, the R.A.F. was too busy saving England. I do not know why the R.A.F. did not execute the ingenious plan later. Perhaps it soon will.

Yes, it was common knowledge in informed circles in Germany in the middle of 1938 that the war was imminent. Not only in the Army Ministry but also in the Air Ministry. It was for this reason that many of the lessons learned in the Spanish war were never put into practice and that many aircraft models were "frozen" at a time when they still could have been improved.

The war was just around the corner. The Luftwaffe was ready—at least for the type of war it thought it would have to fight.

The organization—as always in Germany—was perfect to the last detail. January and February of 1938 had brought about important purges among the generals, especially the resignation of War Minister von Blomberg and Army Chief von Fritsch, and the eclipse of Ludwig Beck, Chief of the General Staff and the brain of the army. It also brought about a purge in the Luftwaffe, in which men like Wilberg, Kaupisch, and Wachenfeld disappeared for good.

By the middle of 1938 the Luftwaffe had as high commander and head of the Air Ministry, Hermann Goering. Erhard Milch was Secretary of State, and chief of cabinet was Major General Bodenschatz. Chief of the General Staff then was Stumpff. Chief of the *Luftwehr* (Air Defense) was General Ruedel of the anti-aircraft artillery, and Ernst Udet was chief of the technical department and Quartermaster General.

At the end of 1937 there were seven air districts (*Luftkreise*)—Koenigsberg, Berlin, Dresden, Muenster, Munich, Kiel, and Brunswick. By the beginning of 1938 they had been reorganized into three air force groups under the air generals: Group I (East) was based in Berlin with Kesselring commanding. Group II (West) was based at Braunschweig with Felmy commanding. Group III (South) was based at Munich with Sperrle commanding. Then there was a Luftwaffe district in East Prussia under General Wimmer. After the Anschluss another district—Austria—was added.

By February 1939, there was a new deployment of the air force which was more or less a mobilization. The groups were now rebaptized air fleets. All these air fleets were subdivided into seven divisions. An air fleet corresponded to an army; that is, it was an organization of mobile tactical units for strategic purposes under a unified command.

As to the actual strength of the Luftwaffe at about the time of Munich, everyone had his own guess. As far as I could learn and have been able to figure out, the number of first-line planes must have been between 3,500 and 4,500. It certainly was not less and it could not have been much more, in spite of the German propaganda.

With the war just in the offing, another urgent problem had to be faced. After all, in a real war with real air fighting, planes are bound to be hurt and repairs are necessary. So the problem of repairs and of supplying spare parts had to be tackled.

In January 1938, Udet had been head of the technical department for two years, and had done valuable work in the development of air weapons. But he had always put off grappling with the dreaded problem of organizing spare-part supply and air repair facilities in the event of war. Now when he was told that in a few weeks Austria would be occupied and in a few months Czechoslovakia and still later Poland, Udet became very worried. His engineers, too, pressed him for a decision.

Nobody, not even an aviation expert, who has not himself handled the organization of supplying spare parts to a big fleet of aircraft of various types and with various engines and equipment, can fully understand the complexity of the problem or problems involved.

One single-engined military aircraft consists of many thousands of different parts. Four-engined bombers consist or more than 30,000 different items. Aero-engines and equipment also require constant replacement and, therefore, adequate stores and supplies of various parts. In order to organize all this, thorough knowledge is a basic requirement. There must be careful, long-range planning and constant vigilance on the part of responsible persons for necessary changes in plans. All this is difficult enough in peacetime. It is a nightmare during war.

The qualities required are patience and a love of detail—in a word, qualities that do not go well with the Nazi mentality (as opposed to German mentality in general). Such qualities, while prevalent in the army, were lacking in the party. Goering probably never knew about these supply problems, and Milch, when he first encountered them during his work in airlines, had despised them profoundly and left their solution to others. That is exactly what he would have liked to do when these ugly problems turned up again in connection with the Luftwaffe. For a long time he simply ignored them.

Then, one evening in January 1938, Udet finally insisted that something had to be done. Milch called a conference for the following week. The meeting—which I consider historic because it was to have greater influence on the outcome of the war than almost any single battle—began with Milch declaring that the problem of supplying the air force with spare parts during the war would have to be solved definitely that night; after tonight he did not want to be bothered any more with these things.

Then Udet talked. He outlined the complexity of the problem, and mentioned that the Spanish war had proved how intricate it was. He proposed to ignore in this meeting the problem of supplying fuel and ammunition—which, after all, should be solved by the General Staff. The same, he thought, was true of supplying mobile formations with new aircraft. This meeting should only discuss and decide upon maintenance and repair—a problem having to do with tools, spare parts, machinery for the various squadrons. Milch agreed and suggested that also the transportation of heavily damaged aircraft which could only be repaired back home should be left to the General Staff, on account of the involved transportation difficulties.

Staff Engineer R. Lucht, the chief of the aircraft division of the technical department, then gave a detailed lecture on the supply of spare parts and on the comprehensiveness of the organization that would—in view of the experiences in Spain—be necessary.

Milch interrupted nervously. He said it all seemed very clear to him. Spare parts and repair facilities had always been a hobby with engineers. He remembered having heard the same kind of lecture in 1933, then made by Bock. He said he knew quite well how complicated the whole problem was, he remembered it from the time he worked with

Junkers. Ever since then it had haunted him. But there was a big difference between the Junkers airlines and the Luftwaffe—that is, between commercial airlines on one side and a dynamic force such as the Luftwaffe on the other. Nothing must be done to hamper movements of the squadrons and prevent rapid changes in tactics and operational orders. They could not load the front formations with administrative work. Also, Milch added scornfully, he would not have it said that officers were dependent upon engineers. That might have been all right in the twenties. But it would never do for a National Socialist organization, it would endanger the morale of the Luftwaffe.

Milch had become more and more excited, and he spoke so sharply and so quickly now that answers were impossible. When he broke off, Udet said in a slightly ironic tone that since Milch refused to consider the classical solution applied by airlines all over the world, what did he order instead?

Milch pulled himself together. The problem was really not that important, he said. The campaigns would be short, damages inflicted by the enemy would either be slight or the airplane would be a total loss. Anyhow, German production was so tremendous that during the short campaigns no repairs would be required at all. As he talked, he warmed up to this idea, liking it more and more. The Luftwaffe, he finally decided, would not carry any spare parts at all. Naturally, there would have to be a few spark plugs and similar items for daily maintenance. But no extensive repair facilities. Damaged planes would be left for salvage and repair at home, after the campaign was won. There his friends, the engineers, could have the time of their lives fussing around with spare parts—for eight or nine months anyhow, until the next campaign began. But

Milch doubted that even that would be worth while. New models would come off the assembly lines so quickly that it would hardly pay to repair the old ones which would be obsolete by then anyhow.

And only the best and most modern planes were good enough for the Luftwaffe. "Am I understood?" he ended, as he usually ended when trying to impress his listeners with his generalship.

By then he really thought he had made a discovery. His eyes were radiant, and a smile broke over his face. Yes, he thought he had really found the solution of solutions. Perhaps he was already thinking of how pleased Goering would be, not to speak of the Fuehrer.

The others, however, were not so impressed. Lucht, for instance, had definite misgivings. What would happen, he ventured to ask, if the campaigns should take longer than expected? And Udet added, "And what if some power should force us into a long drawn-out fight? What if there should be a war of attrition, a war against a coalition?"

Milch raged. The very suggestion, he thundered, that the war would not go according to the Fuehrer's carefully prepared plans was an outrage, an insult to the Fuehrer, to Goering, to himself. He would not allow anybody to talk that way. He had made himself clear. He expected his directions to be executed with expediency in every detail. The discussion was closed. "Am I understood? I thank you, gentlemen. Heil Hitler!"

That is how one of the most momentous decisions having to do with the Luftwaffe was arrived at. Goering, as Milch had foreseen, was immensely pleased and called Milch a "near-genius." The chief of the air staff, General Stumpff, was a bit worried at first but finally he, too, found merit in the decision. After all, it was not his business to keep the planes in repair. If Milch guaranteed enough new planes, the solution would, indeed, give the Luftwaffe a mobility unheard of anywhere before. So he accepted. Hitler, too, appreciated Milch's decision, and told Goering that he liked its simplicity, adding that simplicity was beauty and that it was a typical National Socialistic move.

That is why, early in the summer of 1939, before the expected campaign against Czechoslovakia was loosed, orders were sent to all squadron leaders not to bother about disabled planes. There would be no spare parts, not even spare engines. In case something went wrong with a plane or even only with an engine, the whole plane should be discarded and replaced by a new one. Enough new planes would be available all the time.

The Czechoslovakian campaign, of course, never did take place. The Luftwaffe was ready for it, and Munich was a distinct disappointment to the rank and file and probably even to the higher-ups. Goering, in a speech to the officers of the Luftwaffe, tried to cover up. He said: "The political genius of our Fuehrer has unfortunately seen to it that we will not have the satisfaction of a great war now. But I still hope that one day I will be able to march into Berlin at the head of a victorious Luftwaffe."

The "genius" of the Fuehrer had by no means "seen to it" that a "great war" would not be waged then. A great war was not even in the offing then. The fight against Czechoslovakia would have been a short campaign of two or three weeks, and all that the Fuehrer had done was to make arrangements obviating the necessity for such a short campaign. However, it was for exactly this type of short campaign that the Luftwaffe had been trained, that the personnel of the Luftwaffe had been educated, that the whole organization had been set up—nothing more than short campaigns.

If anybody had dreamed of the possibility of a "great war," Milch's solution of the supply problem would have been criminal nonsense. As things turned out from 1938 on, his· "system" worked for some time. That is, until Russia was attacked and the Reds came into the war, thus forcing the Nazis to fight without let-up, without benefit of pauses between campaigns.

I wonder when Milch and Goering and Hitler first realized that "the typical National Socialist move" was not really beautiful or wise. Perhaps Udet's untimely death was in some way connected with their finding out about it.

PART III: ANOTHER KIND OF WAR

12. *Big Business*

Hermann Goering has always been credited with having built up the Luftwaffe and having led the Luftwaffe to its early victories. I have shown in preceding chapters that, after returning from World War I as a famous flier, he had no connection whatever with post-war aviation, how, when he was Air Minister under Hitler, he left most of the important tasks and problems connected with the Luftwaffe to others. After World War II broke out and as time went on, his position as chief of the Luftwaffe became only nominal.

While his aloofness from 1933 to 1939 can be accounted for by the fact that he really did not know anything about aircraft production, his role afterward can be easily explained by the fact that he knew even less about strategic, tactical, and other military problems. He simply was never meant to be a military leader. But then he wasn't too much interested in all this anyhow—aside from the fun of possessing different uniforms and titles. He was interested in leading a pleasant, luxurious life. He was interested in building up an enormous fortune and a certain power in order to insure this kind of life for the future.

Hermann Goering would have to make a great deal of money to keep up his extravagant standard of living. True, some of his valuables he has never paid for. He is known to have expropriated priceless paintings from museums and even costly stones and jewels to give to Frau Goering. But even apart from these luxuries, he requires a sum of 2,500,-000 marks a year, or roughly one million dollars, for the mere upkeep of his many chateaux and estates, his personal servants, etc. And this is by no means all. For a long time Goering has spent considerable amounts of money for personal publicity by subscribing large sums for public purposes, for instance, for recreational purposes of the Luftwaffe. In one case he gave $100,000 to build a mountain resort for the members of the Richthofen squadron.

When Hitler took power there was a short period in Goering's life when he was comparatively honest. That is, he lived on his "official" income. At that time everybody in Germany and many people abroad joked about and poked fun at Goering's many resplendent uniforms. He was at one time Prime Minister of Prussia, Reichswehr Minister, Commander in Chief of the Luftwaffe, Prussian Minister of the Interior, Commander of the Prussian Police, Head of the Gestapo, President of the Reichstag, Reich Chief Forester, Reich Master of the Hunt, and Field Marshal. Few people stopped to realize that all these titles carried excellent salaries. There was also the salary for his job as Reich Commissar for the Four Year Plan, the amount of which he fixed himself. Furthermore, he held many positions in the party which paid handsomely.

In addition, he earned a pretty penny from the *Reichsluftschutzbund* (Air Defense Association), a newspaper, *Essener Nationalzeitung*, which he had acquired and whose circulation he boosted by none too scrupulous means, a book he wrote, etc.

In spite of all these sources of income, Goering was always hard pressed for money, always had to borrow large amounts from banks, and was never able to pay even the interest on his loans.

He needed much more than those dozen jobs paid him. It was no problem for him to get what he needed. In this respect he was a *true* Nazi.

I have already described how Goering lived from his return from the war to the time he was called into the service of the government. Like Hitler, Streicher, Ribbentrop, and any number of other prominent Nazis, he despised any kind of regular job or honest work for any period of time. For some years he lived on his wife's money. Then he extracted and extorted funds from industrialists and from Heinkel.

It was a racket, but a small racket. Once the Nazis came to power, he proceeded to establish racketeering on an utterly unprecedented scale. Al Capone, at the height of his power, would have been green-eyed.

Not even Goering could organize and operate such a racket all by himself. He needed a large gang and a great number of go-betweens. He found his men mostly among former fliers who had been his personal friends at one time or another and who needed money, though not quite so much money and not quite so badly as he himself. These former fliers, more than thirty altogether, opened offices under one name or another in Spain, Finland, Denmark, China, Panama, Palestine, Iraq, etc. The gang leader was and probably still is a certain Hans von Bahrenfeld. A pilot in the last war, and a reserve officer in the Luftwaffe, he is good-looking, has excellent manners, speaks French and English fluently, and could easily have played a role in international society, accepted as a member of an old family. But he was more interested in money than in society.

After World War I he went to Sweden and ran an alcohol bootlegging ship in the Baltic to Finland, which was then dry. He made a good deal of money, joined the Nazi movement, but soon became disgusted with the party in general and with Hitler in particular and resigned his membership long before 1933. Though few men survive such a change in midstream, Bahrenfeld not only survived but could have entered the party again later if only he had made application. He declined to do so, and Hitler declined to take him back without his undergoing this humiliation.

Nevertheless, he became very rich in the course of the next nine years, and neither Hitler nor Himmler nor the army ever tried to interfere with his financial activities. In this one case, Goering would not stand for any interference.

Bahrenfeld had offices in Berlin, Munich, and Helsingfors. His German company is called *Landwirtschaftliche Maschinenvertriebs A. G.*, and the Finnish firm has the unrevealing name of *Aktiebolaget Suomi* (Finland Company). Both enterprises have or did have branch offices or agents in Stockholm, Prague, Warsaw, Amsterdam, Athens, and Helsingfors. His offices were unassuming, there were only half a dozen employees, most of them stenographers, and his files were slender. Most of his business deals had to do with traffic in arms. Incidentally, one of his most trusted agents was Baroness Reissa von Einem, who specialized in deals with South America, and who also worked as a German spy in Paris from 1937 to 1939. Later she was sentenced to death *in absentia* by French courts, but made a triumphant return to Paris in the summer of 1940.

The goods which Bahrenfeld bought and sold for Goering were mostly rifles from World War I, many of them from stocks which had been hidden or buried in Germany so they would not fall into the hands of the Allied Control Commissions; also stocks from Polish, Czech, and Hungarian factories. The sale of the German-made goods was almost 100 per cent pure profit, since the stocks were taken over by Goering for practically nothing. The many go-betweens who acted in these complicated business deals—to sell to Danzig a number of rifles stored in Holland sometimes meant that not only French but even South American and Chinese agents played a part in the deal—made good money. Still, most of the money came back to Goering.

From the end of 1935 on, China was one of Goering's biggest sources of income. The Chinese then were trying frantically to buy in Europe arms of any make and any vintage. Goering sold them quantities of rifles, machine guns, trench mortars, ammunition, steel helmets, and other equipment. It did not bother him that at that time Hitler and the German Foreign Office were on most intimate terms with Japan, the very country against which these weapons were to be used. Of course, at that time there was still a German military commission at the headquarters of Generalissimo Chiang Kai-shek, but Hitler had already given his word to the Japanese that he would recall it as soon as possible.

At the beginning of 1936, General Oshima, then Japanese Military Attaché to Berlin, also asked that no more arms be sent to the Chinese. Hitler personally promised that he would see to it.

But in October 1938, Oshima came back to him with photos which proved definitely that arms were still being delivered to China.

Hitler went into a rage and called for Goering, and Goering immediately started an "investigation." The investigation "proved" that Krupp as well as the party and the government were entirely without blame. The arms in question had been sold to Finnish firms. How was Goering to know that the Finns would sell them to the Chinese?

What Goering forgot to mention was that the Finnish firm which had acted so indiscreetly was Bahrenfeld's own little firm. But it may be doubted whether Oshima was really convinced. For at just about that time Bahrenfeld founded a new company in Denmark which took over the Chinese business.

Next to the arms traffic, Goering's most profitable racket became the traffic in outdated planes. It was a business on a terrific scale.

This business was made possible only by the execution of the aforementioned plan of Milch's, which consisted of ordering aircraft factories to increase their production for the purpose of gearing themselves for mass production— though at that time only models already considered obsolete from a military point of view could be produced. This was, as may be remembered, the first period of the Milch plan. The aircraft thus produced was destined to be scrapped later on and replaced by planes of military value as soon as the plants could master the mass production methods.

Goering decided not to scrap the obsolete planes but to sell them abroad—even at much less than their cost. Thus he achieved at least three different objectives. He provided the Reichsbank with foreign exchange. He derived a large income for himself. And he all but ruined the foreign market for aircraft companies. After all, the American, the English, and the French aircraft companies were in business to make money. They had to get a certain price. The Nazis took what they could get. They undersold their rivals, and went so far as to promise they would meet any price quoted by others or even undercut the rival price. Incidentally, through such strange business deals Goering also created a certain amount of good will in the countries to which he sold—especially South American and Balkan countries—so that he could really claim that the idea of selling these obsolete planes was in the interest of Germany, too.

In all Goering's deals there is one striking feature which, indeed, is present in most of the private dealings of all the Nazis—that is the desire to commit their crime with some pretense of legality. After all, after Hitler's rise to power, Goering was powerful enough in Germany to confiscate openly whatever he wanted. But he did this only in a very few cases. He always preferred deals, trades, contracts, some kind of legal set-up, even if the pretext was so thin that anybody could see through it. One example of this necessity for a seemingly legal basis is the way Goering derived fantastic profits from the expropriation of Jewish fortunes.

The Four Year Plan of October 18, 1936, which made him a virtual dictator of German economics, provided the ideal set-up. As head of the Four Year Plan, he alone was entitled to issue licenses to those who were allowed to take over and continue to operate Jewish business houses, Jewish banks, etc. Naturally, in almost all cases where big money was involved, he gave the license to one of his stooges. The stooge would proceed to buy a majority of the shares in a bank or a business house for a nominal price which, of course, was never paid. In the case of banks, Goering and Goering's stooge were apt to find in the portfolio of the bank blocks of shares in one or another industrial concern. Again Goering would buy more of these shares in order to hold the majority. There was never any open brute force. It was all done in a very legal manner. But, of course, the other party in such a deal never had any real choice.

This type of business was not to the liking of the President of the Reichsbank, Dr. Schacht, who at one time had also been Minister of Economics. Dr. Schacht, though he was a Nazi, still had some old-fashioned ideas about how business should be conducted. Schacht had long disliked many of the Goering deals—such as his traffic in arms, his sales of obsolete planes—because the Reich was not getting the money and Goering was. Now there was an open breach between Schacht and Goering. The immediate consequence was, though only a few people knew about it at the time, that by the end of 1936 Goering was actually bankrupt. By that time he could no longer obtain large bank credits anywhere to maintain his fantastic standard of living and to continue to send large sums abroad, as he had been doing since Hitler came to power.

It was then that certain industrialists and one well-known banker offered to take care of his debts in exchange for the loan of his name for a corporation to mine low-grade ore. They knew that the name of Goering would mean a great deal as far as business was concerned.

Goering seemed to agree but in the end he double-crossed his advisors and took over the business himself; with five million marks, which the Reich paid, and with a decree (on July 23, 1937) which he could issue as Commissar of the Four Year Plan, he formed the *Reichswerke Hermann Goering, A. G.* He acquired it along with his shares in subsidiary industries. The first production goal was set at ten million pounds of ore. Construction began immediately under the leadership of H. A. Brassert, well-known engineer from the United States. A certain friend of Goering's named Pleiger, a man who before had run a bicycle repair shop, became the president of the vast enterprise.

In 1938, the *Hermann Goering Werke* capital was raised from five million to four hundred million marks—without any money being paid in by anybody. So the industrialists who had held 50 per cent of the original stock were reduced to less than 1 per cent. They were all but eliminated from the company they thought they were controlling.

By that time Goering had gone into coal and oil production, transportation and manufacturing, had established himself as a competitor to Krupp, and was on the road again to making good his promise that his company would be "the greatest industrial enterprise in the world."

When Hitler's army moved into Austria, other opportunities presented themselves to the fat Marshal, especially since he could prevent all his rivals in German industry from arranging equally profitable business deals through the aforementioned license arrangements.

His first concern was the expropriation of Jewish business in Austria. He took over, among others, the Rothschild fortune, which gave him control of the Austrian automobile industry, machine tool concerns, and the majority of shares in the *Alpine Montan Gesellschaft*, which worked the famous Erzberg, an iron ore mountain. There was no more talk of processing low-grade iron ore through the *Hermann Goering Werke*.

In Czechoslovakia, Goering took over half the lignite mines, belonging to the Petschek family, out of which he formed the *Sudetenlaendische Treibstoffwerke A. G.*, the largest synthetic fuel plant in Europe. He also took over the Slovak Danube shipping, fusing it with the Austrian Danube shipping and creating the *Donau-Lloyd*, with which he then controlled all the shipping on the Danube.

Perhaps the most interesting and most sinister of his business deals was the one involving the Skoda Works, in which the French Schneider-Creuzot works had an important control. It will be remembered that shortly before the British Prime Minister declared that England would not move a finger if and when Hitler marched into Czechoslovakia, the British government had granted a loan of eight million pounds sterling to the Prague government. The Czechs used this money in order to purchase the Skoda shares owned by the French. Thus the Skoda Works were entirely Czech state property at the time when Hitler marched into Prague and Goering took over the Skoda Works. If it was feared that under other circumstances the French, then still at peace with Germany, might have protested against Goering's robbery, Chamberlain certainly fixed it so that Goering did not have to fear any protest from the outside.

Perhaps it was only a coincidence. But it was certainly a very happy coincidence for Goering.

In such fashion Goering built up an enormous industrial empire without creating anything himself, without investing his own money. By the summer of 1940—that is, without counting the booty which came into his hands after the occupation of Belgium, the Netherlands, and France—he controlled:

Eight companies in Germany, Austria, Norway, Czechoslovakia, and Rumania in the ore mining business.

Four companies in Germany producing other raw materials.

Four concerns in Germany and Czechoslovakia producing coal.

Seven companies in Germany, Austria, Czechoslovakia, and Hungary producing iron and steel.

Nine various industrial concerns in Germany, Austria, Czechoslovakia, and Rumania.

Four companies in Germany and Austria in the building industry.

Four companies in Austria, Slovakia, Hungary, and Rumania in the shipping business.

Needless to say, he drew big salaries and bonuses from all these companies, and through his men, whom he put into strategic positions, he made still more money in cuts from sales and purchases, in commissions and fees. Finally, there were the dividends and increases of share values which he controlled easily by his manipulations.

All this added together made Goering the man who made by far the most money in Germany, Hitler included. In fact, by the summer of 1940 he was making more money than any single man in Europe and very likely in the world.

By the summer of 1940.... Of course, today, business should be somewhat less profitable for Goering, what with German and other Axis factories being constantly bombed. And how will it be later?

The fact that Goering has been sending so much money abroad seems to prove that Goering must, at some time, have considered the possibility of Hitler's being thrown out of power. Those who know Goering protest that he is much too much a gambler, a daredevil, and an adventurer to try, after the collapse, an escape abroad to live in peace as a rich man.

But there is still another possibility. After all, a Hitler

out of power does not necessarily mean a Goering out of power.

No doubt, the fat Marshal has tried to build up a lot of international good will among capitalists and certain politicians all over the world for just such an eventuality. Those of us who are really anti-Fascist and anti-Nazi have repeatedly had occasion to voice our fears that certain politicians would like to exchange Hitler for Goering. There is plenty of evidence that certain British politicians at one time were very much in favor of just such an exchange, especially those who did business with Goering. It is quite likely that the enormous amounts of money which Goering has sent abroad and with which he has directly or indirectly influenced or helped sympathizers and leaders of political parties all over the world have had something to do with the very birth of such a fantastic scheme. At least, such must have been his ideas before the war.

Of course, there are probably still a few men in Great Britain, in the United States, and in South American countries who would like to help Goering. But their hands are tied today. And they will be even more tightly bound once this war is over and the Nazis receive their just punishment.

It is an utterly fantastic idea that Goering should be able to escape punishment and should be allowed to settle down in some faraway country to live on his income. Not only because the world would not stand for it, but also because it is difficult to conceive of Goering's being satisfied with such a tame end.

Goering is interested in power. He made a lot of money, he pocketed enormous stolen amounts, and he put them away as long as this helped to sustain or even multiply his power. Once the game is over, money will not interest him.

This is a portrait of the man who was and still is in command of the Luftwaffe during World War II. It certainly does not contain any exaggeration. If anything, it is an understatement of what Goering really represents. It must be said that the Luftwaffe has been kept pretty free of the spirit of corruption represented by its leader—which cannot be said of many of the other government departments over which Goering has had control.

But there can be no doubt that a Luftwaffe led by a better man and a man more interested in his men than in his personal welfare would have been an altogether different Luftwaffe. And that means that it would have played an altogether different role.

13. *Victory—Through Air Power?*

When Hitler invaded Poland, and when France and England, to the Fuehrer's great disappointment, declared war on Germany, it was generally expected that the Luftwaffe would start bombing London and Paris immediately. Nothing of the sort happened. The Nazis simply ignored the war in the West. Even when, on September 5, 1939, the British raided the German fleet at the Cuxhaven and Wilhelmshaven bases, there was no reaction or reprisal. The Luftwaffe did not touch the Western Powers before the war in Poland was over. And even then there was a long intermission in which nothing much happened at all, and the world in general and American spectators in particular complained about the "phony" war. This intermission was not phony at all. It was exactly what the Luftwaffe needed. It needed short campaigns with long intermissions in between. It was going to choose its own good time.

In Poland the Luftwaffe carried through everything that had been tried out in Spain—and according to schedule. Poland was an ideal field for the Luftwaffe. The absence of a basic air strategy was no handicap in a country that could be taken in a sprint. The greater part of the Polish air force had been annihilated on the ground during the first few days. Ground facilities, too, had been destroyed. The few remaining Polish planes resisted with great courage, but in vain. There were scarcely any anti-aircraft installations in Poland. Still, the Nazis lost between 2,000 and 2,500 planes (including transport planes) within six weeks. This comparatively high figure can easily be explained in recalling Milch's repair and spare-part policy. Planes were abandoned and were considered a total loss even when they were only slightly damaged. Incidentally, these losses have been kept secret and have not been admitted to this day.

I quote from German official communiqués:

September 1, 1939: Many airdromes have been attacked and destroyed. The Luftwaffe has obtained air supremacy over Poland in spite of the fact that strong forces have been kept in Middle and Western Germany. It has prevented Polish deployment and an orderly retreat, and separated the fighting troops from their command....

September 2, 1939: Numerous Polish planes have been destroyed in air battles. More airports have been attacked. Hangars and planes have been burned on the ground. Important railway lines have been destroyed, trains derailed, the munitions factory of Skarzyske-Kamienna has been blown up.

September 3, 1939: The divisions of the two air fleets have achieved uncontested air supremacy.

September 4, 1939: The Luftwaffe has multiplied its attacks on important points of military traffic. Railway stations have been destroyed, the aircraft factory of Okecie near Warsaw has been severely damaged. Stukas have been to a large extent responsible for the success of our troops advancing from Silesia.

September 5, 1939: More air attacks on marching troops and on railway lines....

The campaign in Poland furnished the Luftwaffe with its first real chance to wage operative warfare on its own. It is true that Goering's desire to fight and win the war decisively with the Luftwaffe alone could not be attained, first because the army would not let him have the whole glory, and second because the political prerequisite of the employment of the whole air force in Poland had not been achieved by Hitler when he failed to isolate this particular campaign. So, naturally the Luftwaffe had to be split up in order to safeguard the West.

There were two army groups, one in the south under Colonel General von Rundstedt, comprising three armies, and one in the north under Colonel General von Bock, comprising two armies. Therefore two air fleets were deployed against Poland, air fleet No. 1 under Kesselring and air fleet No. 4 under Loehr.

Closely following the recipe of Douhet, the operations of the Luftwaffe were to be executed in three different phases.

1. Destruction of the Polish air force on the ground.

2. Destruction, in air battles, of any units of the Polish air force that had been able to take to the air.

3. Annihilation of the Polish ground forces' means of deployment: railway lines, bridges, ammunition dumps, supply organizations, etc., etc.

In addition the Luftwaffe had to provide air co-operation for the army wherever it was needed.

It is true that the Luftwaffe took care of the first two tasks within the first five days. But that was not so much due to the employment of the proper types of planes as to the overwhelming superiority of their number, to their more modern equipment, and to their sudden onslaught without declaration of war. There was nothing unexpected in that success.

What stunned the Polish war machine, the foreign general staffs, and public opinion all over the world was the close co-operation of the Luftwaffe with the army, and particularly the extensive and spectacular use of dive bombers on the actual battlefield. The German High Command, too, stressed that point more than anything else, probably in a deliberate attempt to channel the Luftwaffe from the first more and more into the role of army auxiliary.

The second task of the Luftwaffe—fighting the Polish air force in the air—was expected to be largely unnecessary on account of the destruction of landing fields and ground organizations at the airports. But the day before the Nazis started their attack, the Polish General Staff must have received intelligence as to their plans so that important sections of the Polish air force could be removed in time from the main airports to secret flying fields. However, the Luftwaffe had no great difficulty in finding those fields during the first days of the campaign, and attacking them one after the other. Only by consistently changing fields was the Polish air force able to continue sending at least a few planes into the air for air fighting, but mostly for reconnaissance.

On the ninth of September the German High Command reported that only a few Polish planes were still making an occasional appearance, and on September 18 it was announced that the entire Polish air force had been destroyed.

When one considers the outstanding courage, skill, and disregard of terrible odds for which the Polish fliers in the Royal Air Force have become famous, the relatively poor showing they made in Poland indicates how great the confusion was during those few days of air battle over Poland. Probably, too, the Polish ground organization was not able to cope with the strain caused by the continuous shifting around to different air fields—a serious handicap for the Polish pilots. And last of all, most of the Polish planes were inferior in quality to German planes, so that they didn't have a real chance when they met numbers of the vastly superior German fighters.

Weather conditions in Germany during the first days of the Polish campaign were far from ideal, but the bombers once they had penetrated into Poland proper soon found the going easier. Only the squadrons co-operating with the army met with adverse weather conditions, particularly in the Polish Corridor, and the Stukas had to bomb their targets through nearly closed layers of clouds. Stukas also attacked Polish naval forces in the Baltic Sea harbors and sank most of the ships including two destroyers in Gdynia.

Two commanders of the Stuka squadrons and their aides-de-camp—co-operating with the army—manned the first machines and were made conspicuous by the blue ribbon flying from the staff machine. Their squadrons followed, contemptuous of any danger to be met. So they completed their mission. But weather conditions on the German side grew worse during the day, and many squadrons were hard put to it to find their home air fields. Many aircraft were destroyed in crash landings.

Other formations of the Luftwaffe had already started on the third task, that is, the breaking up of Polish deployment by destroying important lines of communication. Stukas attacked railway lines, derailed military transport trains, and blew up ammunition transports. Low-flying bombers destroyed telegraph and telephone lines, and thus seriously disrupted communication between the troops and the General Staff. Other attacks were made against marching troops and motorized columns, and the few Polish roads were thus made impassable.

After five days, the Polish aircraft industry was out of commission, too. On the sixth day the Polish fighter brigade had only twenty-four planes left, which were mainly used for reconnaissance purposes. So the Polish air force, which to begin with had about 500 planes, went out without having harmed the Luftwaffe to any serious degree.

Poland is mainly a flat country in which vast fields are interspersed with great forests and marshes. Therefore, it became an important task of the Luftwaffe to direct German ground units. Not only did planes direct the motorized spearheads across the country, but they also managed to conduct them far to the rear of the Polish army by guiding them around troop concentrations and fortified positions where they might have met serious resistance. Resistance would have meant a slowing down of the encircling movement, with which the German High Command managed to destroy the Polish units. It was therefore possible for the Nazis to deal with the Poles as they pleased, and thus the Poles never were able to counterattack or to achieve anything but the slightest local success. Needless to say, whenever German planes located Polish units inferior in number and strength to the Nazi ground units they were leading, they saw to it that these enemies were destroyed. Small wonder that the Polish campaign was later described as mechanized butchery.

On September 18, 1939, the German High Command reported that with the disappearance of the Polish air force the Luftwaffe had fulfilled its task in the East and numerous units had already been concentrated for withdrawal.

The number of German aircraft employed in the Polish campaign was about 7,500, including transport planes. The Poles claimed to have shot down 625 of these, and while this figure was doubted at first, the achievement of the Polish fliers later on makes it entirely plausible.

There is no doubt, however, that the Luftwaffe lost

many times that number through emergency landings, crack-ups in taking off, and discarding planes which could not be serviced during the campaign, in accordance with instructions given out in advance. The total loss of about 2,500 planes is not a high one when one considers the lightning speed with which the Luftwaffe managed to destroy Polish resistance and wind up the campaign.

Summing up the performance of the Luftwaffe in Poland, the German High Command stated on September 23: "Our two air fleets have entirely smashed the Polish air force and dominated the air space in a short time. Fortified positions, batteries, troop concentrations, marching troops, and rail transports were attacked without interruption. By their contempt for death, the Luftwaffe men saved an enormous amount of blood for the army.... All in all, about 800 Polish aircraft have been destroyed or captured. A few escaped abroad."

Germany sent its most modern planes into Poland, but no models which had not been known before. There were the bombers Ju 52, Ju 86, He 111, Do 17, Do 215. The dive bombers Ju 87, He 123. The fighters He 112, Me 109. The pilots who had already seen combat in Spain were distributed so that every wing had a few. That helped a lot.

No new tactical experiences were gained in the Polish struggle. For there had been almost no aerial battles at all.

As to the air strategy, there wasn't any. The campaign did not last long enough for the development of strategic goals.

In short, the Luftwaffe learned less in Poland than it had learned in Spain, or at least it did not learn anything new. There were no upsets; nothing unforeseen happened. Everything went according to schedule, according to the plans worked out long before. If anything at all was learned, it was that everything should always be done according to plans worked out beforehand.

This was a fallacy, as the men behind the Luftwaffe were to find out soon enough.

Next came the Danish-Norwegian campaign. It proved —though it was not recognized at the time by neutral observers nor by the Allies, not even by Winston Churchill— that land-based planes are superior to sea-borne planes and that a navy without a canopy of planes overhead is all but defenseless against enemy land-based planes.

In a way the whole campaign was a victory not so much for the Luftwaffe as a strategic unit as for the Luftwaffe as a means of air transport. It is not a coincidence that the operations were conducted by General Milch, expert in air traffic and air transport. It is also not a coincidence that the most effective airplane in this campaign proved to be the old Ju 52, in its old role as a transport plane.

This campaign, indeed, provided the first occasion for troop-carrying aircraft to fly a big force complete with equipment to a country about to be invaded, in advance of the main force arriving on ships which, too, were protected by an aircraft umbrella.

On April 9, 1940, Hitler invaded Denmark and Norway and seized Oslo. The German advance guard arrived in a stream of 300 planes which landed at and seized principal Norwegian airports. Incidentally, no paratroops were used, since no resistance was expected—thanks to the advance work of the Quislings. The only protection used were Nazi twin-engined bombers flying in small formations, especially over Oslo, Stukas climbing and diving while the troops were being landed. When the landings had been effected, the bombers flew off. The only resistance occurred in the

civil airdrome of Tornebu, just outside of Oslo, and at
Kjellar, the military airdrome northeast of Oslo. The latter
was bombed severely, but the small garrison resisted to
the last man. In the meantime a number of German ships
had docked and unloaded troops and tanks, which immediately started to take over. As in Poland, all movements
were directed from the air, and, again as in Poland, dive
bombers acted as an advance guard.

Contrary to the procedure in Poland, it was not intended
to destroy the country. There was no extensive bombing
anywhere. The idea was to take Norway over, and for that
reason the limited traffic facilities had to be carefully pre
served.

Mr. Chamberlain and the whole world were of the
opinion that Hitler had overreached himself, had fallen
into a trap when he invaded Norway. This was soon discovered to be an error.

On April 10, the British navy put in an appearance—
exactly twenty-four hours too late. There is no doubt that
the German navy paid heavily for the landing operations
in Norway—about a third of it was destroyed—but British
navy fliers were not able to achieve worth-while successes
over Norway itself.

British bombers made repeated attacks on German airdromes near the Norwegian and Danish coasts. But the
Germans outnumbered them, and thus all the British efforts to create confusion, to hamper German deployment,
and to prevent consolidation of the Nazi conquest were
frustrated.

On April 15, British and French troops, hastily collected
and ill equipped, landed north and south of Trondheim.
Their ships approached the coast, keeping out of range of
the German bombers, and then during the night they

landed. The landing was successful, but it didn't take the Germans long to reconnoiter the Allied movements, and from then on Allied troops were constantly under bombing attack.

British carrier-borne planes landed on a frozen lake near Aandalsnes, but they were hampered by the absence of ground crews. The Germans attacked immediately and did not let up for twelve hours. After that only five Gladiators were left. At the end of the second day only one was left.

The Allies soon perceived that they would have to get their troops out of Norway to escape annihilation. By May 2, the main evacuation south of Trondheim was completed. In Narvik the Allies stuck it out another week. By June 10, there was no Allied force any more in Norway.

The Allied withdrawal caused Neville Chamberlain's fall. Winston Churchill took over.

The most important lesson of the Norwegian campaign was, of course, that land-based aircraft are superior to carrier-borne aircraft. The importance of this fact, which for once and all was established in Norway, cannot be overestimated. Lieutenant-Colonel Thomas A. Phillips of the United States General Staff was probably right when he drew the conclusion that "land-based air power has made the United States impregnable to a sea-borne invasion."

The second part of the Norwegian campaign, the necessary retreat of the Allied troops, once more underlined the decisive importance of mastery of the air in a battle of ground forces.

But that, of course, has only to do with the question of army co-operation. As far as air strategy is concerned, the Norwegian campaign proved nothing. It also did not prove anything decisive about the value of air power as against sea power. It only proved that in this one very particular case air power was more important than sea power. In any case, the British navy, which has never in its history declined to take any sensible risk, refrained from engaging German ships near the coast, once they were protected from the air. But as I said before, Norway was a very special case.

Erhard Milch was made Field Marshal by the Fuehrer for the successful completion of the Norwegian operations.

The Dutch-Belgian-French campaign was nothing but a repetition of the Polish campaign. Here, too, opposition was negligible. Here, too, most of the enemy planes were destroyed on the ground. Here, too, psychological factors played an important part—Stukas fitted out with screaming sirens, for instance.

As in Poland, the Luftwaffe's first task in the West was to destroy enemy aircraft on the ground. That is not only Douhet's No. 1 point, but it is also prerequisite to a successful blitz offensive on the ground. In other words, air operations must always start that way, whether they are only part of a co-operation plan or an independent operational air offensive. However, as in Poland, the Luftwaffe in the West was not chosen for operative warfare, but again for co-operation with the army. The air battles which had to be fought after mastery of the air had been achieved during the first few days were not strategic enterprises or parts of such enterprises but only actions within the framework of the ground strategy.

The other and most important goal of Douhet's thesis was simply ignored in the West—contrary to what had happened in Poland. The Nazis never even thought of destroying the war industries of Belgium and France;

they had decided to have them work for Germany later on. The cannon factory of Schneider-Creuzot was not hit by one bomb. Neither were any other important industrial works, with the single exception of the Citroën factory in Paris, which was very slightly damaged.

Only a few operative tasks within the framework of army co-operation—such as the wiping out of encircled troops or the cutting off of lines of retreat—were entrusted to the Luftwaffe.

The invasion and conquest of the Netherlands were only part of the German army's entire operation in the West. Specifically, it was an offensive of the right flank of the German army. But from the point of view of the Luftwaffe, and especially from the publicity angle of the Luftwaffe, the conquest of the Netherlands was a war all by itself. It had an immediate and spectacular success. And the Luftwaffe can rightly claim the blitz decision in the Netherlands as a Luftwaffe success. But again it was only a success due to co-operation with the army.

On May 10, 1940, German armies crossed the Belgian and Dutch frontiers. Immediately, air offensives were started against the airdromes of Holland. They were successful and prevented the great majority of Dutch planes from ever getting off the ground. Once this was achieved, the occupation of these airdromes came next. This was done by the landing of troops while the main body of the German army, no longer endangered from the air, followed along rapidly.

As to the landing of troops, a distinction must be made between the two kinds of air-borne troops. The parachutists represent the first line of attack for the purpose of taking airdromes. Then comes the air infantry, that is, specially trained infantry arriving in transport planes and gliders.

In the case of the Dutch airdromes—for instance, of Delft, Zaanvord, and Hook of Holland on May 10—the occupation was executed with utmost precision and with no setback. First the airdromes were bombed by dive bombers. That is, the hangars and the anti-aircraft positions were destroyed; the runway was always left undamaged because it was supposed to be used later by those who were doing the bombing. Fighters machine-gunned the anti-aircraft crews into shelters. Then with or without the help of artificial fog, parachutists jumped to earth unmolested by anti-aircraft fire, for the crews were either dead or holed up in shelters. Then the transport planes or gliders came down. All this took only a few minutes, and in most cases there were no battles in the air at all.

There were, indeed, so few air battles that all in all only 58 Dutch aircraft were destroyed in actual combat.

The Luftwaffe used 800 transport aircraft for the Dutch campaign, which meant that 12,000 men were transported in one flight. Then there were also the planes of the Lufthansa, which were only used in relatively calm regions because they had no armament whatsoever.

In the communiqués of the Nazis, the Luftwaffe continued fighting on and after May 13. Why this should have been the case is hard to understand since the Dutch had only ten of their 250 planes left. Perhaps this was done to cover up for the bombing of Rotterdam on May 14 by hundreds of Stukas, an act of barbarism that had no military or strategic reason. In that bombing, 30,000 died. Two hours before, the Dutch army had capitulated.

Simultaneously with the attack on Holland, air raids began over Belgium and France. The Evers airdrome near

Brussels and the airports at Lille, Nancy, Lyons, Colmar, Pontoise, Metz, etc., were bombed. But they were not heavily bombed.

The sensation of the German air war against Belgium was the capture of Fort Eben Emael, on the outskirts of Liége. It started with a heavy bombing attack. After that the Luftwaffe spread an artificial fog over the fort, and protected by this fog a plane flew over it with a glider attached. The glider was cut loose and the vanguard—engineers with infantry training, crash-landed inside the fort. German reports later said that they immediately took over a part of the fort. It is more probable that they struck from the inside, while motorized advance units hammered the fort from the outside. It was not long before the commander of the fort had to end his resistance.

At the time, this whole enterprise was considered almost a miracle. Experts in neutral countries seriously discussed the possibility that the very appearance of Stukas had so terrorized the soldiers in the fort that they did not think of resisting. Others considered the possibility of a mass hypnosis, perhaps with the aid of some kind of gas let loose by the German planes. Gliders had never been used before for such a purpose, and so nobody thought of a glider. Also very few remembered that, years before, the Germans had built near Dessau an exact copy of the Fort of Eben Emael—German espionage had been effective in securing the necessary plans—and that German troops had practiced landing the glider and invading the fort for weeks and months. Thus, it was not a miracle at all that they effected an entrance into the fort and, once inside, that they knew every foot of ground in it.

After the fall of Eben Emael, the Allies were no longer

able to hold the Albert Line. During the next few days the Luftwaffe co-operated closely with the army without pursuing any strategic task of its own. Between May 14 and 16, hundreds of dive bombers were sent into action around Sedan. They had a very definite part in the successful break-through near Sedan on May 16.

The Luftwaffe continued to play an important part in German communiqués. According to them and to German reporters—there are practically no other reports about this phase of the war—French tanks formed an ideal target for the Stukas. On the other hand, German tanks could be employed successfully because of the close co-operation of the Luftwaffe, that is, the Luftwaffe protection from the air. This, incidentally, made it possible for columns of tanks to advance under Guderian and Rommel, after the break-through near Sedan, to the North with exposed flanks—an utterly unconventional enterprise that horrified staff officers everywhere.

Again according to German reports, the Luftwaffe's part in this feat was not only reconnoitering but also attacking enemy infantry attempting to attack those exposed flanks of the motorized columns. Also German pursuits and fighters shot down dozens of enemy bombers that were trying desperately to prevent the German advance.

In short, the Luftwaffe was everywhere and did everything and accomplished everything highly successfully. It sounds like a fairy tale, it sounds too successful to be true, but there is no reason to believe that it was not so.

The German advance continued into the territory where the A.A.S.F.—the Advance Air Striking Force of the R.A.F.—had its bases. The A.A.S.F. did all it could. The English held out to the last. They abandoned the airports only when the Germans came within ten miles of them.

The last wings of the A.A.S.F. flew back to England on June 15, the ground crew embarked on June 17.

On May 18, sixteen German bombers had bombed Paris without inflicting much real damage. At that time the French were extremely panicky. They had heard that the Germans were bombing everywhere in France, that they were blowing up or burning down everything, that parachutists had been dropped everywhere. Not half these rumors, probably not 10 per cent were true. The fact was that the French High Command and at least part of the French population had lost their nerve completely.

During the following days and weeks there were some advance Luftwaffe operations against Paris and Le Havre, with the army following up rapidly. On June 3, 200 aircraft bombed Paris and dropped 1,000 bombs, leaving 200 dead and 600 wounded. On June 11, there was another bombing on a still smaller scale. On June 14 the Nazis marched into Paris as well as Le Havre.

In the meantime, part of the French army and the British Expeditionary Force had been in constant retreat toward the Channel coast. Then, just at that time, there was a mention in a German communiqué, "the real goal has come nearer." Was it England? Indeed, there were some scattered raids over southern England then On May 21, the Germans reached Amiens and Abbéville, which meant that the English position was no longer tenable. The Luftwaffe, in an attempt to cut off the English retreat, started to bomb the ports on the Channel, specifically Calais and Dunkirk. The idea was to make the embarkation of the British impossible. The Luftwaffe also steadily bombed and strafed the retreating British. The German ground troops following them came up nearer and nearer.

14. *Trouble in the Air*

English troops that had been retreating ever since May 25 in the direction of Dunkirk and then waiting there on the beaches looked in vain for R.A.F. planes. They scarcely saw any. Because the R.A.F. was fighting at their back, trying to prevent the Luftwaffe from breaking through to Dunkirk, and also harrying the advance of the German army.

But a number of German bombers came through anyhow and mercilessly bombed the port installations, but they were not able to annihilate the British soldiers, who had dispersed on the beaches and made a very bad target. By blowing up oil tanks in the vicinity, the Luftwaffe was responsible for the enormous amount of smoke that hung over Dunkirk for many days, thus providing an artificial fog and obstructing their own view.

If the Luftwaffe had achieved its task of annihilating the British in Dunkirk or preventing them from embarking, it could certainly have claimed to have won the war by its own strategy, purely by air operations. But it did not accomplish this task.

Then came another surprise.

Dunkirk provided an opportunity for the Luftwaffe to show that it was up to the famous second task of Douhet's, that is, that in a mighty air battle it could destroy the enemy planes that had not been destroyed on the ground. Neither Poland nor the Western campaign had so far supplied such an occasion. Dunkirk did supply it finally.

That was on May 29, when the R.A.F. fignter group No. 11, under Air Vice-Marshal K. R. Park, left its bases in southeastern England to engage the Luftwaffe before it could break through to Dunkirk. There were Spitfires, Hurricanes, and Boulton-Paul "Defiants." Sometimes they took off four times in a day. They found the Germans, and they trounced them. The reports as to the results in figures differ somewhat. The official communiqué of the R.A.F. on June 3 mentions German losses of 200. But it is well known how conservative the R.A.F. communiqués are. I think the German losses for the nine days from May 26 on—when the embarkation of troops from Dunkirk began— must have been around 350 to 400 with perhaps an R.A.F. loss of 100 or so.

In any case, 335,000 men were evacuated, among them 125,000 Frenchmen. The Luftwaffe had proved itself inferior to its opponent in the first real full-dress air battle that was nothing but an air battle. It had proved itself inferior in speed, maneuverability, fire power, and training of pilots. In a word, it had proved itself inferior in quality.

The leaders of the Luftwaffe had proved themselves inferior because they could not achieve a local mastery of the air. The British could, which proved their genius for improvisation, which later was to play an enormous part in the Battle of England.

Of course, the British had luck on their side, too. The foggy weather helped them and hindered the Germans. And, too, the British had their navy, and a whole fleet of little boats of all kinds was brought over by Englishmen who wanted to help save their countrymen.

All this was of great importance, but the decisive fact was that the R.A.F. had beaten the Luftwaffe.

Even after Dunkirk it seemed to the world at large and certainly to the Nazis that the Luftwaffe could not be beaten. Dunkirk, after all, was only a local affair. Yes, it seemed so to the whole world, which became panicky at the very thought of the Luftwaffe.

At that time and for a long time afterward, the battle of Dunkirk was not understood, digested, nor correctly analyzed either in Germany or elsewhere in the world. The clear analyses by men like Alexander P. de Seversky and William B. Ziff and others came much later. Such analyses have not yet been brought forward in Germany at all.

If that defeat at Dunkirk and, even more, the successes in Poland and France had been correctly analyzed and thus reduced to what they really amounted to, the world might have foreseen the inevitable decline of the Luftwaffe. What those victories in Poland and France really amounted to was just this: the Luftwaffe could achieve spectacular successes if and when it was co-operating with the army in general and with the panzer spearheads in particular, and this only where there was no air defense by an enemy air force working on independent operative principles.

A curious psychological factor added to the great confusion surrounding the true reasons for these victories. Aircraft is more impressive than marching soldiers. In places where victories had in reality been achieved by land armies, after softening up by the Luftwaffe, it looked to not-too-well qualified correspondents and even military men as though the Luftwaffe had won the victory in the first place and the army had come around only when it was all over. Needless to say, such were the ideas of the pilots themselves, too, who in their arrogance did not think much of land armies, anyway.

If there had been a correct analysis of the victories in

Poland and France, it could have been established then and there that the Luftwaffe was definitely not what it had been created to be. It was not an autonomous weapon.

If the defeat at Dunkirk had been correctly interpreted, two things would have been evident:

1. That the Luftwaffe was not capable of defeating an enemy air force that was an operative air force, that is, acting according to its own independent strategy instead of auxiliary to an army or navy.

2. That the Luftwaffe had no staying power—a deficiency that very soon was to show up as its most glaring fault.

Even during and after Dunkirk, the Luftwaffe showed signs of being tired.

The Luftwaffe was built for short campaigns. It was geared to beat the enemy in a few days or a few weeks. Its whole design was based on the idea of a short war. The French campaign, though it involved little fighting, still was long enough to tire a sprinter. The Nazis needed a breathing spell.

By waiting to catch their breath, by resting on their side of the Channel, they gave the British the decisive tip-off. They also allowed them time for reorganization, and thus gambled away what had aided them in all their campaigns up to that time—the moment of surprise.

The Nazis never had realized it. They still don't understand what happened to them at Dunkirk. Goering and Milch probably don't know to this day that the decline began right there over the beaches and waters of Dunkirk.

Finally the big battle against England began. *Der Tag*, about which the Germans had talked so often, had finally come. England had to be defeated. What a chance for the

Luftwaffe! It was up to the Luftwaffe to defeat England all by itself. It was a great strategic task. The army would have to remain in the background, would only come in later—à la Douhet—to mop up and to occupy.

It was, indeed, a great task. Happily for the world the Luftwaffe was not able to bring it off.

There were four different phases in the Battle of England. The first three phases corresponded with the principles of strategic air warfare: destruction of advance enemy bases, ports and airports near the coast; destruction of inland airports, railway stations, factories, etc.; destruction of the capital.

There was only one difference between Goering's Battle of England and any other exact strategy. The latter goes into the second phase if and when the task of the first phase has been completed, and so on. Goering went from one phase into the next without having achieved anything like a victory in the preceding one or ones. And, therefore, it was only logical that he had to add a fourth phase— a phase in which he effected his retreat.

The air offensive started on August 10, according to German communiqués, and on August 8, according to English ones. Convoys, shipping, ports, coastal airdromes were bombed by great numbers of Stukas with fighter escort. In some cases, up to 500 bombers were employed in a single battle.

British fighters offered valiant resistance. Result: 697 German losses, 153 R.A.F. losses.

The first phase ended on August 18. In spite of its having failed, Goering, driven by an inexorable timetable, went into the second phase, which extended to September 5 and which had as its objectives the destruction of the inland airdromes as well as factories, railroads, communication systems, etc.

Goering sent more fighters along with his bombers in order to protect them better, but that did not help. Result: 562 German losses, 219 British losses (132 pilots saved).

There can be no doubt that many German bombers did get through to their targets and that they did enormous damage and destroyed much on the ground that was important to the war effort. However, the operation did not succeed, inasmuch as it had not broken the morale and the will to resist; it had not disrupted important facilities such as railways, water supply, telephone. In a word, none of the objectives listed in the second phase of Douhet's theory had been achieved.

Again Goering simply ignored his failure and went into the third phase, September 6 to October 5, the bombing of London. There was no strategic reason for it. But from the point of view of total warfare, there was every reason. If the goals of the first two phases had been reached, a relentless bombing of London certainly would have meant a complete breakdown of organized government, organized public life, possibly a revolt on the part of the population. For the daylight bombing, Heinkels and Dorniers were employed. Me 109's and 110's came along to offer protection to the bombers. There were 38 daylight attacks. The Germans lost 440 planes, the R.A.F. only 58 pilots.

The heaviest raid took place on September 7. It was directed against the docks in the East End, and 300 to 400 bombers took part. After that day, London's anti-aircraft defenses were considerably augmented and modernized.

But in most cases, it was not anti-aircraft fire nor the sound-detector devices nor the searchlights that proved to be of particular effect. It was the Royal Observer Corps, which did most of the reconnoitering. It was the interceptor activities of the British fighters, which made it difficult, if not impossible, for the German bombers to get through.

Now it became evident and very annoying to the Nazis that they had not been able to accomplish the tasks of the first phases—the destruction of enemy planes on the ground or their airports and ground facilities. If all that had been achieved, nothing would have prevented German bombers from getting through to London. As it was, the resistance against them became stronger and more effective the longer the war progressed.

During this phase the R.A.F. was not only defensive but it undertook a great many night raids over Germany, especially over industrial areas, and also against airfields and ports in Belgium and France from which an invasion might have been started. There was a lot of talk about invasion then. There are experts who believe that an actual invasion was attempted on September 16. In any case, on that day certain invasion maneuvers were observed along the French coast, and R.A.F. bombers and fighters put an end to those maneuvers—a bloody end.

The fourth phase, from October 6 to the end of the month, has nothing to do with air strategy. It was retreat pure and simple. German medium and light bombers all but disappeared from the British sky during the daytime. Formations of Me 109's and Me 110's, trying their luck with a hit-and-run technique, appeared with small loads of bombs. Their forays were of no importance. Bombers still appeared during the night and had very little effect.

By the end of October the Battle of England was all but over. Naturally, it did not end with a gong signal. But it

petered out. It had been a gigantic day-and-night battle
that lasted three months. But the Luftwaffe had lost. According to conservative estimates, the Nazis lost 2,375
planes—damaged aircraft not included. Actually, they lost
at least twice as many planes in that time, since experience
shows that the losses not due to direct enemy action constitute about 50 per cent of the losses at the front. But, of
course, the worst loss for the Nazis was the pilots, thousands of young, well-trained fliers and other crew members
who could not be replaced.

Toward the end of September, Hermann Goering took
a little sightseeing trip. He took off in a bomber and flew
over London, well protected by a great escort of Messerschmitts. He observed for himself the terrible effects of
the bombing of the British capital.

When he returned he immediately reported to Hitler.
He said that England was on her knees, that Churchill
didn't know that he was beaten, and that any day now the
war would be over.

I know from dependable sources that Hitler believed
Goering, at least for a few weeks. If he hadn't, he would
hardly have uttered those confident statements predicting
that he would be in London by October 15, 1940.

But Goering must have had some suspicion by that time
that Hitler would not be in London by October 15. He
must have realized that the Battle of England had been
lost by his Luftwaffe.

The Battle of England, the first great air battle on a
large scale in history—in comparison to which Dunkirk
shrank to a local affair (which does not make it less important)—offered quite a number of important lessons.

The Germans had lost it, in my opinion, on account of

their lack of heavy bombers. The Battle of England proved that you could not carry out the Douhet plan or anything approaching the Douhet plan without Douhet's most important weapon—heavy bombers. The lack of them, perhaps more than anything else, showed unmistakably how amateurishly the Luftwaffe had been built. If military experts had had a hand in building the Luftwaffe, it may be assumed that heavy bombers would have been constructed—or, rather, that there would not have been an all-out attack on England before that great lack had been remedied.

What might have been suspected during and after Dunkirk now became clear beyond any misunderstanding: the Luftwaffe had no staying power. It could not attack with undiminished power over an extended period of time. That had to do not only with the types of planes, but also with the growing repair difficulties and supply problems. German ground crews simply were not able to sustain an attack of such impetus and length. They soon were exhausted, and it became difficult and eventually next to impossible to service planes with the necessary quantities of bombs and fuel, not to mention repairs.

For the first time, the Luftwaffe had come up against really strong defense—and had felt it. England was no Poland, no Holland. London was no Guernica.

Another thing the Germans felt was the superiority of certain British planes, the Spitfires, for instance. In almost no case was there any marked superiority of German types as there had been in Poland and in the Western campaign.

In other words, while in past campaigns the sky had seemed the limit for the Luftwaffe—in every sense of the phrase—it now became evident that the Luftwaffe had very definite limitations. The Luftwaffe had not been able to crush English resistance or even to undermine it sufficiently for an invasion army to come over without encountering strong oppositon. It is still an open question whether any air force would have been able to achieve just such a goal. Perhaps an air force built according to military principles might have turned the trick.

So much graver the setback for Goering and the men around him who were responsible for the whole show. Their failure only confirmed the contempt of the army leaders and it was probably then and there that they must have decided never again to entrust to the Luftwaffe an operational role of any importance.

On the other hand, the lessons of the Battle of England did not become immediately clear to those in charge of the Luftwaffe. It took months before the Nazis in high places were finally willing to face the depressing truth. Even when they knew, they would not admit it.

The Fuehrer was beside himself with fury when he realized that Goering had lied to him. True, there had been a series of small fights between him and Goering—a running fight of many years' standing. But that had not amounted to much. I have good reason to believe that the sensational reports published abroad occasionally that Goering and Hitler had broken off never had any real foundation.

But now, in the fall of 1940, a serious conflict arose between Hitler and Goering. As far as the Fuehrer was concerned, it is understandable enough. The moment the Battle of England was broken off, the decline of Goering's career began. This has never been admitted officially. But among the better informed circles in Germany it soon became an open secret. The fact was that Hitler had lost faith in Goering. The Fuehrer no longer believed anything Goering said, particularly anything having to do with war operations. He never again trusted the Field Marshal's judgment.

It was precisely during the following months that Albert Kesselring, who by then had become Field Marshal, came more and more into the limelight. Hitler decided that Kesselring knew more about air warfare than Goering—which, incidentally, was true. But it was ironic that chance, which so often has operated in Hitler's favor, in this one instance operated against him. When a few months later the question of a Russian campaign came up, and Hitler asked Goering's as well as Kesselring's opinion, Goering spoke against the venture. He doubted that the Luftwaffe would be able to operate on two fronts. Kesselring, however, told the Fuehrer what the Fuehrer wanted to hear. He told him that the Luftwaffe could take the Russians. Hitler thereupon made Kesselring the High Commander of the Luftwaffe in the fight against Russia. Goering protested, but to no avail.

In reviewing the various aspects of the Battle of England, I have not yet referred to the young Nazi fliers themselves. But since the Luftwaffe—like every air force— consists of many human beings as well as machines, it is important to examine the effect of the Battle of England on the Nazi fliers.

Dunkirk had already been a surprise to the arrogant young fliers who had been systematically taught to underestimate the fighting quality of the Royal Air Force. It was more than a surprise. It was the first let-down. It was the first inkling that they, the young Nazis, were not invincible.

The Battle of England indicated to them that Dunkirk had by no means been an isolated local incident. The Battle

of England was for them a horrible blow. Their cock-
sureness, their illusions of invincibility went glimmering in
those days. Something very important to the morale of the
German fliers was lost—and they have never been able to
regain it. They became cautious. They no longer threw
themselves into battle at the risk of their machines and their
lives as they used to do. Many fliers who returned from
England unwounded were nevertheless changed for a long
time. They were not the same as when they had started
flying to England a few weeks before. Some of them had
to be dropped from the Luftwaffe altogether, some of them
even had to be placed in special sanitariums or confined
to asylums.

The question has often been put to me: which did I
consider superior—English fliers or German fliers? And my
answer has always been that in my experience British pilots
are superior—at least in war aviation.

Germans like to prepare everything a long time beforehand, arm themselves against every contingency, and act
according to an established plan. The English often wait
till things happen, and then they are admirable improvisors.
They arrive, with their improvisation or with their intui-
tion, exactly where the Germans arrive with their long
planning and training.

The Germans cannot improvise. An average German
cannot even bear the idea of sitting and waiting for things
to happen. He must plan beforehand. And if something
should happen for which he is not prepared or for which
he has not learned an answer, he is lost. Exceptions, like
Rommel, only prove the rule.

In ground battles it is practically impossible to improvise.
(Again, the desert battles have been exceptions.) Things
must be planned long in advance; the soldiers must be

trained to act according to the plan long in advance. This goes for strategic as well as tactical maneuvers. This is why, in my opinion, the Germans are such good soldiers.

But in the air there is plenty of room—indeed, there is every chance—for spontaneous action, improvisation. Almost anything unlooked-for can happen, and the flier must be geared to split-second reactions to handle the emergency. I think that is why the British have a natural advantage over Germans in the air.

The Nazis took great care to earmark the best human material for the Luftwaffe. Only volunteers were considered. There was never any attempt at drafting for the Luftwaffe. Even of the volunteers, only about 50 to 60 per cent proved qualified, physically and psychologically. Of these again about half had to be retired after the first flights. Of those who were finally sent to pilot schools, a great many never even got so far as to solo, let alone to reach their final flight tests. And the tests, in turn, revealed that some of those who had come that far along had a good technical knowledge but weren't good pilots.

It has been said that the Nazis have shortened the training time for pilots because they need new pilots. I think this is only partially true. The training time was shortened because it is very much in accordance with Nazi psychology to let young people loose before they have calmed down, as they invariably do during a long training period. It has always seemed to the Nazis that enthusiasm, daring— or, as it is always put, willingness to die for the Fuehrer— is more important than anything else.

For the Luftwaffe was always to be a Nazi weapon. That made the selection of human material even more complicated because the young people who were finally admitted had to be politically dependable and even fanatical. Many good prospective fliers were rejected because they showed too much independence of thought to be real fanatics.

This, indeed, became a grave dilemma for the Luftwaffe. Either enthusiastic Nazis constituting excellent material to push a blitzkrieg but not dependable in the long run were taken into the pilot schools, or thinking young men who could be depended upon for the long haul but who could not be counted on to form a party weapon.

Of course, Goering had no real choice. The Luftwaffe had to be a party weapon.

I think that the pilots' intellectual standard did not bother Goering or Milch too much. According to the race theories of the party, they wanted and got the finest biological specimens, selected according to physical and eugenic standards. Moodiness and periods of mental depression were overcome—at least attempts were made to overcome them—by the administration of stimulants such as benzedrine compounds and pervitine, so-called "Stuka tablets," which temporarily increased efficiency and postponed collapse. The fliers were allowed a wide latitude of relaxation and fun, including almost any amount of alcohol and complete sexual freedom—in France, even with girls whose "purity" of race was questionable, and who were made honorary Aryans for the sole purpose of furnishing pleasure to the "real" Aryans, the Germans occupying the country.

Still, in spite of race, in spite of careful selection, the breakdowns among German fliers have increased alarmingly the longer the war has been in progress. There is no doubt that they cannot stand the strain. Fliers everywhere are a highly sensitive lot. They are under great nervous tension when they are fulfilling their tasks in the air at enormous speeds or under risky conditions. But the Nazi fliers are a special case.

I like to think that many Nazi fliers would not break down but would continue to fight if they were less wildly enthusiastic and more quietly sure of their cause and of themselves. It is possible to be intoxicated by words and ideas that are not entirely clear to one; it is possible to do many things while in such a drunken state—perhaps even perform some extraordinary deeds. But in the long run you come out better if you aren't drunk to start with and if you know what you are doing and why you are doing it.

I realize that this sounds unscientific. I know that any number of doctors specializing in aviation medicine can prove that a man breaks down on account of physical causes. Perhaps one must have been a flier oneself in order to know that there are other things that make or unmake a pilot.

15. Ersatz Invasion of an Island

Six months after the Luftwaffe's failure to take the British Isles, it took another island, the island of Crete, in May 1941. At first this looked like and was played up as an enormous Luftwaffe success. In my opinion, it was by no means a success that proved anything of importance.

At Crete, air-borne troops, gliders, and parachutists had top billing in the drama. Parachutists had, of course, already played a certain role during the invasion of Holland and France. But they had not appeared in such large numbers as they did in Crete.

This has given some credence to the notion that the use of parachutists is a Nazi invention. This is not true. The employment of parachutists is strictly an invention of the Soviet—parachutists as well as infantry transported in planes and gliders.

Parachute troops made their first official appearance, as far as the world is concerned, in August 1933, during the Red air fleet festival in Moscow. By that time the institution of parachutists was at least seven years old. It was not a military group, at least not openly, but belonged to the Ossoaviachim Association. The Ossoaviachim had done a lot to make parachute jumping a popular sport in Soviet Russia. By 1938 more than 800,000 men and women had been trained to jump from a tower; more than 25,000 men and women had been trained to jump from a plane.

Since 1933 there had been international discussion as to the military value of this new "sport." Almost everybody, especially in Western Europe, was of the opinion that it had no military value at all—except perhaps in countries with large unpopulated areas and limited transportation facilities.

The Nazis in Germany were opposed to taking up parachute jumping; among the most scornful opponents were Goering and Milch. Some army experts were of like opinion, for instance, Freiherr von Buelow and Major Lehmann of the Army Ministry. The latter said that an attempt to land 2,000 parachutists would result in an enormous mix-up of parachutes, men, and guns—and thus provide an easy target for the machine guns of the opponent. On the other hand, there was the Italian Colonel Bitti, a partisan of Douhet's, who said that under certain conditions parachutists might be a deciding factor in the outcome of a battle.

The Russians must have thought so, too. From 1935 on, parachutists were included in military maneuvers. Parachute tactics were worked out. The classic idea was to land parachutists behind the enemy's front and thus, in effect, accomplish an encirclement. But other possibilities began to be evident, too. For instance, it was found that parachutists could be dropped far behind the enemy's lines in order to commit acts of sabotage or block his ways and means of retreat.

By 1938 Soviet Russia had several brigades of parachutists, trained for actual battle, and a number of smaller parachute units attached to infantry divisions for individual acts of destruction (blowing up of bridges, etc.).

By that time, too, the Nazis had introduced parachutists as a regular part of the Luftwaffe.

In the German case it was entirely a matter of imitation.

It started in 1936 when the British air attaché in Moscow witnessed the maneuvers near Kiev. About 2,000 parachutists took part. And the British air attaché took a moving picture of their feats.

Here was the situation: Kiev was supposed to be in the hands of one party and the commander of the other party had to take it within a short time. This was difficult because he had not been provided with a strong enough force, and Kiev was very well fortified. Therefore, the commander of the forces outside sent a few alleged deserters into Kiev who admitted under grilling that there would be an air bombardment the next day. Naturally, the commander in Kiev accordingly concentrated his forces in the most endangered spots.

The next day the bombers did appear. But they only threw down bombs that gave off a dense fog. The whole town was enveloped in fog. The ensuing confusion was used by the commander outside to drop 2,000 parachutists from his bombers. Eight minutes after the first one had jumped, the whole force had landed and was fully equipped and ready to fight. Their attack came as a complete surprise and the defense of Kiev collapsed.

The German air attaché in London, a former U-boat officer, saw the film of his British colleague. He was immensely impressed and telephoned to Berlin the same night. Goering and Milch at first believed that the whole affair was a Russian propaganda trick. The army's General Staff, in the meantime, had heard of the film or perhaps had seen it, and they decided to act. The generals demanded that something be done immediately in the way of building up a parachutist corps. If Goering still didn't like the idea, the army would take it over.

That decided Goering.

A military man in the Luftwaffe, a certain Kurt Student, who had long recommended the building up of a force of parachutists, was entrusted with the task of organizing and training men in parachute jumping.

I knew Student well. He was the same Student who as a young officer shortly after the war visited the Rhoen Mountains to see us young fellows make our first experiments with gliders.

Student was the son of a Prussian Junker. He had been educated in a cadet school in Potsdam and later in *the* cadet school in Lichterfelde. He became a lieutenant and learned flying before the war; and throughout the war he was a commander of various flying squadrons on the Eastern front and on the Western front. After the war he stayed in the army. When Goering became Air Minister he immediately called Student in—he was an old friend—and put him in charge of the aviation testing stations. In the course of his duties, he had to test parachutes, too, and he early found out—something entirely new at the time—that a soldier who makes a parachute jump does not necessarily have to suffer any nervous strain, and he can go on fighting immediately after he has landed.

So he was the logical man to put in charge of building up the German parachute weapon, and already in March 1939, he could demonstrate before Hitler, Goering, Milch, and a few generals his first flying—or rather jumping—company. Everybody was impressed. Hitler made Student a Major-General and from that time on he had *carte blanche*. Student celebrated his fiftieth birthday—May 12, 1940—by parachuting with his men onto a Dutch airport. He and his troops occupied all the airports in Holland this way, and by landing at the rear of the Dutch army caused the well-known general confusion that helped the German army beat the Dutch and the Belgians in record time.

It must be said that Student did a very good job. While the idea in itself had been lifted from the Russians, the Germans went about the task of training parachute troops with typical thoroughness; and so systematically and carefully was the matter handled that they achieved really extraordinary results. Just like the Luftwaffe, Student's department accepted volunteers only. Once accepted, the young men first received thorough infantry training—a sensible procedure since, after all, a parachutist who has landed must fight as an infantry man.

A special parachute jumping school was built in Stendal, not far from Berlin—and special training methods were worked out. Each man received a parachute which nobody else was ever allowed to touch in order to give him the idea that he alone was responsible for his own safety and life, since he alone was in charge of the one prop upon which his life was to depend later on. The men not only had to study the parachute but they had to spend weeks learning how to fold it the right way. Months were spent doing special gymnastics which limbered up the body in such a way that a fall would not cause fractures or sprained ankles or anything that might for even a short time hamper a parachutist's actions.

Unlike most other systems the German system did not provide for the intermediary of danger-free practice towers, but kept before the men during ground practice the prospect that their first mistake must necessarily be fatal. It trained them on the ground in each single movement of the jumping process and in the procedure of opening the parachute—for weeks and months on end. This was the old Prussian idea of training soldiers for such a long time that every move becomes automatic and the man can be depended upon in moments of danger to make the moves automatically. It was all very thorough, very lengthy, and, as the world was to find out later, very successful.

At the same time, special parachute tactics were being developed for specific purposes in co-operation with the Luftwaffe or in connection with the new tactics of the motorized divisions. The Germans developed jumps from low altitudes, which served to concentrate troops and weapons dropped from the air. After these experiments were successfully concluded, large formations of paratroops were organized. The old Ju 52, which proved a great disappointment as a bomber, turned out to be the ideal transport plane to bring paratroop formations to the tactical or strategical point where they were to be dropped.

Paratroops were first used in Poland, but only in a few cases. In Holland, Belgium, and France they proved to be an international sensation. In Crete they were used for the first time in what then seemed enormous numbers.

During the last days of April 1941, the British Expeditionary Force evacuated Greece. On May 1, Berlin declared that the Balkan campaign was over. Germans and Italians occupied the islands in the Aegean Sea, the British being unable to prevent them from doing so, in spite of British superiority at sea. They could only hold onto Crete, key to the Near East, North Africa, and, of course, Suez.

On May 20, a German communiqué reported that airdromes on Crete had been bombed. This meant that the campaign against Crete must have been prepared a long time before, even before the Balkan campaign had started. This became even more certain the next day, when the

Germans landed air-borne troops on Crete in the neighborhood of the large airports of Rhothymnos and Candia. They were, however, unable to take the airports themselves. Not only parachutists were used but also gliders, the latter particularly in order to land material, light and heavy machine guns, ammunition, provisions, and probably some light field guns. The following day the Germans landed at a third spot, more to the west. This time they were able to take the airdrome of Maleme near Candia. Immediately the Germans concentrated more troops and ammunition there.

It was, indeed, an accomplishment, particularly since the British controlled the sea around Crete. But it hardly proved what so many writers and experts have since contended—the superiority of air power over sea power.

On May 23, the English evacuated their fighters and pursuit planes from Crete. They said that they could not defend the airports because there were not enough anti-aircraft guns on Crete. Churchill made a similar statement in the House of Commons. A somewhat strange reasoning, since the experiences of the whole war thus far showed that flak had never played a decisive part in defense against bombing and that fighters—if not destroyed on the ground —had always proved the best defenders of their own airports or indeed of any territory under them.

The real reason for the English retreat can probably be found in the British General Staff's fear that Suez was in danger—which, indeed, it was, and which, of course, was more important than Crete. And there were not enough British planes around because Churchill had not dared leave the British Isles open to another all-out Luftwaffe attack— which, I think, again was a perfectly sound thing to do.

But even after the British had removed their fighters, they believed that they still had the situation on Crete under control. They thought that the troops stationed there could take care of any parachutists. They still had a superiority of about two to one. But as soon as the British fighter units and the British fleet had retired, the situation changed. The Luftwaffe had complete domination of the air over Crete. Later, the Nazis pretended that they had "gained" this supremacy in the air through fighting. This was not true. But for all practical purposes only the fact of German air supremacy mattered. Hundreds of German transport planes arrived from Greece with only slight interference from British fighters, while the German fighter planes took care of the few British anti-aircraft guns, which put up a marvelous but doomed defense. Hundreds of parachutists whose jumps were timed to the split second bailed out. Guns were parachuted down. Gliders swooped down and spilled infantry, mountain troops, and engineers.

On May 26, for the last time, the R.A.F. sent over a few long-range bombers and fighters, but to no avail. In the struggle that followed, the German ground troops continued to be augmented, and the Luftwaffe played a decisive co-operative part, especially with its Stukas. Rapidly, the tactically important points on the island were taken. British resistance became weaker, while more reinforcements, German as well as Italian, arrived in boats. There was nothing left for the English to do but evacuate on June 1.

German experts were overjoyed by the great success of the German Luftwaffe. Crete and the other islands, they declared, had been since old times the bridgeheads for strategic enterprises against the Near East and now, of course, against Suez. Even a few years ago land-locked powers could not have dreamed of getting hold of such bridgeheads. Now everything had changed.

What would Hitler do? Where would he go next? Would it be Syria; would it be Egypt?

Nothing of the sort happened. In fact, nothing happened at all. Not even more than a year later when Rommel was approaching Alexandria was an attempt made to land air-borne troops based on Crete in the rear of the British Eighth Army. Why?

It is all very simple. Because the victory of Crete did not imply all it had seemed to imply. Because it was not a victory. To be sure, the Germans had taken the island, but with enormous losses. Five thousand men were drowned at sea or during their attempts to land. About 12,000 men, parachutists and air-borne infantry, were killed while floating to the ground, or during the landings of their gliders; 180 fighters and 250 transport planes were destroyed. All that in spite of completely inadequate defense of the island.

So, in the last analysis, the success of Crete was not a strategic success. It proved what the more conservative military experts had always said: that it could not be repeated on a big scale in the face of really strong defense, and never in a country with enough roads and means of communication and airports, such as England or even Egypt. In a word, the conquest of Crete proved exactly nothing.

Of course, Crete did show one thing—what was already known—that is, that land-based aircraft is superior to sea-borne aircraft. This had been established during the Norwegian campaign and was, incidentally, to be established a third time during the Battle of Coral Sea which was won by American land-based aircraft, and still later by the total destruction of a Japanese convoy in the Bismarck Sea, by the same means.

There are those who say that Crete is a milestone in the history of air warfare. I fail to see why this should be so. I concede that Crete was a demonstration of the importance of military aerial transport and that it again showed the enormous advantages of aircraft co-operation with ground forces. But nothing more. It is not strange that the spectacular success impressed people who know nothing about air warfare. It is strange, however, that even experts were fooled—even men like Seversky—though strategic goals such as industries, communications, etc.—strategic goals, according to Seversky—simply did not exist in Crete.

As a weapon, the Luftwaffe achieved nothing at all during this campaign. It never *gained* the air supremacy in a fight, it simply had it. And since there were no strategic goals on the ground, the Luftwaffe had, in the last analysis, neither opponents nor targets, and nothing to prove from a strictly strategical point of view.

Goebbels, of course, told the world what the experience of Crete meant. He immediately claimed, "The conquest of Crete proved that an island could be taken from the air." Therefore, the British Isles, too, could be taken from the air.

That was exactly what Crete did not prove. Crete was conquered because the Nazis were allowed to obtain and maintain mastery of the air during their operations. England was *not* invaded because the Nazis were not allowed to obtain and maintain mastery of the air at any time, and there was no reason why they would be able to do later what they had failed to do in the first place.

I don't think that Goebbels believed a word of what he

was saying. Why then did Hitler not launch a new attack on England after the conquest of Crete? Because he and the leaders of the Luftwaffe and Goebbels and, indeed, everybody knew that such an attack would not succeed.

If they had not known it, why, instead of turning against England, did Hitler almost immediately turn upon Russia?

16. *The Russians Don't Play Ball*

In the Russian campaign the Luftwaffe appeared in a much lesser role than had been expected by those not in the know.

Those who knew were aware that the army leaders had made up their minds after the Battle of England never to allow the Luftwaffe to take the lead again in the war or any phase of the war. The fall of Crete did not impress the generals very much. They knew the exact value of the Crete affair.

The theory has been advanced that the Nazis wanted to take over Russia as it was and therefore deliberately refrained from destructive strategic bombing. It has been said that the Russian war was to be a "war of possession" as distinguished from a "war of elimination" such as was conducted against Poland and the British Isles.

I fully agree that such plans may have existed. But I have reason to believe that the German army's main strategic objective in the Russian war was to annihilate the Red army before winter came. The delay in the Balkans caused by the untimely revolt of Jugoslavia left the Nazis little time.

In an earlier chapter it was mentioned that after World War I the General Staff undertook some elaborate research to discover the reasons and causes for the defeat. Among other things it was found that a victorious outcome could be hoped for in a future conflict only if the struggle were a short one and if the enemy were forced to accept decisive battles near the German frontier. In other words, the enemy should be crushed without Germany's running the risk connected with extended lines of communications. I think that the Nazis' desire to have it all over with in a hurry, without going too deep into Russia, was a decisive factor in the Russian campaign of 1941, a factor that necessarily influenced the role of the Luftwaffe in that campaign.

The Luftwaffe was pretty sure that it could take the Red air fleet by surprise. It prepared its moves with great secrecy and shrewdly camouflaged them. And then, suddenly, it struck. As a matter of fact, it struck an hour and a half before war was declared.

The idea once more was to destroy the Red air force on the ground. Strangely enough the Luftwaffe succeeded in part. Strangely enough, because the Russians should have suspected just such a move. And should have taken precautions.

The lengthy German communiqué of June 29—the week after the beginning of the war—said much about the Luftwaffe and declared that it had gained mastery of the air on the very first day. According to German reports, the Russians lost 1,811 planes the first day as against 35 German planes lost. On the second day the Russian loss had mounted to 2,582. On the eighth day to 4,107.

Fortunately it was not that bad. Russian losses were considerable but not catastrophic. While the Russians had not foreseen and guarded against the German surprise attack, their air fleet was widely dispersed over the width and the depth of the front, and the Germans simply could not hit everywhere.

That was the beginning. What followed was less dramatic.

During the next week or so the Luftwaffe made flights deep into Russia and bombed strategic targets. Kiev, Sevastopol, Kharkov, ports on the Black Sea, airports, railway stations, munitions depots were visited, according to German communiqués, with "definite" success. According to the German communiqué of June 29, there was no Russian air fleet any more. Then on July 1, they repeated the claim. It was all over in the air, the Germans boasted.

From July 5 on, the Luftwaffe was used for tactical tasks in co-operation with the infantry and tank units. Stukas helped mechanized columns to force the Beresina. The Luftwaffe bombed Smolensk, which was to be attacked very soon. Indeed, on July 14, the German communiqué said that Smolensk had been taken, while on August 6 another communiqué admitted that it was not yet quite in the bag—but anyhow almost. In this communiqué was a long report about the Luftwaffe, which, it seems, had helped a great deal. The air fleet under Marshal Kesselring had shot down more than 1,000 enemy craft, not to speak of the railways, mechanized columns, bridges, etc., put out of action.

Exactly four weeks after the war started the first "big" attack on Moscow began. By this time the Luftwaffe was entrusted with new tasks, but again only tactical tasks. It was used on a large scale for reconnaissance: short-range reconnaissance, in order to lead the troops, especially the armored columns, and rapidly guide them through the openings left by the enemy; long-range reconnaissance, in order to find out how many reserves the Russians were bringing up. The enormous length and depth of the front necessitated the breaking up of the air fleets into small units. This, of course, meant that the air force could no longer be used for strategical tasks.

This became evident when the bombing of Moscow started. This should have been a natural task for the Luftwaffe, and, indeed, it was expected that the Luftwaffe would accomplish it. Moscow was so much smaller than London, so much easier to hit, that the effect should have been much more terrific than what was produced on the British capital. But in reality the bombing of Moscow never came off on a big scale.

It began on July 22, when 200 planes attacked the city for five and a half hours. The raids were repeated almost daily till the end of August. But the loss in human lives and the damage to property were comparatively small.

During the month of August the general military situation was shaping up as follows: On both wings the Germans advanced steadily though slowly. On August 14 the siege of Odessa began, and a few days later the situation of Leningrad became critical. In the center around Smolensk the fighting was heaviest. It was here that the offensive against Moscow was to be started.

It was here that the Luftwaffe went into action or, more precisely, was kept in action. Naturally, it played a part in the ground battles near Smolensk. Naturally, too, it cooperated with the armored columns advancing toward Leningrad.

The Russians prepared a counteroffensive west of Moscow and there deployed their reserves. It can be taken for granted that the Luftwaffe knew about this through the activities of its long-range reconnaissance planes. But it is equally certain that the Luftwaffe could not do anything to hinder the deployment of Timoshenko's reserve.

By that time, German communiqués were mentioning the activities of the Luftwaffe less and less. That changed on the first of September again, when Leningrad was attacked and the Luftwaffe once more was used in a concentrated form. Incidentally, the air battles around Leningrad had already begun a few days before. They continued, and Leningrad was bombed regularly for many weeks to come. In the third week of September the Luftwaffe tried to strike a decisive blow. It appeared with a thousand bombers over Leningrad. It selected the living quarters of workers for targets—evidently in order to create panic and bring about a general demoralization. It accomplished nothing of the sort. The Leningrad workers were infuriated, and they took up arms instead.

In the meantime, the bombing of Moscow had all but stopped. Evidently the Luftwaffe was no longer capable of fighting on a big scale in more than one place at a time.

Late in September, Timoshenko's offensive in the Smolensk area had progressed so far that the German army had to throw some of the Leningrad reserves in against him. Still, Timoshenko pushed ahead and made his breakthrough near Gomel.

During all this never a word about the Luftwaffe. If some German air units were fighting there, as undoubtedly they were, they could not have accomplished anything to speak of.

October 4. The picture changed again. Timoshenko's offensive had reached a point where the Germans were forced to do something about him. Consequently, on October 7, an enormous offensive began against Moscow, the Luftwaffe taking part in an extensive way.

The first weeks of October were critical for Moscow, though still not to be compared with the critical situation of London a year before. But the German army could not sustain its attack, and by the end of October it had more or less petered out. By the middle of November a third

and last attack was attempted against Moscow—again in
vain. By that time the great Russian counteroffensive was
well under way. There was no mention at all of the Luftwaffe any more.

Berlin must have felt that the Luftwaffe's performance
had been disappointing. On October 7, there suddenly appeared a very strange German communiqué concerning the
Luftwaffe. Its tone was defensive. It said that the Luftwaffe
really had a great deal to do. That it was fighting from
Egypt to the Atlantic, that it had to cover enormous areas
and enormous fronts. And that in spite of all this the aircraft production in one month was bigger than the losses
of three months. But there was not one word about strategic air warfare in that curious report.

It is an open question whether the Luftwaffe, if it had
been allowed to play an independent and autonomous part
in the Russian campaign, would have been able to bring
about a decision. My opinion is that it would not. Had it
really been allowed a free hand, had it actually been
allowed to play a strategic part, then it would have concentrated on a long-range strategy. It would have bombed
and destroyed the most important strategic points behind
the front—the power plants, the war industries, the air
centers—just as Douhet had set it all down. That was the
logical plan to follow. Instead, the Luftwaffe was used on
the battlefield itself, at least most of the time, as a purely
auxiliary weapon, in a way as an *ersatz* for artillery. Owing
to the vast expanse and extent of the Russian front, it was
simply not able to tackle other jobs. And the longer the war
dragged on, the less possible it became for the Luftwaffe to
attend to anything other than such purely tactical chores.

The strategy of the Russian army—to withdraw but

never to stop fighting and thus always keep the Nazis busy—began to show its effect on the Luftwaffe after the first two months. It was unlike the campaigns in western Europe. The Luftwaffe could not depend on rail and highway communications in Russia, and thus the supply of fuel and ammunitions became a major problem.

Then, too, the Red air force did not prove to be as inferior as many experts—among them Lindbergh—had wanted the world to believe. It soon become clear that the Russian pilots were at least as good as the German pilots. It also became evident that certain Russian machines were on a par with German models. There was, for instance, the MIG 3, a fighter capable of outstanding performance. British experts later pronounced it equal to the Spitfire. The fact that the Russians were able to send bombers over a distance of hundreds of miles to Germany, as well as the performances of the Stormovik dive bombers, also proved that the Red air fleet possessed a number of types that were up to the most modern requirements in design, fire power, and protective armor.

And then came the winter.

Enough has been written about the effect of the Russian winter on the German army in general, so it need not be discussed at length here. I only want to underline that the Luftwaffe in Russia was by no means better off. Those of us who had been pilots during the first World War were not at all surprised. During the winter of 1916 and 1917 in Russia, our engines had often frozen while running under full power.

There were many speculations as to why the Luftwaffe remained so passive. Some experts guessed that there was trouble getting the machines started. There was, indeed, a lot of trouble. Liquid-cooled cylinder heads cracked, and the motors did not start. It is true that the fuel injections of the German aero-engines avoided the usual carburetor difficulties. But since lubricants generally cannot be prevented from dilution by water droplets in the engine itself, they froze, too, and so did the German fuel and coolants. Condensation on spark plugs made the lives of mechanics miserable.

Others thought that the Luftwaffe had become passive because fuel had to be saved for the spring offensive. It certainly had to be saved, spring offensive or not.

Such a relatively small unit as 100 medium bombers flying four hours a day uses up around 200 tons of fuel and oil, and drops at least another 200 tons of bombs, not to mention other ammunition. The German railway system was not—and is not—equipped with many cars of more than ten tons, and heavier cars couldn't have been used anyway on the converted Russian rail lines. That meant forty carloads of fuel, oil, and ammunition had to be shipped in every day to keep even such a relatively small bomber unit supplied—quite a task for a strained and overburdened service as the Luftwaffe was at that time.

Losses in personnel, general fatigue, and overworked staffs, too, began to make themselves felt. Tactical considerations and the exigencies of a blitzkrieg warfare had not allowed for an adequate rotation of personnel and equipment. Theoretically, such a rotation would have been possible and the Luftwaffe might have fought on indefinitely if not more than one-third of the available first-line aircraft had fought at any given time. But, of course, no such plan was adopted, at first because it was contrary to the very idea of a blitzkrieg, and later on because there were simply too many things to do and all the distances were too great.

I have pointed out again and again that the Luftwaffe, even more than the army, had counted on one important characteristic of a blitzkrieg—its short duration which made possible a long rest afterward, a rest to gather strength for a new campaign. Since the Russian war went on and on, there was no possibility of such a rest. Though the army at large felt this keenly, the Luftwaffe felt it even worse.

The Russians realized how matters stood. They never allowed the Germans—including the Luftwaffe—time for a breathing spell, let alone a long rest. They forced upon the Nazis the "war of permanency." There is no doubt in my mind that by pursuing such tactics the Russians harmed the Luftwaffe more than any spectacular defeat in the air would have hurt it. Here a wound was opened over and over again, never allowed to close, and the lifeblood of the body of the Luftwaffe dripped away, much more blood than it could afford to lose.

It is to be remembered that Erhard Milch had not made any preparations for spare parts, repairs, or overhauling because he felt the war would not last long enough to make such preparations necessary. It should be remembered, too, that while the war had been going on for two years before the Russians were attacked, it had really not been one war but a succession of small campaigns with long periods of rest in between—exactly the type of war the "Milch system" needed in order to function. Now it was a different story.

Milch was forced to improvise the repair and overhaul service in the midst of the war. As was to be expected under the circumstances he made a poor job of it. After all, he had no special knowledge of the problems involved. The results were devastating for the Luftwaffe.

Here, too, the winter played a certain role. The incredible cold so paralyzed the mechanics and the ground crews that for months repair and overhaul activities had to stop altogether. And the deep snow made it impossible to ship back to Germany the machines that were in need of more extensive repair.

I have not seen any evidence that the Luftwaffe, since that disastrous first winter, has managed to build up an adequate supply of spare parts and set up repair facilities on a large scale. Milch tried to solve the problem in typical makeshift manner by forcing the aircraft industry itself to organize and set up repair units wherever there was a large concentration of the Luftwaffe. Instead of centralizing, he decentralized—and this in the midst of war. There is nothing to be said against decentralization, which principle has been used by the British with mounting success. However, decentralization cannot be improvised. First, common principles and a common policy must be worked out, after which those principles and policy may be used to direct a decentralized set-up. Naturally, nothing came of this hasty arrangement. The British Eighth Army later on, when it followed the retreating Rommel through Libya, found great numbers of damaged German planes that had been left for repair at such repair branches in the desert. The machines had been lying there untouched for weeks and months without anybody's ever finding time to do anything about them.

In a way, that winter in Russia was not without ironic highlights for the Luftwaffe. It was handicapped in every possible way, particularly through poor communications, the lack of railway cars, the bad roads that cut them off from necessary supplies. The supply problem became such a grave one that the Luftwaffe finally had to become a transport organization for itself as well as for the rest of the army. Hundreds of transport planes were used to bring food, fuel, and ammunition, radio batteries, and all kinds of material to the front, and to transport the wounded back. The Luftwaffe occasionally published reports about these "flying missions." It seems that more than twenty millions of aircraft miles were covered during the winter. That certainly was a triumph—but not the kind the Luftwaffe had hoped to achieve in Russia.

In 1942 the Luftwaffe continued its purely auxiliary role in Russia. Long distance raids were abandoned. Flying units had to concentrate entirely on co-operation with ground troops.

That was to be expected. The Luftwaffe had not been able to stop the Russian counteroffensive during the first winter. It had not even been able to function very effectively in its long-range reconnaissance. Otherwise, it would scarcely have been possible for the Russians to bring up their reserves and to attack the German wings without the Germans having taken appropriate measures against such moves.

True, the Germans could have hoped that the Russian air force would be severely handicapped in 1942, after the severe pounding that Russian aircraft production facilities had taken. They could have expected at least a temporary setback. But that setback was at least partly made up by deliveries from the United Nations.

When the German army started its great offensive in May 1942, the Luftwaffe once more proved to be an excellent co-operative weapon. Hundreds of Stukas and other dive bombers preceded the infantry and the motorized columns on the road to Kerch and to Sevastopol. Kerch was taken.

The whole world was waiting for air-borne troops to cross the narrow channel between Kerch and the Caucasus and its oil. After all, the Luftwaffe had taken Crete.

But nothing of the sort happened this time. The Luftwaffe was not given the opportunity and probably for a very good reason. The Caucasus was still the goal of the summer offensive, and the infantry immediately started moving toward that goal—by way of Rostov. It was there that the main offensive started.

A minor offensive on the part of Timoshenko against Kharkov cost the Nazis some time, but the Germans progressed via Rostov into the Caucasus and from Kharkov toward Stalingrad.

But the Nazis could not get farther than the Crimea. They could not consolidate their successes east and south of the Don. The Luftwaffe could not help them there, either. There was no other attempt to use the Luftwaffe on a large scale, as it had been used before Kerch. It went on co-operating with the infantry—but wherever successes were achieved, even temporarily, it was the ground troops who had to fight for them.

Stalingrad is a good example of how things worked. German bombers attacked the town again and again, until half of it was in ruins. But the defenders of Stalingrad continued to fight from those ruins.

The chief of the Luftwaffe, Hermann Goering, no longer played a very big part. Marshals Kesselring, Stumpff, and Sperrle took things into their own hands. Jeschonnek continued as Chief of Staff.

There were also some personal reasons why Goering had been pushed somewhat into the background. It had become more and more clear that he wanted to make the

Luftwaffe his own, his very personal weapon. When, after the beginning of the Russian-German war, the chances of civil war were debated among high Nazi dignitaries, Goering once was indiscreet enough to make a certain remark concerning the importance of the control of the air in such a civil war. He said, "Victory will be where I shall be."

A remark that certainly must have come to the ears of Hitler soon afterward, and which must have helped a lot to shorten the career of Goering, if not actually to end it.

In any case, with the Russian war going into its second year, he had lost prestige and influence—at least, as far as the Luftwaffe was concerned.

This was not the only major change in the ranking and the influence of the men in the Luftwaffe. As soon as it became evident that things were not going too well in Russia—and up to this very day—hardly a week passsed without changes within the select circle of the Luftwaffe higher-ups. Only occasionally did the world press mention these shifts because while most generals are internationally known, the top men of the Luftwaffe have rarely achieved such distinction. But anyone who knew the inside could not fail to see that beginning with the end of 1941 not only Goering, but in ever growing measure the men belonging to the "Goering wing," lost influence.

There were accidents. . . .

Perhaps there were some genuine accidents, some unfortunate crashes in which the victims were prominent fliers who happened to be friends of Goering's. But the fatal accident involving a man who had been very close to Goering, the death of Ernst Udet, could hardly have been merely an accident.

That was in November 1941. The official German report said that Udet had been killed "while trying out a new weapon." At the same time òfficial Italian sources reported that Udet had crashed.

There had been no official report, however, of the fact that some time previously the Gestapo had arrested Udet. Surely, such an arrest would have been utterly impossible in 1939 or 1940. It proved that Goering in the fall of 1941 was no longer powerful enough to protect his friend Ernst Udet. All he was able to do was to change the "arrest" into a kind of "detention" at his, Goering's, Karinhall estate.

No matter what interpretation may be put upon the way Udet was killed, one thing is sure: in Udet the Luftwaffe lost its best technician, lost him at a moment when it most needed him.

Kesselring, who had outmaneuvered Goering and upon whose advice the Fuehrer had depended for a long time, did not come out too well either. In the early spring of 1942 Hitler finally took his Russian command away from him. A little later Kesselring popped up again as the leader of a German air fleet stationed in Italy. One of his main objectives was Malta, but it turned out that he could not take Malta, try as hard as he would. Kesselring's next job was to co-operate with Rommel, who was on his way to the Suez Canal. For some time he was able to get the transports through to Rommel, but when things went awry for Rommel, they also went bad for Kesselring. He could no longer get his planes through to Africa, most of them being shot down by R.A.F. interceptors. There were some bitter quarrels between Rommel and Kesselring, each blaming the other for the growing African disaster. Later, Kesselring was transferred back to the Russian front, this time in a minor role. At this writing he is back at the Mediterranean.

At the time of this writing I have just received from a confidential source the news that Erhard Milch is out, too. I have no way to check up on this bit of information, which, if true, would constitute the most sensational shake-up inside the Luftwaffe so far. It would, indeed, prove that Hitler has found out that something is wrong, basically wrong, with the Luftwaffe.

When the German troops at Stalingrad finally became, toward the end of 1942 and the beginning of 1943, the "heroic defenders of Stalingrad," when in fact the aggressors had been cut off and encircled, the Luftwaffe once more was called upon to take over the supply service.

There is no sense in denying that it has done this job very well. Thousands of Ju 52's flew to and from Stalingrad in order to keep those German troops alive and to keep them fighting to the very last. The planes transported shells, food concentrates, even water. Heavy losses made necessary the pressing into service of mail planes, passenger planes, trainers.

Yes, the Luftwaffe did a good job there. But what has this to do with strategic operative air warfare? What, indeed, had this to do with war?

Luftwaffe means air weapon. Did the Germans need a "weapon" to transport food and water and shells? I think the Luftwaffe's role in the Stalingrad sector is highly symbolic. Once the Nazis promised their people that the Luftwaffe would win the next world war. Once it had even looked that way to those who were not trained in careful observation. But now even people with untrained eyes and minds could see for themselves. The mighty Luftwaffe, only yesterday the terror of the European continent and the whole world, had become a supply service.

17. *The Receiving End*

The American invasion of North Africa must be considered another defeat for the Luftwaffe—and a very serious defeat.

I do not think that the German General Staff originally had any definite African strategy. At least not for the time when German armies were fighting on another front— or other fronts. This would contradict the basic idea of the German strategy as it was developed after the defeat of 1918 and which stipulated that there be fighting on only one front at a time.

Of course, the Africa Corps had been trained for a long time. But that is not necessarily a contradiction. The Africa Corps was trained and a lot of other preparations were made for African warfare, not for offensive purposes but purely for defensive—even preventive—purposes.

In short, the German General Staff had to prevent the enemy or enemies from getting into Africa and establishing themselves on a springboard from which to threaten Germany's "soft underbelly."

It is entirely possible that plans were changed later, especially after Rommel's first spectacular successes, when it seemed easy enough to take North Africa and particularly Egypt in blitz fashion and to reach Suez.

But whatever Germany's basic or changed African strategy was, one thing is sure: the enemy must not land and establish himself in Africa.

Theoretically, American landings could have been prevented, and, again in theory, such prevention should have been the goal of a strategic warfare on the part of the Luftwaffe. (That the Luftwaffe did not even try to do such a thing does not detract from the brilliance of the American feat.)

There are two reasons why the Luftwaffe could not prevent the American landings.

1. It did not possess sufficient numbers of long-range bombers which could have flown out to the sea and attempted to bomb the American convoys out of existence. In fact, the Luftwaffe hardly possessed any aircraft at all which might have carried through such an operation. The lack of heavy bombers in the Luftwaffe and the reasons for the lack have been discussed in other chapters. It is sufficient to point out that if the Luftwaffe had possessed such aircraft as, for instance, the Liberator or the Flying Fortresses, the landings of American troops in North Africa would have been much more difficult to achieve—if possible at all.

2. The Luftwaffe did not have enough aircraft any more to wage a full-dress battle in Africa. This is not to say that the actual number of first-line planes had diminished—I think it has not yet. Later I shall discuss the reasons for my belief, and shall indicate when I think the actual decrease of planes in the Luftwaffe will set in.

But by the end of 1942 the Luftwaffe's five thousand front-line aircraft were dispersed all over Europe. About 1,000 were based in France, Belgium, and the Low Countries—to take care of the British threat—300 in Norway, 700 in Italy and Sicily, 100 in Greece and Crete, 200 in the Balkans, 400 in Germany proper, and 1,600 at the Russian front. That left roughly 500 for North Africa, which was not enough, not half enough, to do anything really efficient to prevent the American invasion.

This, of course, is not the fault of those who built the Luftwaffe. This is entirely the fault of the political leadership, that is, of Hitler himself, who had promised short campaigns, one enemy at a time, and long breathing spells in between. And, of course, the fault of the Russians, too, who had not allowed the Luftwaffe any breathing spell.

The American invasion was a defeat for the German Luftwaffe in still another sense. It has put the Luftwaffe into a very bad, almost desperate situation. It has put it on the receiving end—as far as the Douhet theory is concerned.

Douhet recommended sending a large force of bombers into the enemy's country to strike at his most vulnerable points. When it is not possible for an air force to follow this strategy, it becomes equally important for the air force to prevent the enemy from ever getting into a position from which he can apply this strategy himself. In a word, the Luftwaffe should have prevented American landings in Africa because North Africa is an ideal base from which to send bombers over Hitler-occupied Europe and perhaps over Germany itself. And while now the Americans are in a position to strike at Germany's heart, the Germans are not in a position to strike at America's heart. This, for instance, is the one advantage the Americans have over the British and the Russians. They can bomb German factories, munitions plants, railway stations, towns, cities. All the Germans can do in retaliation is bomb North Africa, which would not interrupt American airplane production or slow down the American war effort in any way.

No doubt about it, the Germans are now on the receiving end of the Douhet strategy—whenever the Americans feel the time has come to apply the strategy.

The Battle of Germany—the air raids over Germany—
began some time ago. We all know that some cities like
Cologne and Bremen have been bombed more than a hundred times, that others like Hamburg, Berlin, Duisburg,
Duesseldorf, Essen, Hanover, etc. have been bombed at
least fifty times, and that the industrial areas in the Ruhr
have undergone severe punishment. Goebbels' excellent
propaganda and his strict censorship have not been able
to prevent the German population and the world at large
from learning about the serious damage inflicted on Germany, not to mention the loss of life.

All this continues on an ever increasing scale as this
is being written, and it will continue to increase, especially
when the Americans start using their North African base.

The bombing of Germany is an old nightmare of Hitler's. He knew that if Germany's enemies ever made up
their minds, they would be able to do a great deal, perhaps
a ruinous amount, of damage.

He was well aware of this when he came to power and
when Goering began to build up the Luftwaffe in the
greatest secrecy. That goes back to the year 1933, when
Hitler left the League of Nations on the pretext that Germany was not being treated fairly, that she could not
achieve equal rights as to rearmament or disarmament. That
was in October. The following month Hitler, in order to
make wars "more humane," approached the Western powers and suggested the outlawing of "certain weapons and
their use against civil population." What Hitler meant was
that the powers should discontinue building big bombers.

England, however, pointed out that she needed her big
bombers for administrative purposes in the colonies, and
fortunately Hitler's interesting plan came to naught.

That Germany would be relatively defenseless against

bombing in the event of war was, indeed, an open secret among military experts. I quote from the *Militaerische Wochenblatt* of December 25, 1934.

The defense is almost powerless against today's light bombers; that has been established in maneuvers in England, France, and America. In order to protect one single target it is necessary to have ten aircraft for each enemy aircraft. For the attacker has three advantages. He can choose the day and the hour, he can choose the height, and he can choose the target. Victory will come to whomever can hit the enemy the hardest and the fastest and over the longest distances.

Many attempts had been made to transfer German industry underground so that it would function even if Germany were bombed. However, those who sponsored those projects knew quite well that there was a limit to the protection achieved by going underground. You could put a factory underground. But you could hardly force the workers to live underground, too—not to mention their wives and their children. Experience has proved that production can be hampered seriously when workers are killed or even disturbed—though the plant itself isn't touched.

Political protection was much more efficient than going underground; Hitler's attempts to keep the other side from bombing Germany were successful—even after war was declared. He had not been successful in outlawing the bombing weapon in general. But he succeeded in getting Mr. Chamberlain to understand that it would be better for everybody concerned if Germany were not bombed. The R.A.F. wanted to go right into Germany and do its work, but Chamberlain prevented it.

Then there was Goering.

Before the outbreak of the war Goering used to boast

that no enemy bombers would ever cross German frontiers, and that no bombs would ever hit German cities or factories. He made a big show of massing all over Germany enormous quantities of anti-aircraft guns, heavy machine guns, searchlights, and aircraft detecting devices. But, of course, he relied mainly on the offensive action of the Luftwaffe, which was supposed to destroy enemy bombers on the ground—a procedure that, indeed, would have prevented them from reaching Germany.

The very day it became certain that the Luftwaffe had not beaten the R.A.F., it was certain that, and, therefore, only a matter of time before, Allied bombers would appear over Germany. As the majority of experts had predicted, defensive weapons were of little avail against enemy bombing, especially night bombing. The more the night raids increased in intensity and scope and the more uncertain it became where the enemy would strike the next time, the more Goering had to disperse his defenses and the less he could achieve at any particular point.

German anti-aircraft guns today are using up as much ammunition as the guns of all calibers fired during the big offensives of World War I. But that does not prevent the Allied bombers from returning.

No matter how great or how little the damage caused by the raids over Germany, one thing is sure: they have completely destroyed the confidence of the population in the Luftwaffe. Today there are more than one and a half million men within Germany occupied with the task of fighting enemy planes from the ground. And still the Allied bombers have no difficulty getting through. This will eventually help break down civilian morale. It has already not only destroyed public confidence in the Luftwaffe but has changed what once used to be pride in this "unbeatable" weapon into contempt.

The worst defeat the Luftwaffe has yet suffered is its defeat inside Germany.

As to the actual material damage done by the raids, especially the damage inflicted on aircraft production and aircraft accessories production, we can, of course, only try to estimate. According to the soundest and most conservative estimates, production output has not suffered more than perhaps 15 per cent from bombing. Let us suppose then, that the aircraft production has been off 15 per cent for some time. That would mean that Allied bombing has been effective. But I think that that 15 per cent has been easily made up and compensated for by the enforced contributions of French plants and factories in other occupied countries.

How big is German production today and how does it compare with the production in other countries?

When the war broke out, Germany possessed—mainly from the production of the preceding years of rearmament —great quantities of Ju 52 transport planes and Stukas, Ju 87, as well as Me 109's. The Heinkel medium bombers, He 111's, had not been produced in great numbers and can therefore be left out of this estimate. It can be assumed that all the stocks have been used up in the meantime through reckless use in the campaigns themselves, through losses by enemy action in the air and on the ground, through communication work, and in training.

Over the whole three years of war, including the pauses between campaigns and the enforced inactivity of the Luftwaffe during the first winter in Russia, the losses can be assessed at an average of 1,500 planes a month at most.

This figure includes the loss of trainers that have crashed at home and those planes which have been discarded for lack of spare parts.

Total production figures, as they are generally used for comparison, have no absolute value. Four-engined bombers, for example, use up many times the material and the wage hours that go into the making of a single-engined fighter. And a single-engined fighter, in turn, costs many times more material and labor than an elementary trainer. Furthermore, production figures generally include not only the finished aircraft but also parts which are not placed in finished aircraft but are kept in a more or less dis-assembled condition, as spare parts for replacement. But as these practices of computation are about the same in all belligerent countries, we have to use these rather misleading figures for comparison, although it would give a much better picture of production capacity if we were in a position to compare the production based either on total engine output or on pounds of aircraft constructed.

An approximate computation of the German aircraft and engine production facilities leads to an estimate of 2,500 to 3,500 German aircraft which can be produced every month. I know that such eminent American experts as T. P. Wright, who had ample opportunity to study German aircraft production on the spot, lean toward the lower figure. But I think that I have had a better chance to obtain a complete and detailed all-round picture of the German aircraft production potential, not only in the aircraft works themselves but also in the auxiliary industries, the raw material sources, and the bottlenecks, through which the whole volume of production could be more thoroughly checked.

It is thus that I have come to the conclusion that the

German aircraft industry can produce 3,500 fully equipped planes a month, of which one-third may be non-combat trainers and another 20 per cent transport planes for paratroops and air infantry, too.

Of course, there are certain times when the actual production falls off by an amazing percentage, for instance, when new types or even improved types of aircraft are introduced and re-tooling holds up production or stops it altogether. I know there was one period in the summer of 1939 when aircraft production all over Germany nearly stopped in preparation for the new medium bomber Ju 88, which was then considered an outstanding multi-purpose plane.

As to the production of the other Fascist countries and of the United Nations, I can only quote from well-known English and American publications. As to the Russian production, I think that it cannot now be estimated at higher than at 2,000 planes a month, if as high as that.

Thus, the following picture develops.

Axis Nations		United Nations	
Germany	3,500	Great Britain	2,000
Italy	600	U.S.A.	5,000
Japan	1,000 (?)	Russia	2,000 (?)
	5,100 per month		9,000 per month

Considering the relative youth of the American air force, and the elaborate training scheme of the British Empire (and probably of Russia, too), I believe that the allotment of trainers in the total monthly production of the United Nations is considerably higher than on the Axis side. In addition, the fact that Allied production has already overtaken Axis production should not, or at least not yet, be taken as proof that the same applies to the effectives, the

combat planes in active service of the United Nations'
active air forces.

Furthermore, the United Nations have had to disperse
their active squadrons over such widely separated sections
of the globe that except in a few theaters of war the Axis
has had a considerable numerical superiority. This has already changed somewhat, because now the Axis, too, has
been forced to disperse its air forces. And with the mounting quantitative output of the United Nations, this will
change more and more.

Anyhow, the production figure on both sides seems to
prove that production by far surpasses present and past
losses so that considerably stepped-up air activities would
be feasible. This is, however, not the case. Take, for instance, the British "saturation attacks on Germany." The
British lost an average of 5 per cent of their big bombers
in each raid, which is an extremely low figure. But if the
British were to try to repeat their attacks for twenty nights
a month, each time with a thousand heavy bombers, they
would need a replacement of at least a thousand heavy
bombers a month. They are in no position yet to produce
anything like a thousand Lancasters and Sterlings monthly;
nor can America spare the difference between the necessary thousand bombers and the actual British production.
At least not yet.

But there can be little doubt that Hitler is afraid of
the aircraft production capacity of the United Nations,
especially American capacity. When those eight Nazi
saboteurs who came to American shores on a submarine
were arrested, it was found out that they were supposed to
sabotage plants producing aluminum and power stations
on which aluminum production depended. The idea evidently was to disrupt aluminum production to such a

degree that aircraft production itself would be slowed up or stopped altogether for six to twelve months—without attacking aircraft plants themselves, which the Germans thought would be too well protected. (In the last war German saboteurs tried to destroy munitions factories and to sabotage the shipping of ammunition.) On the other hand, the idea of striking against American aluminum production shows that the Germans are afraid we might strike against their aluminum production. It has always been a typically German trait to act on the assumption that conditions abroad are similar to those in the Reich. This should be, and I think it already has been, accepted as a guide for the Boards of Economic Warfare here and in England to strike against German aluminum production.

There is danger that our growing air power and our growing superiority in the air will not have their logical results. Not long ago Hitler announced that he would follow a defensive strategy in order to digest his conquests and to consolidate them. If the United Nations allow him to settle down to another "phony war," and thus to recuperate from serious blows and losses and to prepare a new operative warfare, the Luftwaffe, too, might recuperate and perhaps could even be built up into a real operative weapon.

But Hitler would need time for such fundamental changes. And he would need—or better, the Luftwaffe would have to produce from among its leaders—a man capable of overhauling the Luftwaffe in its entirety—its strategy, its tactics, its equipment. To put it bluntly, he would have to rebuild the Luftwaffe along sound military lines. In such a case, anything would be possible.

I doubt that there is such a man in Germany today. And even if he existed, Hitler would hardly agree to such radical changes at this advanced stage of the war, especially since during the considerable time of transition the conduct of the war would be seriously hampered if not upset. But even if there were such a man, even if Hitler gave him full power, as long as we do not let up on our offensive efforts, as long as we do our utmost to beat Germany and to beat her now, the fate of the Luftwaffe is sealed.

The Luftwaffe in its fourth year of war finds itself equipped mainly with planes whose designs were completed years ago, and with new ones coming along slowly. It has lost its qualitative and at least its wide quantitative superiority. It has definitely lost its best pilots and crews. And, worst of all, it has lost confidence in its ability to surprise, outmaneuver, and outfight any opponent. It has also lost confidence, and certainly the army has lost confidence if it ever cherished any, in the idea that the Luftwaffe will decide the outcome of the war and conquer the world for Germany. And all this results from the fact that the Germans find themselves involved in the very type of war in which they were not going to be involved.

They were not supposed to be involved in any war with Great Britain. They were not to be involved in any long drawn-out war against anybody, let alone against a whole coalition of enemies.

Most important—it must be said again and again—is the fact that the Russians do not allow the Nazis a breathing spell and thus keep the Nazi losses constant. In the first stage of the war, the Nazis were able to make up for losses surpassing production by the simple device of not fighting for as long as they chose not to fight. Now, the decision as to when to fight is no longer theirs. They have lost the initiative.

On the other hand, machines and tools wear out. Labor

in occupied countries, workers supplying auxiliary material and raw material across Europe suffer in growing measure from fatigue, undernourishment, and nervous breakdowns. Also, to a lesser degree, production suffers from the underground warfare, slow-down tactics, etc., which no Gestapo has been able to prevent or stop.

For us, this is only the beginning. For the Luftwaffe, however, it is the fourth year. And this fourth year will find the Luftwaffe pessimistically having to consider everything that has been outlined in these pages. In fact, the Luftwaffe cannot but fall prey to consumption.

18. Tomorrow

The Luftwaffe is doomed. The weapon of which the Nazis have been so inordinately proud, the weapon they thought would conquer the world for them, has been shown up as a failure. The weapon into whose forging they have sunk such unbelievable amounts of money ...

I have often been asked, in this country and in England, to estimate how much money I thought the Luftwaffe has actually cost the Third Reich. The figure at which I arrived—with many reservations—is something like 50 billion dollars, from 1933 to the end of 1942.

Nobody can hope to calculate accurately in dollars and cents what the Luftwaffe cost from 1933 to the beginning of the Polish campaign in 1939. Too many different and unassessable values are involved, such as the cost of foreign raw material, German and foreign patents, purchases in foreign countries either on barter basis or for cash. There is also the fact that in different international agreements Germany has been able to fix the exchange value of its own mark—under the disguise of many different kinds of marks, such as Registermark, Sperrmark, Auslandsmark, etc.—anywhere from ten marks to a dollar to one mark to a dollar.

Furthermore, it is difficult to calculate the wages. A considerable percentage of the ground installations, for instance, was constructed with the help of political prisoners and labor battalions which were paid hardly anything at all.

Few budgets have been published since the Nazis came to power; those that were published were full of holes and inaccuracies. It is safe to assume that even the Nazis themselves would not be able to calculate their expenses. How much has been paid for by the Reich, how much by provincial and municipal bodies? (The latter financed many of the protective ground organizations.) How much land was bought, how much was confiscated? How many industrial plants were purchased, how many were stolen? How many patents were bought, how many were "confiscated"? And the margin of error is widened by the fact that by far the biggest part of the expenses was not paid out of any income of the Reich but by some complicated device of accumulating debts. One can find traces of these debts in the accounts of the so-called employment drive.

Thus the big banking concerns, private banks and savings banks as well as insurance companies, were forced to contribute their liquid assets against "*Arbeits beschaffungs-wechsel*" (Employment Procurement Bills of Exchange) which they had to accept for their portfolios.

Against which particular account the expenses of the Luftwaffe's participation in the Spanish war—just to take one example—were debited, I have no idea. In any case, the published budgets of the Air Ministry for the years 1933 and 1934, when enormous sums were spent for building up the Luftwaffe, quoted figures of only 8 million dollars and 20 million dollars respectively for aircraft construction and for air raid protection.

In 1939, just before the outbreak of the war, Hitler pronounced—take his word for whatever it is worth—that 90 billion marks or roughly 30 billion dollars had been spent for the whole of German rearmament. I think this is one of the few cases in which the Fuehrer has been guilty of understatement.

I have attempted a calculation not of money spent but of equipment manufactured and purchased, of ground organizations built up, of the expenses for upkeep of men and machines from 1933 to 1939, of investments for factories, of fuel and ammunition used up in practice and training, for anti-aircraft artillery, etc., etc. I come to a figure of about 30 to 35 billion dollars for the Luftwaffe alone. But this figure is based on American conditions. That is, according to my calculation, it would have cost Hitler 30 to 35 billion dollars to build up the Luftwaffe if he had to pay according to American standards for his labor, for his raw material, for everything that went into the Luftwaffe—just as, for instance, the American government has to pay for whatever goes into the cost of the American air force.

And I think it is conservative to estimate the cost of the Luftwaffe in the three following years at about another 15 billion dollars. And even this conservative estimate makes sense only for the reason that Hitler's Luftwaffe did not fight more than eighteen months altogether during the first three years of World War II.

Fifty billion dollars is a lot of money. It may be objected here that Germany, by manipulating the value of the mark and using devices as mentioned before, was not actually forced to pay out any such amount. This is true. But on the other hand fifty billion dollars—roughly 50 per cent of the United States budget for 1943—is a much larger sum in Germany than it would be in the United States. So, if one were to set the figure at a lesser amount, this lesser amount within the financial structure—such as it is—of Germany would still mean the same as fifty billion dollars in the United States. In short, it can be said that while the Nazis spent less than 50 billion dollars on the Luftwaffe, they did spend an amount which to them means what 50 billion dollars would mean to Americans.

In any case, it was a large amount of money—not too large an amount of money for an operative weapon that was supposed to win the war. But the Luftwaffe never did become that.

People here and in England have asked me whether it would have been possible at all to build up the Luftwaffe as an operative weapon instead of what it became.

We have seen that the Luftwaffe lacked the main offensive weapon—heavy bombers with a long striking range. I may add that it also lacked escort fighters with the same striking range, at least till 1940. Furthermore, it lacked an organization for sustained attack over a considerable length of time and, last but not least, it was without air transport (for the Luftwaffe itself) from the very beginning.

What would a military aviation leader of real vision have done in the extremely favorable situation the Nazis found when they came to power? There is no doubt that a stronger Luftwaffe on a sounder basis could have been built. But with the same amount of work, and money, such a Luftwaffe could not have been used as early as the Luftwaffe actually was used as an instrument of bluff. It could not and would not have been ready as an instrument of terror by September 1939, or anywhere near such a time. It could have been used only at a much later date and in a much less dramatic manner. In short, it could not have been used in a blitzkrieg manner.

And it was exactly for a blitzkrieg or a succession of blitzkriegs that it was supposed to be used.

I repeat that the Nazis found an extremely favorable situation. In fact, they had the greatest chance in history to prove that an independent air force employing its own operative strategy could decide the outcome of a war. They threw away that chance.

Why was this situation so favorable? Let us review it here briefly:

1. The Versailles Treaty had destroyed all remnants of old-line airplanes, ground facilities, and industrial organization.

2. Germany had, therefore, built up since Versailles the most modern industrial organizations backed by magnificent scientific research facilities and a highly trained technical population.

3. There was a highly trained and war-minded reservoir of officers, with a long tradition of successful warfare, but not so bogged with tradition that they would not have clearly seen the advantages of modern technical development.

4. There were clear political plans of conquest and their strategic foundation.

5. The Nazi system could do away with all cumbersome criticism or delaying parliamentary action.

Therefore the Nazis should have been able to build up and use a Luftwaffe for independent operative air warfare in addition to the tactical air formations required for army and navy co-operation.

Let us review once more why this was not done.

1. There was the opposition of the army to a purely Nazi party weapon and thus the determination of the gen-

erals to make the Luftwaffe a co-operative weapon rather than an independent operative weapon.

2. There was the incompetence of the leading men in the Luftwaffe and their inability to recognize their deviation from the logical course to take, the one originally plotted.

3. There were Hitler's political plans that necessitated the Luftwaffe's early emergence as a weapon of bluff rather than a sound military weapon.

That was why, when the war broke out, the Luftwaffe was really something entirely different from what it should have been in the first place.

This is my point: The Luftwaffe was not built as it should have been built. It was not possible to build, in such a short time, an operative weapon; in view of the geographical strategic position of Germany, and the strategic necessity of waging short wars, more time was perhaps not available.

But all this does not say anything against strategic air warfare as such. I have always been firmly convinced—and I am not any the less firmly convinced today—of the advantages of a strategic air force. I am looking forward to having my conviction fully confirmed by the performance of the Royal Air Force and perhaps by an autonomous American air force victorious at the end of this war.

There is no denying that the Luftwaffe, with all its weaknesses of construction and basic principle, was not very far from winning World War II or from having to win it. As a weapon of bluff, it won many bloodless battles for Hitler, and as a weapon of terror it came close to winning the war itself.

This, of course, is as much to the merit of propaganda

as to the Luftwaffe itself. It has been pointed out how well the propaganda side of the matter was handled. How the rearmament was kept a secret at first and then later how it was over-publicized in order to make the whole world tremble. I have shown how propaganda—with the unconscious help of neutrals and "experts"—brought about the first successful blitzkriegs that seemed almost private victories of the Luftwaffe, thus convincing the world once more of the invincibility of the Luftwaffe.

This is no attempt to minimize the enormous achievements of many men in the German air force and many other institutions or to play down the preparation and carrying through of co-operative operations during the Polish, Norwegian, or Western campaigns or in the Balkans, over Crete, and even in Russia and Africa. But in almost each and every case in which successes were won, they were won not by an invincible Luftwaffe but by co-operative operation—and in the last analysis always, always by the German army, whose strength has never been doubted by the experts and which certainly cannot be counted as an achievement of the Third Reich.

Let us repeat that the army, when it set down the Luftwaffe to the level of a purely co-operative weapon, was by no means acting alone from jealous motives or political distrust of the Nazis. Such motives did exist in the beginning, no doubt. But the generals had very good and sound reasons to insist on not having an operative air force. They did not consider the Polish operative victories a feather in the cap of the Luftwaffe because Poland had been far too inferior in the air. Neither were the German air successes in the next campaigns conclusive, though for a time they prevented the generals from making further inroads into the Luftwaffe. It was thus that the Luftwaffe had its big

chance in the Battle of England. And its complete failure
did away with what doubts the generals might have had as
to its capabilities as an autonomous and operative weapon.

Beginning with the retreat from Moscow in the winter
of 1941, if not before, the German air fleets have been
assigned to more or less tactical tasks only. And they have
been assigned to these tasks by the generals. More and
more, the activity of Nazi fliers confined itself to fights
over the battlefield and attacks on enemy troops. And when
the first Russian winter—for which the Luftwaffe was no
better prepared than the army—killed its initiative entirely,
its fate as an operative weapon was sealed once and for
all. There will be no second chance, no comeback.

The Luftwaffe is doomed. But this does not mean that
we will never hear of it again. We shall still hear a lot
about the German fliers. At this writing they have made
other bombing attacks on London in retaliation for the
successive air raids over Berlin since January 1943. There
will be more raids and perhaps even mass raids over England. To be sure, Hitler can no longer afford such raids
and if he undertakes them in great numbers, and without
regard to the losses, it will simply mean that he has given
up budgeting his forces. In other words, he will no longer
have a concrete or sensible plan as to how to win the war.
He will not even have a plan as to how to win it with a
co-operative air weapon.

But, then, the Nazis announced a long time ago—and
are now mentioning it again quite frequently—that before
giving up as they did in 1918, they would bring the whole
world down with them in flames.

In this connection, bombing raids against America are
entirely possible. They are even probable.

Of course, there is no possibility that the Luftwaffe can conduct an independent operative warfare against the United States or the American continent. The Luftwaffe, feeling more and more the gap between its dwindling effectives and its spreading commitments, cannot possibly undertake such an enormous new task.

Furthermore, for at least the next three to five years, there will not be available any fleet of bombers that can fly from a European base to, let us say, Detroit and return.

We can also rule out the possibility that the Nazis might get a foothold in the Western Hemisphere and, from striking distances, start heavy bombing attacks on American industrial centers.

But there remain the nuisance raids. They could be carried out for purposes of showmanship and in the hope of breaking down our morale or simply with the idea of "bringing down the world in flames," before the Nazis go out. There is, furthermore, the possibility that such raids may be organized in order to obtain better peace terms. (This would be similar to the bombings of Paris and London in 1918 in order to create terror at a time when the German High Command knew that its game was up.)

In any case, such nuisance raids would mean the loss of all the material involved and the probable loss of the crews for the duration at least.

A number of possibilities to help effect such nuisance raids have been under consideration in Germany for some time.

Certain hidden supply bases in the Western Hemisphere could be used, especially bases in sparsely populated spots where fuel and bombs might have been cached. Raiders coming from Europe could make intermediary landings at such spots to refuel and to fill the bomb racks. But only very few planes could operate in that fashion. If any large number were thus employed, the quantities of bombs and fuel stored away in such hidden bases would certainly soon attract the attention of the intelligence service of such a country.

Heavy bombers carrying a substantial bomb load could attempt to fly from the northwest coast of France direct to the American continent. After dropping their bombs, the fliers could land somewhere on the American continent. Here they could destroy the planes, and either try to escape or surrender. They could also return to the sea, where, after landing at an appointed spot where U-boats would wait to take up the crew, the planes could be smashed up or sunk.

I know that the Nazis have worked out plans for such raids.

Finally, there is a possibility of attacks from floating German bases somewhere off the American coast.

These bases could be U-boats that transport planes in folded or dismantled condition. Near the American East Coast, the planes could be assembled and they could set out to raid American centers. Later they could return, be dismantled again, and taken back by the submarines. This sounds fantastic, but it is a fact that the Germans even during World War I built submarine-based planes, and there can be little doubt that they have developed and perfected their technique. But such planes could only be small, could carry only a small bomb load, and would operate only in small formations.

If the Nazis complete the aircraft carriers that are supposedly under construction now, they could also use them for a dash into the North Atlantic with medium bombers taking off against the United States. This would be done only in the last desperate stages, however, since it would involve the loss of the carrier as well as the aircraft and the crews.

Any of these possibilities could be combined. There is also the very remote possibility of using big air ships either as raiders themselves or as carriers for planes.

In short, nuisance raids against the United States are possible and even probable before this war is over. While there is no reason to fear they will change the outcome of the war, they should be expected and prepared for. Until the Nazis are crushed, our vigilance in this respect should never diminish. We must avoid unnecessary damage, a heavy toll of civilian life, and local disruption of industrial production, public services, or communications.

I am satisfied that the American authorities have prepared everything to avoid just those effects.

But no matter how desperate may be the last efforts of the Nazis, they will not give back to the Luftwaffe the decisive moment in history when it seemed to be the chosen instrument for winning world war domination for Germany. The Luftwaffe is no longer the lightning sword striking whole nations down into the dust.

It has fallen into the abyss of military annals.

To bring down the world in flames . . . a gigantic blackmail to get better peace terms in the end.

When the last desperate moment has come, the Luftwaffe can and probably will be used for the purpose of demolishing a good part of Europe.

It will come at a time when the entire Nazi war effort is collapsing, and when the United Nations decline to make peace with Hitler or with one of Hitler's men.

The Nazis then, I am afraid, will resort to actions and

deeds compared to which everything they have done so far
will seem humane.

They will try to murder the four to six million prisoners
of war who are today working in Germany, and who are
more or less at their mercy. (The wholesale murder of
Jews that is going on today is only a demonstration of
what the Nazis are capable of doing.) There is no doubt
in my mind that the Nazis will try to do away with as
many inhabitants of the occupied countries as possible.

The Luftwaffe no doubt will play a big part in this last
horrible tragedy. It will be used not so much for bombing
purposes as for destroying whole towns by means of poison
gas or by creating epidemics by throwing down especially
prepared germ containers.

What could the world do in such a case? I am afraid
I do not know. There is a chance that the German people
would not stand for this kind of sub-human bestiality.
There is a very good chance that the German army would
not stand for it. But I think this is precisely one of the
reasons why the Nazis would use their weapon, their own
private weapon, the Luftwaffe.

And how about the Nazi pilots? Would they stand for
this? Will they go along on that last, horrible mission of
destruction?

The Nazi flier is very different from the German soldier,
the German sailor, or the German man of the merchant
marine. Most of these latter were either grown up or at
least in their late teens when Hitler came to power. The
fliers, on the other hand, are entirely a product of Nazi
education. They believe much more strongly in Nazi ideas
and in the Fuehrer, and it is difficult, if not impossible, to
influence them in any other direction. Men in charge of

prisoners of war in Allied countries can testify eloquently as to the difficulties of dealing with these young Nazi fliers.

These young fliers are also very different from us, the generation of young pilots during World War I. The only thing we had in common was the hunger for adventure and the willingness to sacrifice ourselves entirely for the task.

When the generation of World War I started flying, it did so because here was something that could be built up. When after the war everything broke down, many of us started rebuilding again, in the face of great difficulties. These were idealists—at least most of them.

Perhaps the Nazi fliers are idealists of a kind, too. But they were early corrupted by Hitler and his Nazi ideas. They learned early that there was no particular reason to be decent, there were no moral ideals, there was only the idea of making Germany big and strong and of doing away with Germany's enemies, no matter what the cost—to others. The Nazi fliers were seduced. Seduced so completely that it will be difficult, if not impossible, ever to win them back to any kind of normal life again. Those Germans who went over to Hitler because they thought that Hitler would be good for Germany may be saved from Hitler once they find out that the Fuehrer was definitely not good for Germany. Those Nazi fliers, however, who went over to Hitler seduced and hypnotized and in an indivisible religious, romantic, and mystic belief in the Fuehrer and in Nazism, a belief that withstands any kind of rational argument—they will never admit that they were wrong.

I have indicated that most of us fliers of World War I started to work hard after the collapse in order to build up something new. Some, it may be remembered—like Goering, Loerzer, and Bodenschatz—felt no urge at all to get down to hard work. They wanted to continue the *Herrenleben*, "gentlemen's life," they had been leading during the war. I think that in this respect many Nazi fliers are like their leader, Goering. They will not find their way back to a petty bourgeois existence without the glamour of adventure. In fact, they have never known what such a life is really like.

For this reason, I feel that many of them simply will not want to disband at all. They will want to stick to their comrades, and no doubt will throw themselves into just such adventures and undertakings as many German pilots threw themselves into after World War I—going into Baltic countries, fighting the Poles, fighting anybody, as long as they could fight.

It is possible and even probable that the Nazi fliers will try revolution before they disband and give up their machines.

It is, of course, extremely difficult to find out exactly what goes on inside a young Nazi fanatic of the flier class. Especially since most of them talk like drunkards, with a vocabulary of vague, newly created, mystical words and headline slogans. But I feel sure that most of them would subscribe to an interpretation of their ideas as follows:

"Germany is the first of the great Western nations to pioneer the way to a revolution of better material distribution, to a kind of social justice that all other nations will have to follow. This is the German mission for which we are prepared to fight, suffer, and die."

There is no doubt that the leading Nazis are building up their personal fortunes and leading as comfortable lives as possible. But the young Nazi fanatics, especially those in the Luftwaffe, do not think of gain for themselves individually. They think of revolution, revolution in the direction of communism. They are very much against the older generation—"the plutocrats"—for whose fortune-building they have only contempt. They feel that everything in the world should be redistributed—with Germany not only effecting such a redistribution but also getting the fattest part of the riches of the world.

The young Nazi fliers hope that such ideas will be put into practice after Hitler has won the war, and I suspect that they will try to carry through these ideas even in case Hitler does not win the war.

While the prospect that they will desert Hitler before the end of this war is zero, they could easily do without him once he proved himself incapable of leading them to victory. Somebody like Goebbels might even create a new myth after Hitler's disappearance—effected perhaps by army leaders—a myth in which Hitler would figure the way Emperor Barbarossa figures in old German myths: sitting in a mountain in Germany, waiting for *Der Tag*. The generals or the Junkers might very cynically decide that under such circumstances a dead Hitler would be a better asset to them than a live one because they could always tell the Nazi rank and file that if Hitler had been there things would not have turned out as they did.

I think the overwhelming majority of Nazi fliers will seriously believe in such a Hitler myth. They will really believe that Germany would not have been defeated if the Fuehrer had stayed on. And that, in their minds, will only prove that they themselves were not worthy of the Fuehrer and that they must try again and again in order to become worthy of him.

There is still another possibility as to the future develop-

ment of the Nazi flier. It may well be these young men
who were educated to the belief that they are invincible,
who have not yet come around to the understanding that
other men, men of other nations and races, may be as good
as they are or perhaps even better, that these super-cocky,
hyper-arrogant Nazis, once they look defeat straight in
the eye, will collapse. And collapse completely.

If the Nazi pilots ever lose confidence in themselves,
confidence in their leaders, and confidence in their somewhat nebulous and mysterious half-communistic ideas,
there will be nothing left for them.

The question will be raised as to whether the defeat and
the collapse of the Luftwaffe can be made to help cement
a lasting peace.

There is no doubt that air warfare in itself, in all its
cruelty, should help convince people that it is better to
live in peace—aside from all ideas and ideals—just because
it is so much safer. Air warfare as it is today—not to speak
of the grim possibilities of the future—should bring home to
everybody the idea that there will be no safety any more
for anybody in future wars. There are no restricted fronts
any more; the front will be everywhere. This means that
the homes and families of the men who are in charge of
the war strategy or who provide cannons, airplanes, and
ammunition are equally jeopardized. Air warfare today and
tomorrow means that the time has passed when anybody
could foster wars for no matter what purpose and be safe
himself.

Going a step further, I can even imagine an organization for the preservation of peace—through air power. A
kind of international air force to police the world and
through the sheer threat of such an international air force

to prevent the various countries from fighting each other. It is entirely possible that in the future—I am afraid in a future yet far away—some kind of League of Nations air power could be built up, a set-up that might have better results than the old League could ever hope for.

It is not impossible to visualize future Germans taking part and playing an important part in such an air force. I consider the Nazi fliers of today lost—lost for a future Germany and for a future humanity. But the generations to come, more sensibly educated, could be made to overcome the eternal German inferiority complex by their employment in an international air force where they would have ample opportunity to satisfy their hunger for adventure as well as for self-sacrifice for a worthy ideal.

But what I really hope the future will bring, and this perhaps a not too far distant future, is the rebirth of the airplane in its original role. We have too completely forgotten that the airplane is not primarily a weapon but a means of communication. Perhaps a day will come when it will not be a weapon at all—except for the international police force—but only a means of transport. I hope that a time will come when "air power" means nothing but the power of transporting people and goods across the continents and over the seven seas; when the airplane will help the peoples of the world to understand, not dread each other, and to live and work under better conditions; when, instead of destroying the riches of this world, aircraft will help to distribute them.

BIBLIOGRAPHY

Selected Bibliography

Adler, Der, Berlin, 1938-41.

Adler, Hermann, *Ein Buch von der neuen Luftwaffe*, Stuttgart, 1938.

Aero Digest, New York, 1928-42.

L'Aeronautique, Paris, 1928-42.

Aerophile, Paris, 1928-42.

Aeroplane, London, 1928-42.

Air Ministry of Great Britain, *The Battle of Britain*, London, 1941.

Air Ministry of Great Britain (Bomber Command), *Offensive against the Axis*, London, 1941.

All the World's Aircraft, Jane's, London, 1923-41.

Arnold, Lt. General H. H., *Winged Warfare*, New York and London, 1941.

Aviation, New York, 1934-42.

Barres, Philippe, "Hermann Goering," *Revue des Deux Mondes*, Paris, May 1933.

Blood-Ryan, H. W., *Goering, the Iron Man of Germany*, London, 1939.

Bongartz, Heinz, *Luftmacht Deutschland*, Essen, 1939. "Der Werdegang der deutschen Luftwaffe," *Essener Nationalzeitung*, March 1, 1940.

Buelow, Hilmer v., *Geschichte der Luftwaffe*, Frankfort a/M., 1934.

Crammon, Ludwig v., *Fort mit den interalliierten Kontroll Kommissionen*, Berlin, 1925.

Deutsche Luftwacht (Ausgabe: Luftwelt), Berlin, 1934-37.

Douhet, Giulio, *The Command of the Air*, New York, 1942.

Dutch, Oswald, *Hitler's Twelve Apostles*, London, 1934.

Farago, Ladislas, *The Axis Grand Strategy*, New York, 1942. *German Psychological Warfare*, New York, 1941.

Fischer v. Poturzyn, F. Andreas, *Jahrbuch fuer Luftverkehr*, Munich, 1924-1927. *Luftmacht*, Heidelberg-Berlin, 1938. *Luftbarrikaden*, Hannover, 1926.

Flight, London, 1928-42.

Flugsport, Frankfurt, a/M., 1920-33.

Fox, Ralph, *Genghis Khan*, London, 1936.

Gablenz, Carl August Frhr. v., *D-ANOY bezwingt den Pamir*, Berlin, 1937.

Garnett, David, *War in the Air*, New York, 1941.

Golovine, Lt. General N.N. "Air Strategy." *Royal Air Force Quarterly*, London, April 1936.

Handbuch der Luftfahrt, Berlin, 1936-1939.

Hauge, E., *Odds against Norway*, London, 1941.

Illustrierte Flugwoche, Leipzig, 1919-23.

"Inter-Avia" Korrespondenz, Geneva, 1935-42.

Jacob, Berthold, *Das neue deutsche Heer und seine Fuehrer*, Paris, 1935.

Jahrbuch der deutschen Luftwaffe, Berlin, 1937-41.

Journal, Royal Aeronautical Society, London, 1934-42.

Junkers, Hugo, *Festschrift zum 70. Geburtstag*, Berlin, 1929. *"Illustrierte Technik,"* Munich, 1935.

Junkers Nachrichten, Dessau, 1924-34.

Junkers in World Aviation, Munich, 1935.

Klemm-Merkbuch, Boeblingen, 1939.

Klotz, Dr. Helmuth, *Berlin Diaries*, New York, 1934, London, 1935. *Germany's Secret Armaments*, London, 1934. *Militaerische Lehren des Buergerkrieges in Spanien*, Paris, 1938.

Lachmann, Kurt, *The Hermann Goering Works*, New School for Social Research, New York, Feb. 1941.

Lehmkuhl, H. K., *The Invasion of Norway*, London, 1940.

Lezius, Martin, *Unsere Flieger in Polen*, Berlin, 1939.

Maurois, André, *The Battle of France*, London, 1940.

Meyer, Willy, *Von Wright bis Junkers*, Berlin, 1928.

National Aeronautics, Washington, D. C., 1941-42.

Orlovius, Dr. Heinz, Dr. Ernst Schultze, *Die Weltgeltung der deutschen Luftfahrt*, Stuttgart, Jahrbuch, 1936-39.

Orlovius, Dr. Heinz, *Jahrbuch der deutschen Luftwaffe*, Frankfort a/M., 1936.

Pollog, Carl Hanns, *Hugo Junkers*, Dresden, 1930.

Rangliste, Ehren-des deutschen Offiziersbundes, Berlin, 1926.

Revue de l'Armée de l'Air, Paris, 1929-39.

Riess, Curt, *The Self-Betrayed*, New York, 1942.

Ritter, Hans, *Luftkrieg*, Berlin and Leipzig, 1926.

Royal Air Force Quarterly, London, 1933-42.

Sachsenberg, Gotthard, *Die deutsche Luftfahrt Wirtschaft als Gesamtproblem*, Leipzig, 1932.

Scarfe, Ronald, *In the Norwegian Trap*, London, 1940.

Scheidemann, Philipp, *Memoirs*, New York, 1929.

Seversky, Alexander P. de, *Victory through Air Power*, New York, 1942.

Sigaud, Louis A., *Douhet and Aerial Warfare*, New York, 1941.

Supf, Peter, *Das Buch der deutschen Fluggeschichte*, Berlin, 1935.

Das Tagebuch, Berlin, 1920-26.

Treaty of Peace with Germany. Allied and Associated Powers, Treaties, 1919.

Udet, Ernst, *Mein Fliegerleben*, Berlin, 1935.

Der Waffenstillstand 1918-1919 (Das Dokumentenmaterial).

Wehrmacht, Berlin, 1939-40.

Weil, Kurt H., "Der Leidensweg der deutschen Luftfahrt," *Koelnische Zeitung*, Cologne, 1922. *Technische Erfahrungen im Junkers Luftverkehr*, Junkers Nachrichten, 1926.

Die Weltbuehne, Berlin, 1920-26.

Wentscher, Bruno, *Deutsche Luftfahrt*, Berlin, 1925-26.

Wer ist's? Leipzig, 1935.

Who is Who in British Aviation, London, 1936.

Woodman, Dorothy, *Hitler's Luftflotte startbereit*, Paris, 1935.
    Hitler Rearms, London, 1935.

Ziff, William B., *The Coming Battle of Germany*, New York, 1942.